Disorder and Decline

DISORDER
AND DECLINE

Crime and the Spiral of Decay in American Neighborhoods

WESLEY G. SKOGAN

THE FREE PRESS
A Division of Macmillan, Inc.
NEW YORK

Collier Macmillan Canada
TORONTO

Maxwell Macmillan International
NEW YORK   OXFORD   SINGAPORE   SYDNEY

The Free Press
A Division of Macmillan, Inc.
866 Third Avenue, New York, N.Y. 10022

Collier Macmillan Canada, Inc.
1200 Eglinton Avenue East
Suite 200
Don Mills, Ontario M3C 3N1

Printed in the United States of America

printing number

1 2 3 4 5 6 7 8 9 10

Library of Congress Cataloging-in-Publication Data

Skogan, Wesley G.
    Disorder and decline: crime and the spiral of decay in American neighborhoods / Wesley G. Kogan.
        p.   cm.
    Includes bibliographical references (p.   ).
    ISBN 0-02-929151-8
    1. Crime prevention—United States—Case studies.   2. Inner cities—United States—Case studies.   3. Quality of life—United States—Case studies.   4. Crimes without victims—United States—Case studies.   I. Title.
    HV6791.S57   1990
    364.2′56—dc20   90—3094
                                                                              CIP

To Barbara

Contents

Acknowledgments

I first became interested in disorder when I was part of the Reactions to Crime Project team at Northwestern University's Center for Urban Affairs and Policy Research. Our group was one of the first to shift its attention from levels of crime, and the treatment of offenders, toward a focus on how crime affects the lives of ordinary citizens and the role that they can play in its prevention. Several alumni of the Center, including Terry Baumer, Fred DuBow, Paul Lavrakas, Dan Lewis, Mike Maxfield, Aaron Podolefsky, Dennis Rosenbaum, and Greta Salem have made important contributions to my thinking. Although we set out to study problems of crime, we quickly discovered that people were fearful of neighborhood problems that we did not have in mind. It is difficult to reconstruct where that realization came from, but Albert Hunter was the first to dub these other problems "incivilities"; here they are called "disorders," a term that more clearly denotes the ideal condition against which they offend.

The preparation of this book was supported in part by Grant 85-IJ-IX-0074 from the National Institute of Justice, U.S. Department of Justice, awarded under the Omnibus Crime Control and Safe Streets Act, as amended. NIJ also supported many other research and evaluation projects reviewed in this book. The points of view or opinions presented here are those of the author and do not necessarily represent the official position or policies of the U.S. Department of Justice. The staff of the Police Foundation (Tony Pate, Mary Ann Wycoff, Sampson Annan, and Larry Sherman) freely shared their ideas and their data for this volume, as did Richard Taub, Stephanie Greenberg, and my colleagues Dan Lewis, Jane Grant, and Dennis Rosenbaum. Janet Soule did the graphics. Peter Grabosky and Dan Lewis contributed useful comments on early drafts of some chapters.

Disorder and Decline

1

Introduction

On a cold Saturday morning in October, 1989, neighborhood residents demonstrated outside Priced-Right Liquors, (not its real name), a tavern and carry-out liquor store on the Near West Side of Chicago. They protested that the store and a 35-room boarding house next door, owned by the same person, were destroying their community. Prostitutes reputedly worked out of the boarding house, and drunks and vagabonds gathered outside the tavern every afternoon and evening. Women complained of being accosted as they walked by, and broken bottles were strewn on the sidewalks and in the gutters for a block in either direction. The first available alley stank of urine. The protests came after a series of meetings between the owner and a local block club had failed to alter conditions in and around his buildings, and repeated complaints to the police had produced no action with regard either to prostitution or public drinking in the area.

The residents of this largely black and Puerto Rican neighborhood struggling to regain some control over conditions in their area were not complaining about conventional street crime, although that is certainly also a problem. Their manifesto pointed out how the tavern owner violated criminal statutes and the building code, but their protest was less about "law" than it was about "order." They tried to negotiate a solution first, because they were concerned with setting things right rather than with getting anyone arrested. Arguing that he was understaffed, the district police commander would not promise to do much more about the prob-

1

lem; he also voiced the opinion that the courts would not take any arrests very seriously anyway, for they were flooded with "real" criminals. And, of course, building code violations were not his responsibility.

These residents of the Near West Side were confronting a condition which plagues many inner city neighborhoods. This condition, which we will term *disorder*, has a social and a physical dimension. Disorder is evident in the widespread appearance of junk and trash in vacant lots; it is evident, too, in decaying homes, boarded-up buildings, the vandalism of public and private property, graffiti, and stripped and abandoned cars in streets and alleys. It is signaled by bands of teenagers congregating on street corners, by the presence of prostitutes and panhandlers, by public drinking, the verbal harassment of women, and open gambling and drug use. What these conditions have in common is that they signal a breakdown of the local social order. Communities beset by disorder can no longer expect people to act in civil fashion in public places. They can no longer expect landlords to respect the character of their neighborhood. Sometimes, disorder propels people to act—if they are fortunate enough to realize it is both evidence that their community is in decline, and that it will cause further trouble in the near future.

What is disorder? What are its consequences for neighborhood life? Why is disorder seemingly such an intractable problem, and what can be done to counteract it? This book describes the impact of disorder on the forces which underlie neighborhood stability and change and argues that disorder plays an important role in sparking urban decline. Understandably, communities are troubled when such problems as those listed above appear. Some of the activities are clearly illegal, and residents can hope to get the police interested in those problems. Disorders in this category include public gambling and drinking, prostitution, and the sale of drugs on the street. But, violators of other widely-approved standards of public conduct are not so clearly breaking the law. Into this category fall noisy neighbors, accumulating trash, poorly maintained buildings, and sundry problems relating to congregating bands of youths. Still other forms of disorder seem to present intractable enorcement problems despite their unlawful status. A great deal of disorderly behavior falls into such ambiguous legal categories as "disturbing the peace," "loitering," and "vagrancy." Furthermore, many disorders (the main exception being residential vandalism) do not have individual victims, despite their collective consequences. While these disorders often lead to complaints that the authorities "do something," the source of the public's concern often merely the anticipation of disorderly behavior or the possible consequences of growing disorder for the community, rather than a specific criminal incident. Because of the tenuous legal status of such complaints, and the fact that many disorders are not conventionally defined as serious problems, getting the attention of the police or other municipal agencies can be difficult. Sociologist Albert Reiss (1985) of Yale University captured the flavor of disorderly conditions lying near the edges of the law when he dubbed them "soft crimes."

But, legal distinctions and organizational encumbrances have little to do with the considerable impact of these problems on community life. In a report issued by President Johnson's Crime Commission more than 20 years ago, Albert Biderman and his fellow researchers (1967) argued that popular impressions of any area derive from the "highly visible signs of what [people] regard as disorderly and disreputable behavior in their community."

Those impressions deserve to be taken seriously, for they plainly have objective consequences. Researchers have found that perceptions of disorder have many ill effects on urban neighborhoods. Disorder not only sparks concern and fear of crime among neighborhood residents; it may actually increase the level of serious crime. Disorder erodes what control neighborhood residents can maintain over local events and conditions. It drives out those for whom stable community life is important, and discourages people with similar values, from moving in. It threatens house prices and discourages investment. In short, disorder is an instrument of destabilization and neighborhood decline. The following chapters document these conclusions and take a close look at strategies for dealing with disorder.

THE IDEA OF DISORDER

After more than 70 years of empirical research on the processes involved in maintaining social order, relatively little systematic work exists on its obverse—disorder—other than what we know about common crime. This neglect may be partly due to the limited amount of easily-accessible official statistics on other kinds of disorder. It may also reflect the fact that "order" itself is a slippery concept, once one leaves the well-defined domain of criminal law.

Research on disorder begins with a quest for important distinctions. What is disorder, and what isn't? Grouping building abandonment and public drinking under the rubric of disorder may at first seem too wide-ranging. But what they have in common is how neighborhood residents *react* to their appearance. Disorders vary in the extent to which they have been scrutinized by researchers—there is a great deal of research on vandalism and housing abandonment, for example, but very little on littering. And how people react to these problems has not been much considered. The present study investigates public responses to two general classes of disorder: social and physical. Social disorder is a matter of behavior: you can see it happen (public drinking, or prostitution), experience it (catcalling or sexual harassment), or notice direct evidence of it (graffiti, or vandalism). Physical disorder involves visual signs of negligence and unchecked decay: abandoned or ill-kept buildings, broken streetlights, trash-filled lots, and alleys strewn with garbage and alive with rats. By and large, physical disorder refers to ongoing conditions, while social disorder appears as a series of more-or-less episodic events.

Social and physical disorder are considered here as different problems with different cures; indeed, every problem we discuss has interesting features of its own. But, these differences are not important for many of our purposes, since the disorders in question usually engender the same *reaction*—be it fight or flight—from neighborhood residents. These reactions, and their larger consequences for urban communities, are what really interest us here. This book will also present some evidence that disorder needs to be distinguished from the ordinary crime problems facing the same communities. While disorder is clearly associated with common crime, the two turn out to be distinct issues.

Of course, a concept to be useful must also be clearly defined. It cannot encompass every nuance of behavior. Disorder violates widely shared values, but the social order is not defined by everything people agree upon. Order is defined by norms about public behavior, and these norms are only a subset of the manners and morals of the community. They prescribe how people should behave in relation to their neighbors or while passing through a community. This is still not a neat bundle of rules. Unlike criminology, which avoids many complex conceptual issues simply by pointing to the statute books to classify behavior, the study of disorder necessarily examines conflicts over an uncodified set of norms. The only real difference between crime and many disorders is that politicians have not enacted some widely agreed upon values into law. But, because many norms of public behavior are uncodified, the potential set of standards which may be violated is larger and more amorphously bounded than behaviors prescribed by the criminal law. One of the aims of this book is to work through the untidiness of disorder, and to discover what its true dimensions are.

All claims about how people should behave are subject to the charge that they are relative judgments. If disorder largely rests "in the eye of the beholder," does it simply reflect narrow-mindedness? Does the concept of disorder represent anything other than intolerance for all but conventional middle-class views of how people ought to behave? In the case of common crime, a large body of research indicates that there *is* in fact a value consensus. People of all races and classes agree we should shun theft, violence, sexual assault, and aggression against children. They give very similar ratings to the seriousness of various kinds of offenses, and they agree to a surprising extent on how stiff the punishments ought to be for violations of the law. The issue of what is criminal has been settled politically in debate over the criminal code, and within law-abiding society there is broad consensus on such matters. These middle-class values are just about everyone's values.

But there is no equally widespread agreement about what is disorderly, and there are conflicting claims. Urban historians report that American conceptions of the appropriate level of public order have changed dramatically over time. At important points in our history these conceptions have been the subject of intense political conflict; this experience suggests that the popular view of disorder is not immutable, and that it has reflected ethnic and class cleavages in society. In addition, urban utopians argue that city dwellers have a positive *taste* for disorder, and that it is an aspect of life worth celebrating.

Over time, American society has witnessed what historian Samuel Walker (1983) dubbed a "revolution in public expectations about the quality of life," clearly indicating that what is "disorderly" depends on the historical context. Before the mid-nineteenth century, daily life in American cities was more unpleasant than it is today, and almost as insecure. A marked decline began in the 1870s, both in the level of predatory crime and in social problems such as public drunkenness, vagrancy, disorderly conduct, and simple assault (Monkkonen 1981). Urban historian Richard Wade (1969) of New York University offers numerous reasons for this, for example, the emergence of a modern system of social control that featured well-organized municipal police forces, the first social welfare programs, and compulsory schooling. Also, the growing taste for order in American cities (in 1900, urban rates of violence were lower than in rural areas) may well have reflected, not just the demands of industrial life for regular, docile, sober behavior, and a willingness to accept supervision, but also the emergence of new social norms reflecting the conditions of modern city life (Lane, 1980). Close-packed, mutually-dependent city dwellers appear to have lost their earlier tolerance for interpersonal violence, drunkenness, and truancy. Historical evidence suggests that ''over a long term urbanization had a settling, literally a civilizing, effect on the population involved'' (Lane, 1968).

This civilizing process was not smooth, and the values it represented were partly imposed by force. History suggests that disagreements over norms about order reflect fundamental social cleavages; in other words, ''conventional'' norms can favor the interests of some over others. After the Civil War, police focused their attention on minor offenses against public order. This led to skyrocketing arrests for public drinking, vagrancy, suspicion, and loitering. Levels of arrests for these offenses peaked about 1870, but after the turn of the century they dropped dramatically. During the unstable period, widespread strikes and a wildly fluctuating economy pushed large numbers of people out of the labor force, and Americans took to the highways and rode the rails in unprecedented numbers. It became the task of the police to bring tramps and unemployed workers back into line. They also imposed conventional norms on the seemingly endless waves of immigrants, who brought with them alien ways of life. Historian Sydney Harring (1983: 199) argues that many offenses against public order (including public and Sunday drinking, lounging at corners, recreational violence, and consorting with prostitutes) were in fact ''working-class leisure-time activities,'' and that criminalizing them was part of ''the task of bringing immigrants into conformity with the labor discipline of industrial society.'' The police intervened in civil affairs to keep the bottom layer of society from drifting outside the economic system and forming a "dangerous class" that might threaten the hegemony of industrialists.

The claim that a measure of disorder is actually *good* for us can be found in the writings of urban utopians like Jane Jacobs, Harvey Cox, and Richard Sennett. They illustrate the sometimes shadowy boundary between consensually agreed-upon order and tolerable levels of diversity. Jacobs argues that people choose to live in cities in order to savor the variety and richness of the urban experience. Lively and challenging city life is created by the mingling of people with contrasting life styles. "[C]ity areas with flourishing diversity sprout strange and unpredictable uses and peculiar scenes. But this is not a drawback of diversity. This is the point, or part of it. That this should happen is in keeping with one of the missions of cities" (Jacobs, 1961: 238). A stimulating neighborhood environment may have collective as well as individual benefits. Jacobs is perhaps best known for her theory that a diverse environment attracts the kind of public attention that keeps it safe. The passing parade draws attention to the street, and encourages its use by the general public both during the day and after dark. "The greater and more plentiful the range of all legitimate interests (in the strictly legal sense) that city streets and their enterprises can satisfy, the better for the streets and for the safety and civilization of the city" (Jacobs, 1961: 41). Our discussion of the impact of disorder on the watchfulness of neighborhood residents will show that both communal watchfulness and individual efforts to promote neighborhood security are undermined when disorder overtakes a community.

Harvey Cox and Richard Sennett both advance variants of the medieval rule that "city air makes man free." Cox, a theologian, endorses the secularism of modern urban society. Cities promote and support unconventional lifestyles, which in his view is a good thing. Urban living provides what he characterizes as "a liberation from some of the cloying bondages of preurban society." It provides people with a chance to be free. "[F]or many people it is a glorious liberation, a deliverance from the saddling traditions and burdensome expectations of town life and an entry into the exciting new possibilities of choice which pervade the secular metropolis" (1965: 47, 49). Cox calls for a "theology of anonymity" which celebrates the ability of secular people to (as would be said two decades later) "do their own thing."

In *The Uses of Disorder*, social philosopher Richard Sennett actually suggests that we *impose* disorder on ourselves. Sennett argues that people segregate themselves by class and lifestyle in order to "cocoon" themselves in comfortable, unchallenging, residential environments. An undesirable political consequence of such segregation is the opportunity it creates for urban planners and bureaucrats to maintain control over a diverse and class-ridden society simply by policing the interstices between these segregated areas. As a result, members of a mass society live in the "self-imposed tyranny" of "safe and secure slavery." Sennett (1970: xvi) wonders "how dense, disorderly, overwhelming cities can become the tools to teach men to live with new freedom." He wants more disorder. He proposes to promote it through mixed and uncontrolled land use, high-density living, accelerated racial and class desegregation, locally controlled neighborhood institutions (such as schools), and a radical decentralization of political power. In his resulting "anarchic city," people would be forced to struggle for their own interests as they would then more clearly see them. Disorder would free better-off segments of society from the false sense of security that their currently segregated lifestyle promotes, and would force everyone to try to take command of their lives.

We will attempt to turn some of these claims about order norms into researchable questions. To be sure, this enterprise also involves making value choices; even to attempt to define disorder involves arguing for the preeminence of one set of values over another, as when one chooses to focus on public intoxication rather than on stock market swindles, or selects the problems community residents will be surveyed about. This raises some empirical questions: How widespread, really, are varying tastes for order? Is there real conflict, or substantial consensus, over the issues at hand? What social cleavages do any apparent conflicts represent? Are minority views concentrated among the young whose views will probably change as the youths show more regard for the consequences of what they do? The implications are far different, however, when minority views represent the economic condition or lifestyles of significant racial and class groupings. We will examine these issues of consensus and cleavage, concluding from the evidence that residents of urban neighborhoods are normally in overwhelming agreement about the nature of their problems.

If norms about order are widely shared and violations of them have common consequences, this stems in part from the nature of the problems being considered. Certainly, there are conditions in which Jacobs' kind of diversity widely is not only tolerated but even attracts a crowd. Peddlers and street musicians, sidewalk drinking, and dense late-night foot traffic can be tolerable in the right places, just as the antics long associated with Mardi Gras and Halloween are appropriate at the right times. Urbanologist William H. Whyte (1988) argues that they can also be good for business. Whyte observed patterns of foot traffic in retailing areas of Manhattan and came away with the impression that colorful, interesting, festive street life attracts shoppers and encourages people to linger downtown after work. However, we will be examining the impact of less benign disorder—including vandalism, drug dealing, street harassment, physical decay, and public prostitution—in areas that are solidly residential in character. The surveys, field observations, and experiments in policing and community organizing described here cannot test the historians' claim that urbanization and industrialization have shaped people's taste for order, nor the utopian's that urban diversity is preferable to suburban or village life. Our empirical research is necessarily confined to the here and now, and to phenomena that vary from place to place. But the evidence suggests that these disorders are not experienced differentially, that people agree on the extent of the problems they face in their communities, and that major economic, social, and lifestyle divisions in urban areas are not reflected in real differences over appropriate levels of order.

DISORDER AND COMMON CRIME

This book is not about common crime—most disorders do not fall clearly into that category. There has been a great deal of research on "garden-variety crime"—murder, rape, robbery, burglary, and the like—and hundreds of studies document how levels of crime vary from place to place. These studies link levels of crime in a given area to virtually everything. There seems to be no social handicap or environmental pathology that is not correlated with crime rates for cities, neighborhoods, or blocks, including such diverse factors as average building height, the tuberculosis rate, air pollution levels, and distance from the downtown area. From the opposite perspective, some research has also examined the impact of crime on other neighborhood problems. In these studies crime is treated as the causal variable, one that has consequences for individuals and neighborhoods. For example, high rates of crime are related to inner-city depopulation, declining property values, and high expenditures on the police. We will take a similar perspective on disorder, focusing on its consequences.

Our concern with common crime is limited to whether disorder is a cause of it. As we shall see, neighborhood levels of disorder are closely related to crime rates, to fear of crime, and the belief that serious crime is a neighborhood problem. This relationship could reflect the fact that the link between crime and disorder is a causal one, or that both are dependent upon some third set of factors (such as poverty or neighborhood instability). In an important article that appeared in *The Atlantic Monthly*, academic policing experts James Q. Wilson and George Kelling (1982) maintained that disorder actually spawns serious crime. They alluded to a sequence in which unchecked rule-breaking invites petty plundering and even more serious street crime and theft. However, the precise relationship between crime and disorder remains unclear. It is an important question, for research has not identified many neighborhoods that are high in disorder but low in crime; whatever the link between the two is, it is powerful.

According to Wilson and Kelling, disorder undermines the processes by which communities ordinarily maintain social control. Where disorder problems are frequent and no one takes responsibility for unruly behavior in public places, the sense of "territoriality" among residents shrinks to include only their own households; meanwhile, untended property is fair game for plunder or destruction. Further, a neighborhood's reputation for tolerating disorder invites outside troublemakers. Criminals are attracted to such areas because they offer opportunities for crime. Areas that tolerate (or cannot effectively counter) rowdy taverns, sex and drug-oriented paraphernalia shops, public drinking, prostitution, and similar disorders, will almost certainly be plagued by crime. Where disorder is common and surveillance capacities are minimal, criminals will feel their chances of being identified are low, and may be confident that no one will intervene in their affairs. Gambling and drinking lead to robberies and fights; prostitution and drug sales attract those who prey upon the consumers of vice. Wilson and Kelling suspect that a concentration of supposedly "victimless" disorders can soon flood an area with serious, victimizing crime.

We will reexamine Wilson and Kelling's argument in the light of data on levels of disorder and crime in 40 urban neighborhoods, and will focus on the consequences of both crime and disorder on fear of crime, community stability, and the ability of neighborhood residents to do things to protect themselves and their families. We will also document our finding that the effects of disorder on community morale and cohesion are independent of the effects of crime, and that both make a difference. This conclusion provides a rationale for focusing new resources on problems of disorder, for it can no longer be taken for granted that "more cops" and other standard responses to crime problems will deal with disorder as well.

DISORDER AND COMMUNITY CHANGE

One of our major concerns is the impact of disorder upon neighborhood decline. Most neighborhoods are stable social systems; which is why they are identifiable as "neighborhoods," with names that serve as useful labels, sometimes for generations. Their present condition generally resembles their past. At various times this stability may be threatened, but old patterns persist. Analytic models of such stable systems feature "negative feedback loops," or mechanisms which react to destabilizing events, set things right, retard change, and keep most problems within bounds. In residential neighborhoods, these feedback mechanisms can include both unconscious and conscious efforts at community renewal. Through individual initiatives and collective action, residents of stable areas find ways to fight unwanted change and preserve their community's character.

The unconscious forces largely reflect the housing market. Numerous and uncoordinated efforts by property owners to rehabilitate and upgrade their buildings can counter decay. Conscious action may be inspired government and police programs and community organizations. In stable neighborhoods, an emergent disorder problem—say, the appearance of after-hours drinking in the alley behind a tavern—would swiftly disappear as these feedback mechanisms exerted their influence. Residents would demand police action, meet with the tavern owner and perhaps threaten to challenge his liquor license, organize teams to drive through the alley with their headlights set high, spotlight the alley from their backyards, and even march (as we saw at the beginning of the chapter) to draw attention to their cause.

"Stability" does not mean that things remain the same, of course. Dynamic social systems never rest. Even in places which on the surface appear tranquil, families move away, buildings age, and macro-economic forces continually affect the price of housing. However, if approximately the same number of people move in as move out, and if the new arrivals resemble those who left, the area can be counted as stable. Areas remain stable when the housing stock is continually repaired and renewed, and when people can sell and buy or rent homes there at prices that are appropriate to the quality of the structures and the social class of the area's residents. "Stability" means that the neighborhood reproduces itself as a social system.

However, dramatic changes can ensue when the process of neighborhood renewal is disrupted. Numerous factors can trigger that disruption, including large-scale construction and demolition projects undertaken by local governments; disinvestment by mortgage lending institutions; block-busting efforts by real-estate entrepreneurs who buy homes cheaply from fleeing whites, and resell them dearly to newcomers desperate for good housing; demagogic politicians capitalizing on the racial fears which fuel "white flight"; and the impact of regional and national economic forces on interest rates and local employment (see Skogan, 1986b). Unstable systems lack steering mechanisms capable of making mid-course corrections. When stabilizing mechanisms fail, other forces can be loosed which *accelerate* further changes rather than slowing them down. One problem leads to another. Systems characterized by this kind of "positive feedback" can change rapidly. The changes do not necessarily increase crime or lower the quality of life in those areas. Neighborhoods undergoing rapid gentrification or extensive upgrading of housing are both examples of destabilized systems that improve rapidly once they pass a critical threshold of investment by early "pioneers." However, when they go wrong, neighborhoods can decline quickly, and as we shall see, disorder can play an important, independent role in stimulating this kind of urban decline.

Once a community slips into the cycle of decline, feedback processes rapidly take control. The problems that emerge can include more serious forms of disorder, as well as escalating crime—consequences that further undermine the community's capacity to deal with its problems.

For residents, disorder and crime lead first of all to withdrawal from the community. Daily experience with disorderly conditions creates anxiety; the prospect heightens fear. When communities finally become unpleasant to live in, and encounters leave people feeling uneasy and unsafe, many residents will try to leave (Smith, 1988). Studies indicate that neighborhood crime problems are strongly related to residential dissatisfaction and the desire to move (Kasl and Harburg, 1972; Droettboom et al., 1971). However, moving is selective. Families and members of the middle class tend to leave first, often to be replaced by unattached and transient individuals (Stark, 1987; Frey, 1980; Duncan and Newman, 1976). Those who cannot leave physically, withdraw psychologically, finding friends elsewhere or simply isolating themselves (Kidd and Chayet, 1984). Such withdrawal tends to reduce the supervision of youths, undermines any general sense of mutual responsibility among area residents, and weakens informal social control. Withdrawal also undermines participation in neighborhood affairs, presaging a general decline in the community's organizational and political capacity. More, it contributes to the deterioration of local housing and business conditions, neighborhood elements that have already been affected by population change. Fewer people will want to shop or live in areas stigmatized by visible signs of disorder; these problems feed upon themselves, and neighborhoods spiral deeper into decline. Leo Schuerman and Solomon Kobrin (1986), sociologists at the University of Southern California, have tracked communities in Los Angeles over a 20-year period; they find that, in the worst areas, crime has shifted from being an effect of social and economic conditions to being a cause of those conditions as well.

The population drops precipitously in areas on the edge of collapse. Street prostitutes move on, for the trade depends on customers feeling they can cruise safely. Uncollected litter blows in the wind. In cold weather, men gather around fires in trash cans. Unattached males, the homeless, and the aimless live in seedy residential hotels and flophouses, or squat in boarded-up buildings. Taverns are the only commercial establishments open after dark. Abandoned buildings serve as "shooting galleries" where drugs are distributed and used. Vacant lots are filled with the rubble of claw-out demolition. Residential and commercial buildings stand scarred by arson, and where they burn the city develops a hollow core, These areas have reached the bottom of the cycle of decline, and may no longer be recognizable as neighborhoods.

DEALING WITH DISORDER

Although disorder may seem almost as unpredictable and uncontrolled as the weather, there is hope that we can do something about it. Three long chapters in this book examine ways of dealing with disorder. Some of these rely on police, and in Chapter 5 we examine special neighborhood-policing programs in Houston and in Newark, New Jersey. Community organizations are another important means for tackling disorder. Chapter 6 describes such projects in Chicago and Minneapolis, and considers what they tell us about the advantages and disadvantages of relying on voluntary efforts. Chapter 7 explores community economic development strategies for dealing with disorder problems. In these chapters we will point to some successes, but will also acknowledge some clear failures and try to learn from them as well.

Policing Disorder. Wilson and Kelling suggested that police agencies should identify areas in jeopardy—places that are "deteriorating but not unreclaimable"—and assign police officers to those areas to support local efforts to control disorder. This would contrast with the usual practice in American cities, which is to pour police resources into traditional crime-fighting activities in the highest-crime areas. Wilson and Kelling believe the worst areas are beyond salvation, and they appear to call for a kind of "triage" which condemns some areas to the urban scrap heap. However, our review includes policing programs that enjoyed some success in areas that were in fairly bad shape, so it may be too soon to say which areas are beyond salvation.

Rather than calling only for more traditional policing in worthwhile areas, Wilson and Kelling advocate that police take the initiative in targeting and counteracting disorder in accordance with what they call "communal needs." However, they do not spell out just how the police could know what various neighborhoods want in the way of order. In the absence of a guiding legal code to enforce in traditional fashion, police would have to develop ways of discovering the problems and priorities of local residents. As many of the concerns of neighborhood residents would involve events and conditions not clearly within the purview of the criminal law, this would inevitably lead the police into uncharted territory, where their training and experience would not offer them much of a guide to action. In the course of maintaining order, it would also call for them to make important discretionary decisions. Wilson(1968) himself has spelled out how efforts by police to maintain order can become a source of racial and class discrimination, when the definition of who is "orderly" lies largely in the hands of the police.

It is the nature of disorder that many problems fall outside the traditional police mandate, but an accumulating mound of evidence from research on police since about 1980 (summarized by Sherman, 1986, and Skolnick and Bayley, 1988) suggests that there *are* strategies that can bring police closer to the people. Collectively known as "Community Policing," these strategies include foot patrol, team policing, administrative decentralization to local storefront offices, and other efforts to build two-way communication into neighborhood police work. When they succeed, such programs function in two ways: they open informal channels for the flow of information and demands for action from the people to the police, *and* they facilitate police action on that basis. These programs differ from traditional police community-relations units. In the main, community relations bureaus have been concerned with education efforts in schools, with representing departments in meetings, fielding questions, and engaging in public relations efforts. Community Policing is a line rather than a staff responsibility; unlike traditional bureaus, the officers involved in community policing have the capacity to respond in significant ways to neighborhood problems. Also, reflecting our concern with disorder, effective Community Policing requires that this information flow and action be broadly focused, and not just "crime"-oriented.

The several innovative Community Policing projects we examined in Houston and Newark involved foot patrol, neighborhood storefront offices, community organizing by police officers, and local newsletters. These projects were evaluated by a team from the Police Foundation and Northwestern University, which found good evidence that Community Policing can significantly reduce disorder. The programs were highly visible and very well received. Compared to similar areas where no new programs were set in motion, residents reported lower levels of social and physical disorder, less fear of crime, and greater confidence in the police. In Newark, Community Policing could be contrasted with a traditional enforcement program aimed at suppressing street disorder. Aggressive street sweeps, roadblocks, foot patrol, and crackdowns on disorder on mass transit also reduced street disorder there, but unlike Community Policing, they had no additional benefits.

However, there was also disturbing evidence that the benefits of Community Policing were largely reserved for white and better-off residents of the target communities. Evaluations indicate that they had knowledge of the programs and participated in them, but that minorities and the poor did not. Thus, most of the desirable results were confined to one segment of the community. This evident "class bias" could be traced to the way in which Community Policing activities were organized. In order to move quickly, police in most of the areas allied themselves with existing community organizations, often finding it easier to work with homeowners in the better parts of the target neighborhoods. The consequent unequal distribution of benefits goes against some of the assumptions of Community Policing. It can be risky for police to open themselves to "input" in communities that are diverse, for it appears that when police move beyond enforcing the criminal code, and become involved in negotiating the character of local order with other community elements, policing becomes a more overtly political process.

Community Organizations and Disorder. During the past decade there has been a great deal of interest in remobilizing communities to deal with disorder and crime on their own. An increase in disorder and crime reflects the declining strength of informal control in urban neighborhoods that are caught in the cycle of decline; hence, the logic goes, efforts to reinvigorate informal control mechanisms may reverse the trend to disorder. While there may be other means of doing this (by attacking unemployment for example, or upgrading the schools), organized community groups have emerged as our primary hope for reshaping the destiny of threatened urban neighborhoods.

Dan Lewis, Jane Grant, and Dennis Rosenbaum (1988), crime researchers at Northwestern University, have summarized the theory behind community-based strategies for reversing neighborhood decline. They found that organizations typically attempt to control disorder and crime through activities that make people aware of opportunities to join in crime prevention activities, and that stimulate actual participaiton in them; that enhance feelings of efficacy about individual and collective action, and also increase personal responsibility for these actions; that stimulate actions to regulate social behavior in the neighborhood by promoting feelings of "territoriality" and a willingness to intervene in suspicious circumstances; that act to prevent victimization via individual and household crime prevention efforts; and that enhance neighboring, social interaction, and mutual helpfulness.

Community organizers have devised a number of tactics to promote these ends, including inspirational meetings, block-watch groups, neighborhood patrols, property marking, home security surveys, escort services for the elderly, educational programs, leafletting, and marches to "take back the night." The monumental problems involved in making such programs work are detailed in Chapter 6, where we examine two efforts to mobilize communities in Chicago and Minneapolis to tackle neighborhood problems. The Chicago project involved established, successful, professionally staffed community organizations that had previously focused on housing, land use, and community economic development. The Ford Foundation sought to gauge the effects of turning the expertise of such groups to the problems of crime and disorder, and the Lewis, Grant, and Rosenbaum team evaluated their success in doing so. In contrast, the city of Minneapolis attempted to create new block clubs in previously unorganized areas. While plainly a more problematic venture, it was perhaps more likely to benefit disenfranchised neighborhoods. Professional organizers spent two years building networks of block clubs in 21 target areas, while a research team from the Police Foundation and the Minnesota Crime Prevention Center evaluated their efforts.

Unfortunately, neither of these programs showed much success. In Chicago, local organizing efforts actually *increased* fear of crime. In every case, most residents of the target communities were aware of the programs, and a significant number were involved in activities similar to those described above; but this awareness and involvement had no measurable effects. The evaluations concluded that community-based programs are very difficult to launch in low-income, heterogeneous, high-turnover, high-crime neighborhoods. Whether the programs were self-initiated or fostered by outside agencies, it seems that the more these programs were needed, the less successful they were. This was true even though the organizing *effort* was disproportionately dirrected toward neighborhoods in need. Our analysis of the Chicago and

Minneapolis projects challenges some of the underlying assumptions of the community-based approach to controlling disorder and crime. As happened with some of the policing projects, there was evidence that those neighborhood residents who were better off were more likely to gather whatever benefits the programs were able to deliver.

Will Anything Work? While much of this book could appear to be yet another "nothing works" report on social policy, this would be inaccurate with respect to Community Policing. There is no doubt, however, that I am skeptical of traditional community approaches to controlling disorder. The concluding chapter extends the policy net somewhat more widely, and describes other promising ways of tackling disorder; these include developmental strategies that could empower communities to regain control over local conditions, and environmental design tactics that could yield smaller but significant victories over particular kinds of disorder. But while they appear promising, these approaches remain untested. And if one message can be drawn from evaluations of policing and community organizing programs described in this book, it is that well-meaning programs may not work, and may even have unwanted consequences. It seems as if one of the "iron laws" of policy evaluation is that, the more we know about a program, the less confidence we have in it. This should not be a surprise, since American public policy tends to be formulated and applied in a context that ensures that most of it will have only a marginal effect on significant problems. There are no "silver bullets" in social policy because (a theme we will take up in Chapter 7) the political system deflects them, the social system rejects them, and the legal system protects us against them. Our nation's cultural and political diversity, coupled with its strong orientation toward individual rights rather than collective responsibilities, should deter us from expecting too much in the way of engineered social change. Even so, the programs we examine here, while not all successful, do merit serious consideration.

A BRIEF LOOK AT THE DATA

The Surveys. Parts of Chapter 2 and all of Chapters 3–6 rely heavily on surveys of selected urban neighborhoods. Most research on crime-related neighborhood problems has employed official offense or arrest data and census figures for blocks or census tracts. However, these statistics greatly underrepresent and somewhat distort the true distribution of many types of crimes, and police records are totally inadequate for helping us understand disorder problems, since such problems by their nature largely escape formal action.

To counteract this problem, most of our research is based on interviews with city dwellers. The data utilized in Chapters 2–4 represent the combined results of surveys of 40 residential neighborhoods; they were conducted as part of five different studies of neighborhood crime problems between 1977 and 1983. Such surveys help overcome the limitations of police figures on crime, since the interviewers went directly to people's doorsteps and inquired about their victimization experiences. They were also asked about the extent of various forms of disorder in their immediate area, as well as their satisfaction with the neighborhood; whether they intended to move; their fear of crime; and other questions directly related to theories about neighborhood stability and change. Slightly under 13,000 adults were interviewed in all.

The responses were collated to produce statistics at a neighborhood level. While measures of important neighborhood factors were not exactly comparable, they were assembled for most of the 40 areas. The appendix describes how the statistics were combined to form neighborhood measures, and also describes the 40 neighborhoods surveyed. They were diverse with respect to race and class, and the extent to which they were troubled by disorder and crime. Four of the six cities studied—Chicago, Philadelphia, San Francisco, and Newark, New Jersey—are Northern industrial cities marked by racial transition, declining populations, and shifting economic fortunes. Two others—Atlanta and Houston—represent the Southeastern and Southwestern cities that prospered and grew during the 1970s. The data are limited by their emphasis on inner cities. Although suburbs are not immune from disorder— most big cities in the East, Midwest, and Mid-Atlantic regions have old, close-in suburbs facing similar problems—the emphasis in the data is on inner cities. This book also concerns itself exclusively with residential neighborhoods; it does not deal with the issue of disorder in declining or rebounding downtowns or in nightclub districts; and it is not about subways. However, there were no strong city-specific patterns in the areas examined here. They differed mainly with respect to the level of disorder—with

Newark often coming out worst—but they did not differ with regard to how disorder and crime were related to social, economic, or environmental factors. Thus, it seems likely that the patterns identified here would apply to other big cities as well.

Chapters 5 and 6 are based on surveys of selected neighborhoods in Chicago, Minneapolis, Houston, and Newark. These surveys were fielded to help evaluate special policing programs and community-organizing efforts. In each city, neighborhood residents were interviewed both before the projects began and after they had been in operation for some time. Each evaluation involved program target areas and sets of matched comparison neighborhoods. No new programs or activities were undertaken in the comparison areas, in order to provide benchmarks against which to compare changes over time in the program areas. The programs all involved several organizing or policing tactics, and between them they provide rigorous tests of the viability of such efforts for intervening in the process of urban decline.

Field Observations and Interviews. Chapter 2 makes extensive use of observations and interviews by field researchers working in 10 of the 40 study neighborhoods. These 10 neighborhoods (4 in Chicago, 3 in Philadelphia, and 3 in San Francisco) were canvassed as part of a Northwestern University study of how individuals and community organizations react to crime problems. The site observers noted conditions and events in the study neighborhoods over a one-year period, and conducted hundreds of unstructured interviews with community residents, organization leaders, merchants, police officers, and local officials. This field research was completed just before surveys were conducted in the neighborhoods. The teams recorded some 10,000 pages of field notes; they are the source for the quotes and observations concerning disorderly conditions.

2

Disorder and Neighborhood Life

What is disorder and what are its implications for neighborhood decline? Visible social disorder provides direct, behavioral evidence of community disorganization, and the most highly-ranked neighborhood problems fell into this category. Survey respondents ranked public drinking highest, followed closely by loitering youths, and reports of drug use. There was considerable variation, of course; in some areas they were not regarded as problems at all, while elsewhere they were ranked as very serious. Problems with noisy neighbors were rated less highly, and various aspects of street life, including panhandling and harassment, were considered minor annoyances everywhere. While very few people thought panhandling was a major problem in their area, it was strongly linked with concern about public drinking; lounging drunks, and being solicited for small change, turn up as problems in the same places. Neighborhood concern about street prostitution and sexually-oriented enterprises varied considerably, ranking low in most places but toward the top in a few. These are problems that neighborhoods either do or do not have, and since those that do are quite different from the others, they are considered as a separate cluster of problems.

Public Drinking

Across the 40 study neighborhoods, the most highly-rated form
of disorder was public drinking. Complaints about drinking typically involved either groups of young people or "skid row" vagrants. None of the study areas included a traditional skid row, yet
in some of them many residents rated "people drinking in public
places, like on corners or in the streets" as a big problem.

A great deal of public drinking takes place in and around parks
nestled in residential areas. The problems this creates were described by an informant in the Sheffield neighborhood of Chicago.

> I live right on Lakewood, and this playlot is across the street.
> We have a number of teenage guys, and they drink out
> there, especially during the warmer weather. They park in
> their cars and vans; they drink; we call the police. . . . The
> police come, and do nothing at all. How do you keep that
> playground free for the little kids? [Sheffield, Chicago]

One of the things I learned at a public hearing at which park
officials announced their plans for the construction of a neighborhood playlot was how threatening a park can be to a neighborhood. Everyone who came was against the idea. Parks are places
that no one controls; people you do not know come into the
neighborhood to use them; youths drink and use drugs there; it is
difficult to find legitimate reasons or the means to push undesirables out; you cannot protect or control your own kids there. In
disorderly neighborhoods, parks are places you keep your children out of.

Businesses along the arterial highways on the edges of neigh-
borhoods can also create a great deal of trouble for area residents.
Customers use their parking places, and drop litter on their lawns.
In addition, drinkers also gather on commercial strips, often in
front of liquor stores and taverns. This was a big problem in the
Mission district of San Francisco.

> One problem is that there are bars with drunks hanging
> around on the sidewalks and doorways. That bothers
> merchants who have businesses around them. Women
> shoppers aren't going to go plowing through
> down-at-the-heel, scruffy-looking individuals who are
> drunks making cracks at them. They don't block the

sidewalks, but it is a deterrent for shoppers. [The Mission, San Francisco]

The wino types present a problem. You find them smashing bottles on the front steps of houses. Or they are pissing in doorways and stuff like that. They are pretty obnoxious. [The Mission, San Francisco]

Cities traditionally have tolerated public drinking on the fringes of downtown, where drinking coexists with liquor stores, flophouses, rescue missions, and other well-known features of skid row life. This segregation spares most city dwellers from the problems associated with vagrant drinking, including panhandling, public urination, and the sight of disreputable-looking people rummaging through trash cans and sleeping in doorways. However, many of these areas appear to be on the way out. They stand in the way of downtown expansion, offer cheap land for urban renewal and parking lots, and are being gentrified into fashionable bohemian quarters (Miller, 1982; Lee, 1980; Ward, 1975). Such well-known tourist destinations as Larimar Square in Denver and Old Town Sacramento were notorious Skid Rows; Chicago's largest skid row is now a glittering middle-class housing complex. While there always is casual outdoor drinking by neighborhood residents, Ward and others speculate that people who frequented skid rows now have dispersed to scattered sites in many cities. There they are more visible—and upsetting—to residents of the areas upon which they descend.

Corner Gangs

Problems with bands of loitering youths tied in over-all importance with public drinking, and presented the most highly ranked problem in a few areas. The Philadelphia term for them is "corner gangs," a frequent reference in the notes of field observers there. Corner gangs range from casual groupings engaging in a bit of drinking and social conversation to organized fighting squads.

The least threatening corner groups are just a nuisance. They are young, bored, and restless.

[Observer: What about the gang hanging out in front of the drugstore?] As far as I know they have no name. They are neighborhood kids and they sometimes make a nuisance of themselves. Actually they stand there because they have no place else to go. . . . Corner groups stand on corners because there aren't enough places for them to go in a high-density area. They are young, 12 to 15 years old, and have nothing to do. [South Philadelphia]

Older, rowdier corner gangs seem more threatening. Gangs like this were a highly visible problem in West Philadelphia.

[Observer: Are there areas you would avoid because of danger?] 52nd street from about Market to Pine or Spruce, you won't catch me there by myself. . . . Because of the crowds hanging on the corners. There's always men hanging out on those corners. And the language coming out of there . . . ahhh. And then the smoking and drinking. They're either drinking or smoking dope. [What ought to be done?] Put the cops back on the streets walking. Foot patrols. And, don't allow loitering on the corners or outside of places where people have to go in and out. Public places—post offices, stores, restaurants—all of these are places where you see people hanging out and it shouldn't be. [West Philadelphia]

Corner gangs establish their territorial dominance by testing the fringes of the normative order; they control areas where they can cow residents into putting up with their activities.

Sometimes I walk out of my house and start to try to walk down the street, and a gang will cross the street and try to scare me and my mother. A gang used to sit and drink beer and smoke pot in front of our stairs. My mom used to come out and tell them to get off; they would, and then when she would go into the house they'd come back, sit back down, and look at us. Actually we're afraid to walk around in the neighborhood after it gets dark. I stay right in front of the house where my parents can see me. [Wicker Park, Chicago]

Just when a group constitutes a corner gang, and when it poses a disorder problem, are matters of judgment. These groups are troublesome to the community when they persist in activities that are annoying or threatening activities, as is the case when their presence is combined with drinking, drug use, and harassment of passers-by. Police find it difficult to deal with simple ''corner loungers'' and those they cannot catch with contraband. Mostly, policing of congregating youths consists of driving by, rolling down the window, and telling them to move along. Not surprisingly, they reassemble easily, and often are there the next night as well.

Not all gang activity necessarily threatens community residents. Gangs have traditionally played a role in protecting their neighborhood ''turf'' against encroachment by near-by ethnic and racial groups. Among our 40 study neighborhoods, this role was taken most clearly by white corner gangs in South Philadelphia. This area, dominated by blue-collar white ethnics, is rimmed by black neighborhoods and dotted with enclaves of blacks in public housing projects. Racial boundaries in South Philadelphia were patrolled by white youths who kept a careful eye on anyone crossing them.

> [Observer: Are there any dangerous, unsafe areas in South Philadelphia?] What you have here are black and white areas. There are certain parts—white neighborhoods—where blacks don't go. There are other areas where whites won't go. There are also neutral corridors which are used by both. You are safe as long as you stay in your area . . . [How do you get this clear-cut division?] There is an all-white gang called ''The Counts.'' They have the blessing and support of their parents and of their community. The job of this gang is to keep the blacks out of the area. . . . The Counts are responsible for most gang killings in the area. . . . This gang is as close to a teen-age vigilante group as one can get. It is a fairly active group as they keep standing on street corners, and if anything comes up, the word goes out that the gang is moving into action. They will strike back against the blacks no matter who the culprit is. When there is trouble, they assume it's the blacks. There is always a show of strength as a response to crime. [South Philadelphia]

Clearly, for white residents of South Philadelphia, these gangs are not ''disorderly'' at all. Rather, they are an unofficial, extralegal, yet institutionalized arm of prominent parts of the community. They are fighting a rearguard action against neighborhood ethnic succession, adding muscle to more genteel mechanisms for maintaining area stability—such as discrimination in the housing market. As this book was being written, a ''turf-maintenance'' murder in the Bensonhurst area of New York City brought new attention to the role of youth gangs in maintaining clear racial boundaries between neighborhoods. While that incident and South Philadelphia's Counts lie at the extreme, we shall see at several points in this book where vigilance easily translates into racial divisiveness and threats of vigilante action, in places where problems of disorder and crime appear to overlap with threatening racial change.

Street Harassment

Street harassment is intimately linked to the problem of loitering bands of youths, although it is less frequently cited as a major neighborhood problem. In overt as well as subtle ways, corner gangs exercise control over legitimate users of the streets and sidewalks. When their activities fall short of criminal assault or robbery we class them as "disorderly," but for their targets this may be too subtle a distinction.

Two major victims of street harassment are women and the elderly. Women report street encounters involving catcalls, lewd comments, obscene gestures, and other forms of harassment. These uninvited intimacies are always annoying, and often offensive and embarrassing. They can lead their victims to avoid areas or activities that expose them to such "street remarks" (Gardner, 1980). Street harassment was associated with public drinking in The Mission.

> For a couple of ladies at the meeting, their priority was prostitution, drug addicts and winos, and people who just hang around on corners yelling obscenities at women. You know, like "hey, baby" and all that. These ladies didn't dig it, these guys hanging aroud on the corners. [The Mission, San Francisco]

Carol Gardner has focused attention on such forms of harassment, which involve a "breach of the norm of civil inattention between unacquainted persons." Individually, these breaches can seem to be relatively minor, as in Sheffield:

> Mostly it was just people that were annoying, people being obnoxious. But nothing serious. You know . . . when a babe

gets off the El to go home she doesn't want some drunk making comments to her. [Sheffield, Chicago]

But although many of these encounters are limited to verbal innuendo, the context within which they take place and the threat they communicate have considerable cumulative effects. Other forms of harassment can escalate beyond these street remarks, to overt physical harassment—what Andra Medea and Kathleen Thompson (1974) dubbed "little rapes."

> I was walking down 24th over there and there were five boys walking down the street towards me. They were spread out the length of the sidewalk so I had to walk through them. I thought maybe I should walk across the street or something but I figured that would just attract their attention, so I just kept walking. Well, they separated when I walked past but one of them all of a sudden reached out and grabbed my breast. [The Mission, San Francisco]

It is easy to harass the elderly. Rifai (1976) reports that in Portland a large porportion of victimizations recalled by the elderly involved nonphysical, verbal harassment by teenagers. In The Mission,

> There are always 13 and 14-year-olds pretending to be thugs. There will be a group blocking the street, and an old lady will walk around them. She probably has arthritis, which makes it hard for her to handle the curb, but she has to endure the indignity of it as well as the pain so that she can get around those kids without getting into any trouble. [The Mission, San Francisco]

The elderly also were targets of incidents in South Philadelphia.

> Old ladies who come to the [community] center were harassed by kids out on the street but couldn't call us for help, so we gave them whistles. They found the whistle was better than a freon horn—easier to handle. The elderly felt the need for that. This is an area where people express a great deal of anxiety. [South Philadelphia]

The elderly are very vulnerable to street crime, which they reasonably fear in areas where they are fair game for harassment. It is not only their money they may lose; they can easily suffer an injury (like a broken hip) from which they may not recover. Surveys reveal that the elderly are by far the most fearful of crime even though as a group they are the least likely to be victimized. One reason may be their sensitivity to the threat implied by lower-level street disorder, when it is aimed at them.

Other forms of street harassment are much more pointed, and not at all subtle. One function of verbal harassment is to reinforce the racial balance of power in neighborhoods and to maintain boundaries between groups. Street harassment tells people where they do not belong. It can be a tool in the exercise of power; where groups feel dominant, they can act to maintain their status through threats and intimidation. Threats of violence were used to define neighborhood racial boundaries in South Philadelphia.

> [Observer: Do you have problems like racial tensions in the community?] Yes. You have all ethnics here. It's just ready to start. As soon as it gets warmer, baseball bats are starting to be used and there is trouble. Now that the school year is almost over, at least the school buses won't have trouble, with white kids hollering at them and throwing things, but now they will all be out there. Actually, it's not just kids, you have grown-ups too, hollering and screaming and there is a confrontation. The color depends on where you travel. [South Philadelphia]

Another example of harassment linked to ethnic turnover was reported by an older white male from the Wicker Park neighborhood in Chicago. Wicker Park was a traditionally Polish working-class community which in the years immediately preceeding our interviews experienced a large influx of blacks and Hispanics. In time, Hispanics—principally Puerto Ricans—became the dominant group in the area.

> No place in this area is safe, really. We used to walk from here to St. Al's to church every day. We used to walk back and forth, you know. But not any more. These past four years we can't. We've had to take the bus to St. Stephens. [Observer: What is the problem between here and St. Al's?] Why, you get shouted at, and people throw things down at you. Its frightening. [Wicker Park, Chicago]

In another incident in Wicker Park, young men "feeling their oats" had a bit of fun while expressing their new dominance of the area.

> She works at night, for the telephone company, and comes home late. She used to ride the bus, but not anymore. Since the neighborhood has changed, she can't walk from the bus stop anymore. A woman who works with her now drives her home to the front door. She calls her husband from work before she leaves, to tell him when to expect her home. I asked her if anything ever happened to make her so fearful? One evening, she responded, after coming home from work in a car full of passengers, some young Puerto Ricans blocked the street and forced the car to stop, and then proceeded to rock the car. The passengers inside were quite helpless and frightened. [Wicker Park, Chicago].

Such confrontations can reshape important aspects of people's daily lives. Fearful of harassment, they drive rather than walk, avoid public transportation, and go out only with an escort when they can. In the surveys, personal precautions of this type were highly related to neighborhood levels of social disorder. They were also linked to perceptions that neighborhoods were in a decline, and to reports that residents wanted to move away.

Drugs

Another highly ranked problem in these neighborhoods was the sale and use of drugs. Drug-related rumors and the fears they stir up permeated many of the rougher study areas, and our field observers interviewed many people who had first-hand experiences to report.

> I came back home one night from work and parked my car outside in the back. I started to come toward my house, and I saw these boys sitting right behind my house. I went back to my car and watched them. They had the powder, the match, the needle. They lit the match and got it ready. They were just going to put it in a vein when I got out and came over and told them to get away. When they saw me they panicked and ran away. I don't want them doing that around here. They could be an influence on my boys. [West Philadelphia]

I have been seeing drug dealing going on for years. They
pull up in a car and one guy goes up the street and then
comes back and hands out little packages to all of them.
Then they take off. It's been going on for years. . . . Kids use
the church steps to smoke pot on. I usually know the kids
too, but I don't want to say anything. . . . I'm scared to
death to report anything. Never know but what they may
come back and get me for telling. [Visitacion Valley, San
Francisco]

Studies of drug distribution sites—"copping zones"—indicate
they are located in poorer parts of town, on busy arterial streets
where transit stops, bars, pool halls, and wherever general night-
time activity levels are high, and street dealing (and even drug use)
therefore is less conspicuous (Fields, 1984; Wiedman and Page,
1982; Hughes and Jaffe, 1971). No one feels especially responsible
for transitory areas like these, so the trade can be conducted without the resistance it might encounter in residential neighborhoods.
Users, and most dealers, tend to live nearby, and frequent the
areas on a regular basis. During the day they coexist easily with
shoppers and other passersby; when approached with the query,
"want some dope?" those who don't studiously ignore them.
Wiedman and Page report that peer and police pressure confined
to the hours of darkness most of the violent and bizarre behavior
that they saw associated with the drug business. In Fields' "weed-
slinging" (marijuana-selling) area, drug dealing was but one of
many illegal enterprises going on; the area was an open-air bazaar
where dealers and users were joined by youths buying and selling
stolen goods. They all drank and socialized in a festive way, to the
sound of loud portable cassette players. In other cities, certain
drug-dealing blocks operate like fast-food restaurants—drive-
through customers (some apparently from the suburbs) get curb-
side service, while the whole operation is guarded by young look-
outs at each end of the block. Near one of the study neighborhoods
(Chicago's Edgewater, where I live), the community's solution to
this problem was to demand that the phone company take out the
phone booth on the corner, so that suburbanites could not call in
advance to place their order. The phone company did so, and
cocaine dealing on that block dried up.

Rumors concerning drug sales and use in residential ares are
disturbing for a variety of reasons. People fear the crime which

they believe goes along with drug use. They know that some of the customers finance their purchases through burglary and theft. They also feel that drug users are unpredictable, threatening, and cannot be counted upon to even be rational criminals—they do crazy things, and are unnecessarily violent. Most of all, like this resident of South Philadelphia, they fear that their children will become involved:

> The young people need money for drugs. They will do something violent to get the money. There are also drug pushers here who hook the kids and make a fortune that way. There used to be one very rich pusher who lived here—he had a green Cadillac; his nickname was the Jolly Green Giant. It's like a trademark. When the kids saw the car they would run to meet him, as if it were an ice cream truck. [South Philadelphia]

> We have a pusher in my neighborhood—he comes right up my street, a regular huckster, no sense of shame. He is a young man who delivers vegetables from a truck. He also has drugs at the back of the truck. All the kids know him. He has a loudspeaker and you can hear him two blocks away. He specializes in selling pot to very small kids. [South Philadelphia]

Our informants were frightened and angry when drug dealers and users took over corners, parks, and other public places, closing them to respectable users while at the same time tempting the young and generating neighborhood crime.

> The most dangerous area in my community is around the park. Members of gangs spend their time there and there is a lot of drug pushing going on there. . . . It is very dangerous even in broad daylight. Not too long ago a friend of mine was almost shot because they thought he was a member of a gang. Another girl friend of mine was jumped by this dude because he mistook her for his wife. Man, all kinds of crazy things happen in this little park. [Wicker Park, Chicago]

> All those kids from the schools from around here came to this street because one of the biggest dealers was living here. Oh, we knew who it was. Those kids would come and sit

out on the stoops and check out all the houses. They'd sell
their drugs and smoke them and whatever else they do. You
know it was so bad you couldn't walk out on the street at
night. [The Mission, San Francisco]

Here we see again the problems presented by public places.
Ordinary citizens usually do not have legitimate grounds to intervene in events taking place in parks, and when drugs are involved
it is believed that there are special dangers in intervening. In a
disorganized and demoralized place like the Mission, out-of-
control kids even successfully challenged residents for control of
their front porches.

Noisy Neighbors

Some of the street life that is characteristic of disorderly neighborhoods involves significant criminal intent (for example, drug
sales). Other disorders (including street harassment) probably are
malevolent at least some of the time. Some simply reflect conflicts
over what James Q. Wilson (1968) dubbed "standards of right and
seemly conduct." People can have different views about the appropriate use of public space, as in these two examples:

The filthy streets—garbage everywhere! The youngsters sit
on the steps at all hours during the night smoking reefers.
The smell is so strong you can get high just passing by. They
also litter the sidewalk with greasy fish bones and french
fries and ketchup. Oh, it is terrible. Then there is also that
loud music that they play, right on your doorstep.
[Woodlawn, Chicago]

We have problems like the bongos. Some young Latino
bongo players have adopted Dolores Park as their practice
area. . . . The area around there is a middle income
residential area. You know—nice, well-kept homes—and the
people around there are complaining about the noise and
trying to get [the area organization] to drive them out of
there, but the bongo players think they're entitled, and
they've made a kind of power issue out of it. [The Mission,
San Francisco]

Another example of this is complaints about "noisy neighbors,"
which fell near the middle of our list of social disorders.

The kids were playing ball and bouncing the ball off our wall. Can you imagine what it's like trying to sleep with that noise? Bang. Bang. I was inside sleeping because I worked night shift that week. My father said, "OK, boys, that's enough." They got real mad and said, "He called me 'boy.'" [Logan, Philadelphia]

These confrontations can mirror lifestyle preferences. The conflict may be between intense users of public space—"stoop-sitting" families, or men repairing their cars at the curb—and those who prefer more private activity. Outsiders who do not know the rhythm of life in a community also can mistake the intensive use of public space for disorder. Where there is real conflict it can reflect the temporal rhythms of different workplaces. In cities, not everyone lives on the same schedule. Disputes over noise and loud parties often occur between families of 7:00 A.M. to 3:30 P.M. factory workers and 5:00 P.M. to midnight building janitors and food service workers. The latter often can be seen "hanging around" during the day, perhaps appearing shiftless and threatening to those whose lives follow a more traditional work schedule.

New Forms of Disorder

In the last few years a new problem has come to public attention: the disorderly appearance and activity of apparently homeless and seemingly mentally ill street people. In the heart of many great cities it is common to see people sleeping on hot-air grates or under layers of cardboard boxes; shopping-bag ladies carrying their wordly possessions; and men and women dressed in layers of dirty, tattered clothing scrounging through waste receptacles in search of cans and cigarette butts. Many who observe such highly visible street people infer that homelessness and mental illness go together. This makes them understandably edgy when they come across the mutterers, cursers, and ranters who wander along many downtown streets. Yet, studies of shelter residents indicate that homelessness is also a real economic phenomenon. The difference between these two assessments may be due to the fact that homeless women, children, and those who are desperately poor are much less visible than denizens of the street. However, the extent of mental illness among the homeless generates more disagreement than most other topics, for it lies at the heart of the politics of the issue. A recent study by sociologist Peter Rossi (1989) concluded that between one-quarter and one-third of homeless people suffer from chronic mental illness, a proportion much higher than may be found in the poor population as a whole. The surveys examined here, which were all completed by the mid-1980s, did not ask about these problems. Thus, our reliance on measures of what has been judged disorderly in the past does not address questions concerning the impact of these "new" social disorders, and of others yet to emerge.

COMMERCIAL SEX

Research in street prostitution and "adult entertainment" establishments has generally been confined to prominent red-light districts. These are typically located on the edge of the downtown, in lightly populated areas with a great deal of street traffic. They offer a range of opportunities for excitement, as they always have. Today's topless bars, film and video stalls, and live sex shows were yesterday's burlesque parlors and taxi-dance halls; yesterday's brothels now masquerade as massage parlors. Street-walking has changed a lot less (Symanski, 1981; Shumsky and Springer, 1981; Reckless, 1932). Historically, cities controlled the extent of the excitement through segregation. Brothels, burlesque, gambling, and late-hour drinking were condoned—with appropriate payoffs to police and public officials—in particular areas of town. Chicago's most prominent vice district, the Levee, was founded on the South Side when a coalition of Protestant revivalists and political reformers managed to drive these activities out of the heart of downtown. Even today, red-light districts are officially tolerated in a few cities; they include Boston's famous "Combat Zone," and "The Block" in Baltimore. Other unofficial but well-known red-light areas include San Francisco's Tenderloin, Chicago's Rush Street, and New York's Times Square.

Street prostitution also flourishes away from downtown, along busy arterial streets in poorer, transient, and heterogeneous areas, and there it becomes a disorder problem. Away from the red-light area, prostitutes rely on a distinctive dress and demeanor to advertise their availability; they frequently wear platform shoes and hot pants, and wave in friendly fashion at passing cars. Residents of neighborhoods behind the arterials are likely to encounter newly-acquainted couples transacting their business in parked cars, or in the vestibules and hallways of apartment buildings. They are particularly distraught when their children are exposed to the problem.

A closely-related problem arises when "legitimate" sexually-oriented businesses operate in residential areas—residents are unhappy about it. The most severely affected of our 40 study neighborhoods was the Mission in San Francisco, located just across Market Street from the Tenderloin. Residents frequently brought up its impact on their children:

> Why should it be in our neighborhood? Why don't they put it near their homes? . . . Children have to walk by on their way to school, and they see that sort of thing. Certainly it's not out in the open, but it's not too hard to peek in as you walk by. We don't want our children exposed to that sort of thing. [The Mission, San Francisco]

Since many sex-oriented enterprises are in fact legitimate businesses, their opponents cannot rely on the police to control their operation. It takes organization and considerable political savvy to bring that about:

> We talked to the bookstore and movie operators and told them we didn't appreciate their operation here and the element they draw to the neighborhood. And we've done what I guess you could call informational picketing or walk-bys. And we've gone to the owners of the property and asked them to sign agreements not to rent to such businesses. . . . Our real concern is that it lowers the level of the quality of life to have these sort of businesses around. They're gaudy and ugly and vulgar and they attract the sort of people who enjoy that sort of thing. [The Mission, San Francisco]

Residents of ten neighborhoods were asked about "pornographic movie theaters or bookstores, massage parlors, or topless bars," and in six others they were also quizzed about "adult theaters and bookstores." (The questions about adult entertainment establishments were included in the Houston surveys because I couldn't help noticing beer halls in several neighborhoods, with flashing neon signs announcing "Naked Girls Dance!") Adult bookstores, movies, and other sexually oriented businesses

were ranked as problems in the same neighborhoods where prostitution flourished. They are equivalent to the "vice resorts"
which accompanied prostitution in the past. In his study of the
location of brothels and streetwalkers in Chicago in the early
1920s, Walter Reckless (1926) found them alongside "saloons,
gambling-dens, fortune tellers, dime museums, and lady bar-
bers," and noted their particularly close correspondence with the
distribution of burlesque theaters. Adult entertainment continues
to be associated with other kinds of problems, as in West Philadelphia:

> There's a bar, the Foxy Lounge, on the corner. The people
> on Frazier Street are upset about it. They have go-go dancers
> half naked. Minors are being served—they're 13, 14, 15 years
> old. They get older kids to bring out the beer and give it to
> them. . . . And I heard there was dope sold there too. [West
> Philadelphia]

Street prostitution and sexually oriented businesses were not
among the most highly rated problems in our areas. An examination of disorder in these neighborhoods indicates that patterns of
street prostitution and the prevalence of commercial sex establishments are different from the others. These problems go together
distinctively; a few areas scored high on both, while most reported
having few problems with either. They also were not related to
other kinds of disorder. These problems did not bother the same
set of people who had experienced concern about the others; as a
result, this cluster of problems will be considered separately in the
following chapters.

PHYSICAL DECAY

Unlike social disorder—which often involves specific events or
activities—physical disorders are enduring, day-to-day aspects of a
neighborhood's environment. Some of these disorders are illegal,
but most are not. Legal disorders involve "perpetrators" rather
than "offenders," for many of them are simply acting in a busi-
nesslike way to maximize profits on lawful investments, and minimize the effort they put into preserving the commonweal. However, all disorders leave visible marks on the community, marks
that stigmatize it in the eyes of residents and outsiders alike.

We found considerable variation in the extent of decay. The study areas ranged from communities blotched by derelict or abandoned buildings and clawed-out vacant lots to heavily gentrified neighborhoods where aggregate housing values might rival the Gross National Product of some small nations. Everywhere, vandalism was the most highly ranked problem, followed closely by litter and trash, garbage handling, and junk-strewn vacant lots. Dog litter also was pervasive; no neighborhood gave it a low rating. Building abandonment was not much of a problem in some places, and fell near the bottom of the list overall, but there were also neighborhoods where abandoned buildings and junk-strewn vacant lots were the *most* highly rated problems.

Vandalism

Vandalism is a common fact of life in many neighborhoods, and indeed it was the most highly rated kind of disorder. Legal definitions of vandalism use words like "wanton," "willful," and "malicious" to describe the damage it entails. Individual offenses may be minor; the difficulty is that their effects persist and often accumulate. Vandals upset, dent, smash, slash, and spray-paint their targets, which may be street signs, vending machines, park facilities, schools, or businesses. Relatively little vandalism is directed at private homes. Even in highrise public housing, most vandalism is aimed at common space rather than at individual apartments (Mawby, 1984; Wilson, 1978). Unclaimed and impersonal space is the favored target of graffiti artists (Ley and Cybriwsky, 1974). In one survey, fully one-half of the vandalism involved parked cars (Chambers and Tombs, 1984). Schools, bus shelters, and other public facilities are also frequent targets. This damage may be the most enduring, for bureaucratic snarls often delay the repair of public facilities.

There has been more research on the perpetrators of vandalism than on any other form of disorder, probably because most offenders are young and relatively easy to reach through classroom questionnaires. Their own reports reveal that vandals have little parental supervision and are poor achievers in school. They typically get into various kinds of trouble and frequently associate with other trouble-makers. A great deal of vandalism is carried out by bands of youths. The fact that young vandals operate in groups suggests that they gain prestige among their peers by showing off and taking risks. Vandals come from poorer, high-density residential areas where there are many children, and they inflict most of their damage close to home (Mawby, 1984; Webb, 1984). (*See also* Gladstone, 1978; Wilson, 1978; Cohen, 1973.) They have diverse motives for selecting their targets. Some vandalism is *tactical* in origin; in Chicago's Sheffield, graffiti was often used by gangs to mark out their turf:

> [At a community meeting, someone asked] . . . if anyone knew anything about the "Born Angels," a new gang in the area. There is spray paint all over. They used to just do the sides of buildings, but now they have graduated to cars. You can see "B-A" all over. [Sheffield, Chicago]

Rival gangs vying for control of the contested turf often inscribe "obscene amendments" (Ley and Cybriwsky, 1979) to the marks of others, proclaiming their dominance. Graffiti also marks the borders of racially delineated neighborhoods. Ley and Cybriwsky (1974) report that graffiti that aimed racial epithets and obscenities at newcomers were common along "zones of tension" between diminishing white and growing black areas of Philadelphia, marking the spots where breeches were occurring in the walls between blacks and whites.

Damage that looks like vandalism can be a *tactical byproduct* of another crime, one which leaves a visible stain on the neighborhood. In Wicker Park,

> Auto burnings are a real problem. People steal cars and strip the tires, radio, etc., and burn the rest of it. They figure if they burn it the city will haul it away. We once found a Volvo lying on its side with gas poured out of the tank on the ground. We turned it right again and soaked it down, but the cops didn't take it away. Two hours later we got a call—someone had burned it. [Wicker Park, Chicago]

Vandalism also can be *vindictive* in nature. Some vandals seek revenge against their real or symbolic enemies or sources of frustration. The vindictive nature of some of these acts is suggested by studies of school vandalism, which find that overcrowded and deteriorating buildings, with obsolete facilities and equipment and low staff morale, are the most commonly damaged (Cohen, 1973). In the Woodlawn area of Chicago, one informant indicated that vindictive vandalism was "kind of a practice" because rents were just getting ridiculous, and a lot of people couldn't afford to pay that rent, especially when no repairs were being made and the service in the buildings was lousy anyway. She mentioned a building that used to be in real good repair. But what happened was done by the residents of the building. The landlord was going up on the rent and the residents were really upset about it because none of them could afford to pay for it. So when they had to move out of the building, they came back and just totally destroyed the building. They tore out all the electrical work, they broke all the windows in the building. The landlord? She guesses he just go tired of trying to fight them, and just gave up. [Woodlawn, Chicago]

Vandalism can be an expression of *intergenerational conflict.* Retaliatory vandalism (ranging from "trashing" lawns to setting fire to garages) is one way for youths to lash back at adults who complain about their behavior. This can happen anywhere, but in neighborhoods marked by racial or ethnic transition, younger residents often come from encroaching groups. As a result, perceptions of boisterous (or malicious) mischief on their part, and adult reactions to it, reflect lifestyle and cultural differences between older and newer residents of the area.

[Observer: That's a beautiful garden you have.] Yeah. Except they destroyed everything. Those little back———. They came in and tore up the chard and the potatoes. See that tree over there? It always has fruit. Well, those little black kids just come in and tore everything up. They are all kids, too! The other day I saw a little one about 13 or 14 and said, "why don't you ring the bell and ask me for some. I'd be glad to give you some." They just said, "you mother f—— whitey." Blah, blah. It makes me sick. [The Mission, San Francisco]

A final explanation for the spread of vandalism is that it is "infectious"—where it appears and is not quickly erased, its presence stimulates still more vandalism. The *contagion* theory of vandalism is widely acknowledged, as in West Philadelphia:

I asked at the corner bar how they kept their place so clean. They showed me. Inside behind the bar is a bucket of paint and brushes. As soon as the kids mark the outside, they

> come out with the paint and paint it over, right away. That's
> the only way. [West Philadelphia]

But even rapid repair does not always halt the assault, and some
finally give in:

> Like the house across the street. They had new siding on the
> building. But kids wrote all over it with paint. So they had it
> repainted, but they came right back and wrote on it again.
> So people feel defeated; it just doesn't pay to fix things up if
> it's going to be damaged the next day. [Wicker Park,
> Chicago]

Research suggests that even accidental damage or normal wear-
and-tear may stimulate vandalism if it is not repaired (Webb, 1984)
Apparently, visible disrepair undermines inhibitions people may
have against leaving their mark. The inhibtion level may vary by
neighborhood. Philip Zimbardo (1970) conducted an experiment
to test this proposition when he purposely "abandoned" similar
cars in New York City and near the Stanford University campus in
California. He found that the anonymity provided by New York
City encouraged the rapid destruction of the car after he initially
"spoiled" its identity by removing the license plates and leaving
the hood raised. However, the destruction of the other auto took
longer, and it was also necessary to "provide more extreme re-
leaser cues" (Zimbardo is a psychologist) by initially smashing it
up a bit. One consequence of the contagion effect is that publicity
about vandalism—even anti-vandalism campaigns—may have the
unwanted effect of encouraging even more of it (Whittingham,
1981; Cohen, 1973).

Dilapidation and Abandonment

The presence of abandoned buildings may be the most dramatic
indicator of a neighborhood's unhealthy condition. Abandonment
is a clear signal that in that area it is no longer worth the effort to
keep housing or businesses open. Neighbors fear the consequences of even low levels of abandonment, which are numerous.

An "abandoned" building is off the market; it is not just await-
ing sale. Rather, the heat and electricity have been cut off, it is not
being maintained, the property taxes are not being paid, and

sometimes the owner has officially relinquished title to the city or the mortgage holder. If the neighbors are lucky the building is securely boarded up, but sometimes it is put to disorderly uses.

Large-scale housing abandonment is a relatively new phenomenon in American cities. Until the mid-1950s, relatively few residential buildings were abandoned, and they were the most outmoded segment of the housing stock. Often they were without private baths or kitchen facilities, and through abandonment they dropped out of the housing market. However, there has been a tremendous increase in the abandonment of sound, modern buildings since then. The reasons are many, for the deterioration and abandonment of housing stock in America's central cities is intricately interwoven with a broad spectrum of urban problems.

Briefly, abandonment reflects the structural depression of central-city housing markets, especially those tied to Northern industrial "Rust Belt" economies. The flood of immigrants, first from Europe and then from the American South, that stretched the housing supply in those cities to the limits has now subsided. Population growth (which fuels demand) has recently been largely confined to the suburban ring. City-suburban class and racial segmentation has brought to inner cities a concentration of those who can least afford newly constructed units or support a housing rehabilitation market. This in turn discourages investments by landlords, banks, and insurance companies, who can often shift their capital to safer, more profitable locales. Finally, a number of federal policies—some explicitly concerned with housing, and others indirectly affecting the housing market—have made the situation worse. Government-sponsored FHA and VA mortgage loans stimulated suburban development after World War II, a move made possible by new, federally funded highways. Federal subsidies and tax policies favored new construction over rehabilitation. The depression of the housing market can reduce the true worth of aging inner-city buildings to below their insured value; as a result, burned as well as simply vacant buildings dot the urban landscape.

From a resident's point of view, abandoned buildings blight the neighborhood in several ways. First, they harbor decay:

> We have an abandoned house that's full of trash. It's falling apart, there are rats in the attic, they come out on the ground. I can't let my children go outside around my own block for fear they will be bitten. [West Philadelphia]

Tramps sleep in abandoned buildings, and squatters may move in more permanently:

> They get in there and use the house. What's to stop them?
> There's a bunch of them who sit up on the front porch of a
> vacant house, just up the street. They sit out there and drink
> wine. They play the radio and make all kinds of noise all
> hours of the night. They say all kinds of things to people.
> The poor woman in the house next to that is afraid to sit on
> her front porch. See, there she is now [pointing]. She's
> sitting on the back porch. That old couple never sits out on
> their front porch; they're afraid to do it. [West Philadelphia]

Frequently, empty buildings are heavily vandalized, for no one is protecting them or repairing the cumulative damage. An empty building can be stripped of valuable copper plumbing, electrical fixtures, and architectural ornamentation. The neighbors also fear it will be set afire:

> Chidren broke in and tore the wiring out. There was a party.
> I saw children in there with matches. There could be a fire
> and all the houses next to it could go up in flames. [Logan,
> Philadelphia]

Buildings do not have to be abandoned to become notorious as "shooting galleries" where drugs are sold and used, but empty buildings often acquire that reputation. Abandoned buildings also may serve as a hangout for local predators, and people are afraid to walk near them:

> The kids here are dangerous. Do you see this vacant
> building? The neighbors are asking the city to knock it
> down. It has been boarded up, but the black kids break in,
> hide in there, then at night they jump out and attack people
> on the street. [South Philadelphia]

Problems with severely dilapidated buildings may fall some-what short of abandonment, but reflect the same market forces:

> The landlords were doing nothing. We were fixing [the
> buildings] up for the damn landlords. So you would have to
> pay the rent, pay for the maintenance of the property, and
> paint it. This is what you had to do if you wanted to have a
> little decency in the house. Every time you fixed it up the

landlord would raise the rent. . . . The people tried to pressure the landlords to fix a toilet, to fix a window, and the slumlords just said to hell with it. They just rent out and collect the profits. . . . It gets worse and worse. Mobility in the area gets greater. [Wicker Park, Chicago]

The cumulative impact of dilapidation and abandonment will depend upon how many buildings stand deteriorating or empty. Like vandalism, abandonment may in part be self-generating. Two studies by the Department of Housing and Urban Development (HUD) during the 1970s indicated that abandonment is contagious. Scattered abandonment is bad enough, but concentrated abandonment speeds the withdrawal of investment capital and promotes the collapse of a neighborhood's housing market (Department of Housing and Urban Development, 1973a). While it may begin with the worst structures in an area, abandonment can undermine the attractiveness and profitability of sound buildings nearby. The tipping point appears to be low—better-off residents begin to move from an area, and potential investors become concerned, even when as few as 3 to 6 percent of buildings stand abandoned (Department of Housing and Urban Development, 1973b).

The extent of visible abandonment partly reflects local policy. Chicago moves fairly quickly (as municipalities go) to tear abandoned buildings down, so its worst-off neighborhoods have many junk-filled empty lots. On the other hand, Newark—a city with a high abandonment rate—long has pursued the strategy of boarding up rather than immediately tearing down abandoned buildings. Newark has done this because demand for housing by the poor remains high; the city hopes that future federal programs, and subsidized rents that poor people can afford, will make it possible to rehabilitate structures that now stand abandoned. Meanwhile, there are a large number of abandoned buildings all over the city, and during the early 1970s a substantial porportion of Newark's reported crime took place in or near them (Sternlieb and Burchell, 1973).

Rubbish

Other forms of physical disorder may undermine the morale of residents and signal that a neighborhood is out of control. Building deterioration and abandonment may be the most substantial sign of physical disorder, but in the 40 neighborhood surveys one of the most frequently cited problems was the widespread presence of litter and trash on streets, sidewalks, and alleys, and mounds of discarded appliances, torn mattresses, and other junk in yards and vacant lots. The manner in which residents dispose of their garbage—a related problem—was also identified as causing relatively high concern.

Problems of this sort present unusual difficulties, for they are an example of the "free rider problem." While every member of a community may enjoy the benefits that flow from the extra effort required to keep a neighborhood looking nice, there are few ill consequences for any individual who takes the easy route in disposing of debris—as long as everyone else does it the proper way. But of course they do not. The amount of debris that accumulates is a function both of how fast it is put down and how fast it is picked up. Like vandalism and abndonment, littering appears to be contagious. Observations of city blocks indicate that, controlling for other factors (including age—youths are by far the most frequent offenders), the presence of debris in an area seems to stimulate yet further "trashing" of the environment (Finnie, 1973). A large volume of trash strewn around a neighborhood partly reflects upon the level of city services, for it is obviously not being picked up; but if the pick-up effort is at a reasonable level, an accumulation of trash signals disorder problems. In West Philadelphia it was a sign that kids were out of control:

> The kids are destructive. At the park I brought over a large barrel with the word "trash" written on it. The kids just rolled it around. When I went back a few days later, it was gone. So I gave up. The kids are so destructive! Just the other day I caught a boy picking up bottles and smashing them on the street. [West Philadelphia]

As with vandalism, people who complained to the field interviewers about littering often described the problem in terms of the unseemly behavior of encroaching groups. In Wicker Park,

> The Puerto Ricans are dirty . . . they throw garbage out of their windows, they don't put trash into trash cans but throw it all over the alley, they don't keep up their property; it used to be a beautiful neighborhood, but it is all changed now. [Wicker Park, Chicago]

I was talking to [a friend] when I first met him, and he said
that the people in the Mission, who are mostly Latinos, have
a feeling that the Mission is a dirty place to live in so they go
on putting their garbage on the street without considering
the consequences of what they are doing. Like the building
across from here; everyone knows it is an eyesore. Kids
throw things out the window and they live there. Nobody
has ever gone to their parents to ask them to restrain their
kids. And they are throwing all kinds of shit and trash all
over the place. [The Mission, San Francisco]

A second theme is demoralization; littering problems are taken
as symptomatic of the widespread sense that no one in the neighborhood cares about it:

There are papers all over the place; people dump garbage;
it's just a mess [Question: Why is that?] People want to save
money so they don't do what they should. There is also a
lack of city services. People don't care. There is not much
pride in property. People are just letting their houses go.
With absentee landlords who don't care, people say, why
should we worry? [The Mission, San Francisco]

A teacher in San Francisco recounted his reaction to decaying
conditions around his school:

[T]he place is always dirty. Wherever you go there is
garbage and litter. The district is always cutting back on
maintenance crews. Those guys work their ass off, and still
they can't keep [up] with all the dirt and vandalism. The
schools are asking to be defaced. Nobody cares about their
school when everyday you see it dirty. . . . You come to
school in the morning and you see it dirty and you don't
want to spend any more time than you have to. [Question:
Is there a spillover to the neighborhood?] You bet. It extends
to the neighborhood. Houses are defaced, cars ripped off,
houses are burglarized. The Board [of Education] receives
a lot of homeowners complaints. [The Mission, San Fran-
cisco]

Responsibility for trash and garbage problems does not necessarily lie just with the *residents* of the area. Businesses do their part
also:

There's a problem with a fish store on the corner. He just

throws his old fish heads and trash on the other side of the
railroad fence there [pointing]. He keeps his fish overnight
in an old van that isn't refrigerated and the rats can get right
in there. They are getting to be pretty big [she spreads her
hands about a foot apart]. It was getting so that the people
that live right there in the house nearest the store couldn't
even sit on their front step. [Logan, Philadelphia]

Waste problems arise routinely in residential neighborhoods
that lie behind commercial strips. A study of the relationship between residential neighborhoods and nearby commercial areas by
McPherson, Silloway, and Frey (1983) found that residents regard
as major problems the trash, noise, after-hours drunkenness, and
other fallout from nearby stores and taverns. In Chicago, which is
represented by 17 neighborhoods in this study, the city does not
collect garbage from residential buildings with more than 4 units.
Instead, the owners of larger buildings must employ a private
pick-up company, whose crews come in less often when the profitability of buildings declines. Finally, as disposing of refuse become more difficult as well as costly, "fly dumping" plagues some
neighborhoods. Contractors with construction debris to dispose
of, or manufacturers faced with mounting inventories of noxious
or even toxic wastes, may find it expedient to open the back of
their truck in a vacant lot and pass the cost of removal on to
someone else.

A final problem—rats. Concentrations of abandoned buildings,
junk-strewn vacant lots, and unbundled garbage provide hiding
places and levels of nourishment that ensure heavy rat infesta-
tions. Studies in Newark and elsewhere have documented that
complaints about rats and reported rat bites are highly correlated
with other forms of physical decay, including trash, discarded
appliances, abandoned buildings, and uncovered refuse contain-
ers (Margulis, 1977).

THE CONSEQUENCES OF DISORDER
FOR NEIGHBORHOOD LIFE

The disorders described here had several things in common. All
involved public displays of incivility, for the concept of disorder
does not stretch to cover such private problems as intra-family

conflict. They may or may not have been illegal (a lot of them involved unruly youths), but whatever their legal status, these disorders were an affront to widely supported community values. They were all directly attributable to individuals (or gangs), and most could not be excused by writing them off to large-scale social forces or bureaucratic nonfeasance. The sole exception may be the rubbish problem, but research suggests that the rate at which people litter varies more from place to place than the rate at which street cleaners pick it up. Finally, many (but not all) disorders are produced by people who are themselves considered disreputable or vaguely threatening.

Two frequently expressed consequences of disorder were *anger* and *demoralization*. The anger came from being crowded out of community life. Residents of disorderly areas find it uncomfortable or even dangerous to be in parks, in shopping areas, or even on the streets near their homes. This seems unfair, and they are indignant about it. Residents also often noted the demoralization in others. Those interviewed frequently commented that "no one cares," and expressed a certain degree of hopelessness about their situation. They were clearly frustrated by their seeming inability to do much about mounting disorder.

Fear was also a frequent response, mostly discernible in regard to social disorder. Disorderly people are unpredictable by everyday standards, and some are potentially violent. Those seemingly crazed by drugs or drink *might* do anything (recall the man mistakenly almost shot in his neighbrhood park, or the woman who was assaulted there). Abandoned buildings may harbor predators; corner gangs can be menancing, especially for women and the elderly. Another cause for fear was that some disorder came from *inter-group conflict*. Sometimes that conflict was racial; at other times it was between generations, or between home owners and renters, landlords and tenants, and others with conflicting economic interests. The potential for violence can smolder behind these divisions. It is also important to note that people report being afraid for their *children* as well as for themselves. They fear their children will be the victims of violence or the targets of drug pushers, and feel in particular that they should not be exposed to blatant commercial sex or public drinking.

Visible physical decay may spark fear of crime, because Americans have come to associate it with higher levels of risk. Like observable social disorders, physical decay is taken by many as a "sign of crime." Arthur Stinchcombe and his colleagues (1980) argue that one of the things that differentiates fear of crime from concern about many other risks (such as being run over at a street crossing) is that Americans identify the incidence of crime with environmental cues. They dubbed these "the signs of crime," and their presence is taken by many as an early warning of impending danger—"we fear crime in stituations that give off danger signs in advance." Graffiti marking a gang's turf, burned-out buildings, and abandoned cars provide just this sort of signal. Being wary in their presence may indeed be wise; we shall see that robbery rates and other indicators of the extent of neighborhood crime are strongly related to the level of perceived disorder.

The effects of disorder may be even more general, however. It is not just that people fear that disreputables may actually harm them or their chidren. Disorder may also serve as an indicator that community self-controls no longer protect residents and passers-by; witness the report of an informant in Wicker Park:

> There was a mother less than ten feet away, and one of her kids walks up to an old woman. There was an old woman working in the front yard and the kid walks up to her, and—this is where the sidewalk is higher than the yard—the kid proceeds to pee on the old lady. [Wicker Park, Chicago]

Visible physical and social disruption is a signal that the mechanisms by which healthy neighborhoods maintain themselves have broken down. If an area loses its capacity to solve even seemingly minor problems, its character becomes suspect. Dan Lewis and Greta Salem of Northwestern University describe the importance of the "moral reliability" of a community in the eyes of residents:

> When the moral reliability of a community dissolves, local residents are no longer sure that the behavior of their neighbors will conform to what in the past were uniformly acceptable standards, and fear of crime appears. . . . Because of the heterogeneity of the population, city life puts a premium on moral reliability. City dwellers learn to distinguish between those they can trust and those they cannot. The trustworthy, those who share our values, serve as the building blocks for our lives, while the untrustworthy are to be avoided. Thus, people can be relied on to the extent that they share expectations about each other's behavior and

can be disciplined when those expectations are violated. Those people whose behavior is not subject to the moral order are dangerous both because they cannot be relied upon and because they will not accept discipline (Lewis and Salem, 1986: 99–100).

Thus, even though disorders are not in themselves life-threatening, fear may be a rational reaction to them.

Another consequence of disorder is *more disorder*. The problem is contagious. Wilson and Kelling's article (aptly titled "Broken Windows") attributed a great deal of importance to the role of observable decay in stimulating neighborhood decline. They implied that deterioration lowers the inhibition level of (primarily young) residents and passers-through, because things are already "smashed up."

> [I]f a window in a building is broken *and left unrepaired*, all the rest of the windows will soon be broken. . . . [O]ne unrepaired broken window is a signal that no one cares, so breaking more windows costs nothing. (It has always been fun.). . . . Untended property becomes fair game for people out for fun or plunder. . . . (Wilson and Kelling, 1982: 31)

This view is consistent with research on vandalism, littering, and building decay and abandonment, all of which appear to be contagious. Researchers and neighborhood residents agree that certain disorders are self-propagating—once they appear, they generate more disorder unless they are quickly and energetically stamped out. The contagion proposition implies that levels of disorder across urban neighborhoods may be only partly explained by such factors as poverty. To the extent to which disorder becomes self-generative and feeds on itself, current levels of disorder produce future levels of disorder. It will not be possible to document the magnitude of this process using the data available here, since we are dealing with one point in time in the development of each neighborhood. However, this position has important policy implications, for it suggests that intervening directly to attack specific disorder problems is indeed striking at its "causes."

Finally, disorder also has implications for the future of a neighborhood through its impact on *non*-residents, for it stigmatizes both the area and the people who live there. No one driving through Chicago's Woodlawn could avoid the impression that the

community was deeply troubled. As one of our observers described it,

> [M]ost of the stores along 63rd Street were just empty shells.
> The interiors had either been torn out or they were plagued
> with fire or vandalism. We passed several buildings that
> were falling down, and next door to these buildings I
> noticed a second-hand store. A man was busy outside of the
> building putting bars on his store. [Woodlawn, Chicago]

Thus in addition to its effects on the morale of residents, disorder signals signals about neighborhood problems to potential residents and investors. Is this a good area to move into? Will my
mortgage be safe there? The answers to these questions lie partly
in the reputation a neighborhood develops among outsiders; how
it looks can play a large role in the development of those perceptions. Confidence is hardly bolstered by the spread of boarded-up
buildings, burned-out storefronts, poorly maintained homes and
lawns, garbage spilling out of waste cans, and junk and trash
strewn about. Such areas will also not attract shoppers or potential
employers, to the further detriment to the community. In short,
where things begin to look bad, the economic factors which underlie neighborhood stability can take a turn for the worse.

3

The Extent of Disorder

How much disorder is there? Where is it concentrated, and why? Given the variety of cities, the mix of problems, and the legal and illegal activities involved, official records are not of much use; surveys on the other hand provide a way of turning directly to the public for reports of what is happening in their communities. In all, residents of 40 communities were asked how big a problem various disorders posed in their area, with an average of 325 respondents in each neighborhood (described in an appendix). Although the surveys asked about a somewhat different mix of problems in different cities, they all covered most of them. People's assessments of conditions in their area turned out to be consistent enough that their ratings could be used to give each neighborhood a single index of disorder.

The index is the average of two components: one for social, and one for physical disorder. The first measure combines average neighborhood responses to six questions concerning problems with groups of loiterers, drug use or sales, vandalism, gang activity, public drinking, and street harassment. The second component combines responses to three questions about building abandonment, garbage or litter on the streets and sidewalks, and junk and trash in vacant lots. It turned out that physical and social disorder correlate very strongly; there were few differences in how they were related to other neighborhood factors. Both forms of disorder were most common in poor, unstable, and minority areas, and they were also tied to indicators of neighborhood cohesion and morale. As a result, one over-all disorder index was formed from the evenly weighted components.

The 40 areas varied considerably in the extent to which residents were troubled by disorder problems. Four of the six worst neighborhoods were in West and South Newark, while the two nicest were "in-town suburbs" in Chicago (Portage Park and Beverly). The third most disorderly community was Chicago's Woodlawn. Woodlawn has lost almost 40 percent of its population in the last 20 years. There are abandoned buildings everywhere, and rubble-strewn vacant lots where the city has clawed out the most decayed structures. Woodlawn's commercial strips are dominated by taverns, cheap shoe stores, and vacant buildings. Across the street from Woodlawn (in Chicago, neighborhood boundaries are well known and sharply drawn) lies the 6th least troubled community, Hyde Park. This is the home of the University of Chicago, which has invested millions in community development and housing, and maintains an extensive police force (Taub, Taylor, and Dunhman, 1984). Two of the three San Francisco neighborhoods (Visitacion Valley, which lies in South-central San Francisco, and Sunset, which is located at the foot of Golden Gate Park) fell well below the median, but interviewers recorded numerous complaints from residents of the more troubled Mission district. All three Philadelphia areas were among the dozen most disorderly. Chicago's Edgewater, where I live, ranked a comfortable 28th, but is a world away from the highest income neighborhood in this survey, Chicago's Lincoln Park (37th).

IS DISORDER A REAL PROBLEM?

We have already noted the "cultural relativism" of disorder. Historians indicate that our standards have changed over time with respect to some forms of disorder, and that they have been the source of political and class conflict. Some suggest that conventional definitions of order merely reflect the distribution of white, middle-class views about public deportment, and that other contemporary subcultures are far less concerned about many of the same conditions. And, of course, the poor have many other social and economic problems to be concerned about; unlike better-off city dwellers, they may not fret as much about these issues. As a result of their differing priorities and interests, it may be that membe̵s of the middle class overreact to local disorder, while the poor downgrade its significance. The survey data can shed some light on this.

The surveys used here all measured disorder in virtually identical fashion; people were asked "how big a problem" various conditions were in their neighborhoods. This approach implicitly combines questions about the *presence* of conditions or events with respondents' *judgments* about them, and the assessments are clearly affected as much by the standards and values of the beholder as by "objective" conditions. Neighborhood residents doubtless differed in their expectations about public conduct and conditions, and in the tolerable degree of deviation from those standards. Residents could report public drinking as "no problem" if its frequency or character was not distressful, or as a "big problem" if they viewed its frequency or character with dismay.

Since we are ultimately interested in the impact of disorder on people's beliefs and behaviors, their reactions to the social reality of their environment are as significant as the independent views of outside observers. But it would be informative to know how far these disorder measures reflect "external" conditions and events, as opposed to people's "internal" judgments about them. If disorder ratings mostly reflect environmental variations, we can think of neighborhood residents as *informants*, reporting on surrounding conditions. If, on the other hand, people viewing the same conditions come to significantly different conclusions, the respondents should be thought of as *critics* passing individualistic judgments. Of course, a finding that the former view is more accurate would not rule out the relativism of those perceptions, either historically or in relation to what people from radically different places might think of great American cities. But, for the purposes at hand it would be fair to call those survey reports measures of the prevalence of consensually-defined urban "disorder," without discounting them as merely "perceived."

One way to choose between these two views would be to match the respondents' impressions against carefully structured observations of the same areas. This was not done here, as there is little research anywhere on the correspondence between perceived social disorder and independently observed neighborhood events. Neighborhood conditions such as litter, graffiti, and building abandonment are easier to quantify and compare to residents' perceptions, and Temple University sociologist Ralph Taylor and his colleagues (1985) have conducted extensive surveys and observational studies of neighborhoods in Baltimore. For one project, student observers made carefully controlled counts of litter, graffiti and building abandonment in 66 areas. These observations correlated substantially with survey measures of litter, abandonment, and dilapidation as perceived by residents,[1] suggesting that survey respondents' reports *can* be considered fairly accurate measures of the "objective" conditions around them.

Likewise, the National Housing Survey conducted by the U.S. Census Bureau elicits responses on a variety of neighborhood problems, including run-down housing, abandoned structures, and trash. A Census Bureau study (Dahmann, 1985) found that reports of these problems formed a separate strong cluster that was only weakly related to other problems *not* on our list of disorders, including street noise, heavy traffic, air pollution, and poor street lighting. The disorders included in the Housing Survey questionnaire were heavily concentrated in larger inner cities, and clearly form a distinct dimension on which Americans bore evaluations of their home communities.

There are also statistical approaches to judging the contribution of "internal" and "external" survey components. One first controls statistically for the home neighborhood of each of our 12,813 survey respondents, and then assesses how much of the remaining variation in judgments may be linked to such factors as race, education, and income. If some classes of people are more sensitive to (or intolerant of) disorder (that is, if their assessments of disorder reflect a largely "internal" set of standards), people living in the same neighborhood will report substantially different levels of disorder. This method provides one test of the "class bias" hypothesis: If disorder strongly reflects distinctively middle-class standards of public deportment and owners' interest in the value of their property, then home-owning, better-off, more educated people should be more frequently offended by violations of those standards. On the other hand, if respondents were reporting on what they had seen and heard, and agreed in their judgments, the big difference among them should be based on where they live, not who they are. In this case, blacks and whites, owners and renters, and others in the same neighborhood would largely agree on the extent of disorder.

The most important overall factor seems to be environmental; neighborhood of residence is a much more powerful determinant of disorder reports than are personal factors. The survey included ten race, class, and lifestyle factors that frequently divide neighbor from neighbor, but they explained little additional variation in disorder ratings while area of residence alone explained a substantial amount. About 95 percent of the explainable variation could be attributed to differences between neighborhoods, and only 5 percent to differences between people. This was also true for the separate measures of social and physical disorder as an analysis of individual disorder further indicated. Reports of public drinking and street harassment had the largest "individual" components, and the three measures of physical decay the least; but in every case, almost all that was explainable was accounted for by neighborhood.

The strongest individual determinant of perceived disorder among survey respondents was age. One might reasonably anticipate that older people living in these neighborhoods would be less tolerant of deviance and more often unsettled by disorder than their younger neighbors. Surprisingly, older residents consistently reported less (but not much less) physical and social disorder than younger people living in the same area. (This result will be examined in more detail below.) In sum, therefore, statistical analysis suggests that respondents in the 40 neighborhood surveys were acting by-and-large, as informants rather than critics, and that their reports can be treated with confidence as indicators of actual conditions.

A more graphic means of addressing the concensus/dissensus issue would be to compare reports from either side of major social cleavages in the same area. If the respondents agree in their assessments of neighborhood problems, there is evidence of community consensus and further evidence that real area conditions—not tolerance of disorder, group politics, culture, lifestyles, or economic interests—are reflected in the survey. For this purpose, area disorder scores were calculated for major social groups, then compared using plots and correlations. If there was high agreement *across groupings within neighborhoods,* the reports would cluster tightly, and perceptions of local conditions would not then differ greatly by race and class.

An example of this analysis, presented here in Figure 3–1, compares levels of disorder reported by homeowners and renters in each of the 40 study areas; the former are plotted across the bottom axis, the latter up the side. Each symbol identifies an area on those

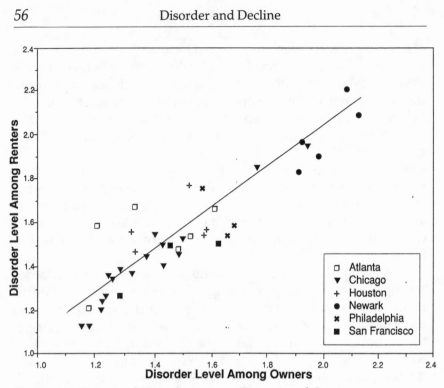

Figure 3–1 Perceived Disorder Among Renters and Owners

two ratings. If owners and renters generally agreed about conditions in their areas, the two sets of ratings would go together
tightly. In fact, the two sets of ratings are very highly correlated
(+.90), for people to a large extent agreed about what their neighborhood was like. A similar plot, dividing the reports of higher
and lower-income respondents, looks the same; the two measures
were correlated +.88.

The same can be said concerning comparisons of black and
white residents of the study areas. (Hispanics and Asians were
excluded from the calculations.) Blacks and whites agreed in their
views of their communities to a surprising extent; the correlation
between their views was .87, when three neighborhoods with only
a few black or white respondents were removed.

Finally, a comparison of the neighborhood ratings of younger
and older residents of the 40 areas revealed that younger and older
residents generally agreed on where they ranked their community
with respect to local problems; the two measures were correlated
+.92. Recall that age was the strongest individual-level correlate

of perceived disorder, once area of residence was taken into account. Younger respondents perceived somewhat higher levels of disorder in every area, probably because they are out more often and in contact with more diverse elements in the community.

WHERE IS DISORDER A PROBLEM?

While we are principally concerned with the *consequences* of disorder for urban neighborhoods, it is important to understand where it is concentrated, for some of the apparent consequences of disorder (including crime, fear, and neighborhood dissatisfaction) are strongly influenced by demography. Research also suggests that neighborhood economic status affects the influence of disorder on the real-estate market (Taylor et al., 1986), so analyses in the next chapter will control for important neighborhood social and economic factors. This section first examines their direct connection to disorder.

The surveys gathered a wide range of personal information, including data on education, income, race, employment, marital and family relations, and the like. Most of these factors were related to disorder, but they were also related to each other. Because there are only 40 neighborhoods to examine, it was useful to reduce this list to a smaller number of summary measures that reflect the important elements of all of them. This was done using factor analysis. This statistical procedure examines a large set of variables, and extracts what they have in common. It identifies a smaller number of basic dimensions that summarize all of the original information, and gives each neighborhood a score on these dimensions.

Table A-3–1 in the appendix reports the results of such an analysis of the 40 neighborhoods. There were two dimensions, or clusters of variables, in the set. One cluster reflects *neighborhood stability.* Areas with high scores on this factor had a larger proportion of long-term residents, more older people, a higher percentage of households that were single family homes and owner-occupied, and relatively low unemployment levels; those with a low score fell at the opposite pole on each of those measures. The second cluster of variables reflected *neighborhood poverty.* Areas with a high score on the poverty factor had higher levels of unemployment, a smaller porportion of adults in the labor force, lower

family incomes, and fewer high school graduates. These two dimensions describe combinations of stable and unstable areas that
were both poor and better-off.

Figure 3–2 illustrates the relationship between neighborhood
stability and disorder in the 40 areas. Points on the plot indicate
how high or low each community lies on each of two measures; in
every figure the presumably "causal" factor (here, stability) lies
across the bottom, and its "effect" (here, disorder) is presented
above the side. When the two factors are negatively correlated
(−.49), as they are in Figure 3–2, the neighborhood points go
generally from the upper left to the lower right-hand corner of the
figure. (With 40 cases, a correlation of .30 is statistically significant
if these are treated as a small sample of the universe of urban
neighborhoods; statistical matters are discussed in the appendix.)

Figure 3–2 indicates that most stable neighborhoods enjoyed
low levels of disorder. Areas with older, long-term residents, and
with more single-family and owner-occupied homes, were more
successful at maintaining acceptable standards of public conduct

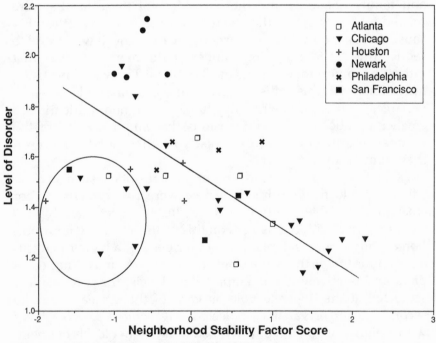

Figure 3–2 Neighborhood Stability and Disorder

and housing conditions. However, there is also a cluster of low-stability but *lower*-disorder areas evident in Figure 3–2, in the lower left-hand quadrant. There was less disorder than we would expect, based upon their low stability, in those areas in Chicago, Atlanta, Houston, and San Francisco.

As this indicates, there are other factors at work besides stability. The second major correlate of disorder was area poverty. Residents of low-income, high-unemployment, low-education areas were far more likely to report extensive problems with disorder in their community; the correlation between the two was + .58. Tim Hope and Mike Hough (1988) of the Home Office Research Unit in London found the same pattern in British public housing estates, which include people with a broad range of incomes. Affluence helps explain the position of several of the anomalous low-stability, low-disorder areas identified in Figure 3–2; they were "yuppy" areas like Lincoln Park in Chicago, where young, single (e.g., short-term renter) professionals gather.

A third important correlate of levels of disorder in these 40 areas is race. There was a strong relationship between levels of disorder and the concentration of racial and ethnic minorities in these communities. The measure of the latter combined blacks, some Hispanic respondents, and a small scattering of Asians (many in San Francisco and Houston). It indicated that where racial and linguistic minorities predominated, levels of disorder were higher (the correlation was + .62).

It should not be surprising that race and the economic and social factors examined here also are interrelated. The two factor scores are independent of one another, but neighborhood minority concentration is positively related to poverty (+ .47), and negatively related to neighborhood stability (− .30). This may in part explain why race seemingly is the strongest correlate of disorder; it may "carry with it" effects of those factors as well. Simple causal models can be used to probe whether poverty, stability, and race are all independently linked to levels of disorder, or whether one or two of the measures actually reflect the effect of a third.

Figure 3–3 indicates how all of these factors may be related to one another. It also presents estimates of the relative strength of each of the causal paths, and a summary of the effects of each of the variables in the model. The path coefficients associated with each of the arrows that point to disorder in Figure 3–3 indicate the relative importance of each measure in predicting neighborhood

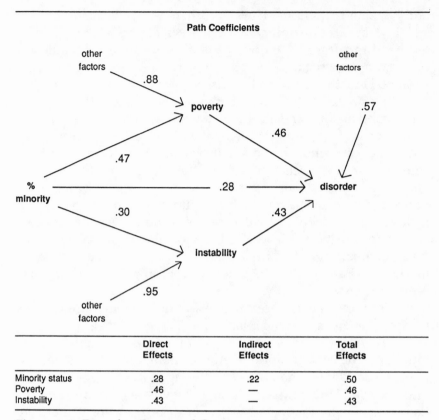

Path Coefficients

	Direct Effects	Indirect Effects	Total Effects
Minority status	.28	.22	.50
Poverty	.46	—	.46
Instability	.43	—	.43

Figure 3–3 Disorder, Race, and Community Economic Factors

levels of disorder (for a discussion of this technique, *see* Asher, 1983). All of them are statistically significant, indicating they were not likely to have arisen by chance—not a trivial issue with only 40 areas. Figure 3–3 indicates that poverty, instability, and race were all independently related to disorder, even when relationships between them were taken into account.

Figure 3–3 also summarizes the *indirect* as well as the direct effect of each of the variables. The direct effect of each equals the path coefficients sketched in the model, while the indirect effect of neighborhood racial composition stems from its causal relationship to area poverty and instability. The direct-effects column indicates that stability and poverty had effects on disorder of almost the same magnitude; neighborhood racial composition was directly related to disorder, but less strongly so. However, race also was linked to disorder *through* poverty and instability. The arrows from "other factors" in Figure 3–3 indicate the relative importance of other neighborhood variables and measurement error in explaining those in the model. Those paths are largest for poverty and instability; the unexplained portion of disorder is smaller. Together, these three factors explain 67 percent of the variance in disorder. The largest component is due to the effects of race.

These findings parallel those of one of the few observational studies of physical decay. In Taylor, Schumaker, and Gottfredson's (1985) study of Baltimore neighborhoods, observed litter, dilapidation, and abandonment were most common in black, lower-income, lower-education, and high-rental areas. By far the strongest correlates of disorder across these neighborhoods are area unemployment and education. The proportions of households consisting of married couples and living in single family homes follow closely behind. All of these are also strongly linked to the racial composition of these areas. The "bottom line" is that racial and linguistic minorities in these 40 areas report the most significant disorder problems.

WHAT ABOUT COMMERCIAL SEX?

As indicated earlier, the distribution of neighborhood problems with commercial sex—street prostitution and the appearance of adult book stores and X-rated movie theaters—was quite different from that of the other problems considered here.

The major reason for this may be that, unlike the other disorders (the exception being drug sales), these are businesses requiring locations where they can operate safely, attract paying customers, and survive local protests. These are not likely to be either the best *or* worst neighborhoods in town. During the late 1970s, Bernard Cohen (1980) drove the streets of Manhattan every night, observing the distribution of street prostitutes. He noted where stable zones of prostitution could be found, who the typical customers were, what other kinds of people could be observed in the area, and the effects of passing patrol cars as well as intensive crackdown efforts on the relocation of clusters of street walkers. All of the areas where he could predictably find prostitutes were located in stable, low-to-moderate crime areas. Cohen concluded that street prostitution could not persist in neighborhoods where there was vocal intolerance or organized resistance to prostitution, and it also could not flourish in dangerous or disreputable areas where customers were unwilling to go:

> Apparently, unlike juvenile or gang delinquency and street crime, visible street deviance involving prostitution is not as likely to emerge and persist in deteriorated, transient, and slum neighborhoods. Poor, unsavory conditions, including the presence of crime, repress visible street prostitution, especially the type that attracts clients city-wide, because it intimidates clients and prostitutes, who are anxious about their personal safety. Also, clientele fear minority neighborhoods. These neighborhoods have a heavy police presence, which represses visible street prostitution too. This is another reason why stable conditions of female street prostitution do not usually develop on streets where drug sales or muggings are prevalent (Cohen, 1980: 120).

Prostitutes and others involved in commercialized sex have a stake in keeping their turf clear of competing disorders. Cohen observed numerous instances of prostitutes chasing away alcohlic derelicts who attempted to share their sidewalk. (Women who were not involved in the trade shunned these blocks, to avoid unpleasant encounters with cruising customers.) Specialized micro-economies developed around areas where prostitutes worked, contributing to their stability. Hotels and coffee shops, parking lots, saloons, massage parlors, peep shows, and topless bars coexist with street prostitutes in a money-making environment which depends upon excluding disorders that might drive away customers and undermine their covert economy; and they act to protect it.

Cohen's observations in New York City are consistent with the data available from our neighborhood surveys. Questions about commercial sex were included in only 16 of the neighborhood surveys, so our conclusions are tentative; but, unlike other forms of disorder, these problems were not reported in the poorest or the most unstable areas. Commercial sex problems ranked highest in racially heterogeneous areas, but in largely black or white areas they were not seen as serious problems at all. As in New York, problems with commercial sex were most common in areas with fairly *low* levels of threatening crime (as measured by both the robbery rate and a scale of perceived area crime problems), and in places that were only moderately disorderly in character. The best areas in Atlanta and Houston, and the worst areas in Newark, shared the same low level of concern about prostitution and sexually-oriented business establishments. On the other hand, neighborhoods in Houston and Atlanta lying at the middle of the disorder scale scored the highest. Cohen was right—commercial enterprises need to locate in places which will attract paying customers, and this extends to the sex business as well. As a result, these types of disorder are concentrated in other areas of the city.

4

The Impact of Disorder

What are the consequences of disorder for city neighborhoods? Does it goad them into action, or do they give up in the face of mounting problems? Three aspects stand out in the process of community change. First, disorder undermines the mechanisms by which communities exercise control over local affairs. It fosters social withdrawal, inhibits cooperation between neighbors, and discourages people from making efforts to protect themselves and their community. Second, disorder sparks concern about neighborhood safety, and perhaps even causes crime itself. This further undermines community morale, and can give the area a bad reputation elsewhere in the city. Third, disorder undermines the stability of the housing market. Disorder undercuts residential satisfaction, leads people to fear for the safety of their children, and encourages area residents to move away. Fewer people will want to move into the area; the stigmatizing effect of disorder discourages outside investors, and makes it more difficult for local businesses to attract customers from outside. All of this erodes the value of real estate in disorderly communities, contributing to the further deterioration and abandonment of residential and commercial buildings.

Theories of neighborhood change need to be dynamic, featuring factors which affect one another over time. For example, the link between disorder and neighborhood residential composition might come into play slowly, through the accumulating effects of differential migration to and from problem-ridden communities.

Theoretically, some relationships are reciprocal in nature as well; that is, neighborhood factors might even affect themselves over time. The process of contagion described in regard to littering, vandalism, and abandonment shows how disorder begets future disorder. However, there has been virtually no research on disorder or individual reactions to crime over any length of time. Longitudinal studies by Leo Schuerman and Solomon Kobrin (1986) have used census figures and officially recorded crime for areas of Los Angeles, for these data are available for different periods. Their work suggests that in small urban areas important changes can take place rapidly; neighborhoods apparently can move from low to high-crime status during the decade between censuses. Unfortunately, fear of crime, residential dissatisfaction, and other factors, that in theory provide the linkage between disorder and community decline, are better measured through interviews. Surveys concerning crime problems in cities or in particular neighborhoods so far have provided only one-time views of their residents' fears and intentions. As a result, we can only make cautious inferences about change within neighborhoods judging from differences between our 40 study neighboroods. Differences between neighborhoods which score high or low on a particular factor are taken as suggesting what happens when areas go from high to low over time.

COMMUNITY CAPACITY TO EXERCISE CONTROL

There are competing views about the relationship between people's concern about a problem and their willingness to take action. The two could be related positively, negatively, or in curvilinear fashion, and this relationship may differ from one form of action to another. The *positive* view is that concern stimulates action. French sociologist Emil Durkheim argued that crime has an integrative function—it shocks the sentiments of ordinary people by threatening their lives, families, property, and their views of appropriate behavior. This affront to their values leads them to act individually and—more important—collectively to "do something" in response. The positive view was expressed in this interview in San Francisco:

[Observer: I asked him to tell me some of what the block

clubs are doing presently, and this is what he told me.] The
16th street area is organized to control the porno shops in
the area, with the eventual goal of eliminating them entirely.
Their second goal is to bring new money into the area by
influencing banks to provide low interest loans to interested
homeowners and small business people. . . . Their success
in keeping the porno shops out are numerous. The Roxie
theater, which was one of the more sleazy porno theaters in
San Francisco had its lease revoked by the owners and is
now run by progressive members of the community.
Landlords of existing porno bookstores have agreed not to
renew the leases of the stores in their buildings. [The
Mission, San Francisco]

During the 1970s, the belief underlying several federal crime
prevention programs was that people living in high-crime neighborhoods would, with only a little encouragement, form neighborhood organizations for their own protection (Lewis, 1979). Other
attempts to frighten people into protecting themselves—for example, into fastening their seat belts or quitting smoking—are based
on a similar hypothesis.

The *negative* view is that concern actually discourages constructive responses to problems. There has been little research on the
consequences of disorder, but fear of crime does not appear to
stimulate positive responses to crime (Tyler, 1984; Lavrakas, 1981).
In fact, surveys and experiments generally indicate that high levels
of fear reduce people's willingness to take positive action when
they see crimes being committed—many balk even at simply calling the police. Past research suggests several reasons why disorder
might undermine a community's capacity to act collectively.

First, perceptions registered in surveys that "neighbors help
each other" appear to be an important indicator of morale in urban
communities, and are related to a variety of positive actions
against crime. Without such support, people feel powerless, impo-
tent, and vulnerable in the face of crime. In past studies, high
levels of disorder appear to undermine the belief that problems
can be solved locally; they increase people's sense of personal
isolation, and spread the perception that no one will come to their
rescue when they find themselves in trouble (Lewis and Salem,
1986).

Second, perceptions of disorder, like fear of crime, may shrink the circumference of the turf that individuals feel responsible for defending. When the boundaries of their watchfulness are wide, neighborhood residents monitor the behavior of more youths, keep an eye on more strangers, and investigate more suspicious sounds and activities. Where territories encompass only people's own homes and families, untended persons and property are fair game for plunder. Territoriality is an important component of the larger process of surveillance, which may be an important mechanism for controlling crime. Surveillance entails both "watching" and "acting." Acting is facilitated by personal recognition; hence the importance of knowing your neighbors. It is also facilitated by the sense that local standards about appropriate public behavior are widely shared; this legitimizes individual intervention. There is some evidence (summarized in Shotland and Goodstein, 1984; Goodstein, 1980) that crime is encouraged by low levels of surveillance of public places, and reduced by people's willingness to challenge strangers, supervise youths, and step forward as witnesses.

However, in neighborhoods in decline, mutual distrust and hostility are rampant, and antipathy between newcomers and long-term residents prevails. Residents of poor, heterogeneous areas tend to view each other with suspicion (Taub, Taylor, and Dunham, 1984; Greenberg et al., 1982; Taylor et al., 1981). Sarah Boggs (1971) found that black central-city residents were less likely than other Missourians to think their neighbors would take responsibility for neighborhood safety, and less likely to think their neighbors would call the police if they saw a crime. Criminologist James Hackler and his colleagues (1974) found that residents of affluent areas were most likely to indicate (in hypothetical questions) that they would intervene to control juvenile misconduct. Numerous studies have concluded that crime-prevention programs requiring social contact and neighborhood cooperation are less often successful in heterogeneous areas and in those with high levels of fear. City surveys conducted by the U.S. Census Bureau during the 1970s indicate that respondents who thought that local crime was committed by "people in the neighborhood" were more fearful than those who thought it was the responsibility of "outsiders." Such perceptions are corrosive, for they undermine trust among neighbors. They certainly violate one of the assumptions behind Neighborhood Watch and other programs that attempt to promote mutual cooperation to prevent crime—it may not seem wise to inform the neighbors that you will be out of town when it is their children whom you fear (Greenberg 1983). We can sense this kind of suspicion of neighbors in the following report from the Mission district of San Francisco:

> [Observer: What do you think will happen to this area?]
> Well, whites associate Puerto Ricans and blacks with decay. As soon as they see them moving in, they think that's it for the neighborhood. And then the only whites who will live in the place are poor whites . . . You can always tell a neighborhood is going down the drain when the big apartments start taking transient residents, and start getting their money from the welfare department. That means that the worst people are coming in—people who don't have a stake in the neighborhood and are poor, too. [The Mission, San Francisco]

A greal deal of research supports the view that there is a negative relationship between area disorder and community capacity to maintain control; where disorder is high, capacity should be low. A somewhat more complex *non-linear* hypothesis is that excessive levels of concern are debilitating, but moderate levels of concern actually are constructive. Those who think their area is virtually problem-free would have few reasons to engage in problem-solving activities, while at the high end of the scale demoralization and distrust may prevail; in this view, community capacity would be highest in places facing middling disorder, where there are visible problems but they are not overwhelming. There is a great deal of interest in neighborhood watch programs in Britain, and a national survey there found just this pattern: middle-range levels of concern about disorder and crime—but not high or low levels of concern—were most strongly related to support for neighborhood watch (Hope, 1988). This suggests that the effects of disorder are curvilinear. We should look for instances in which individual or collective problem-solving goes up at first, and then—at some "tipping point"—drops again in the face of mounting levels of neighborhood deterioration.

Finally, *both* the positive, negative, and non-linear views might be partially correct. Some research on the impact of disorder and crime on community social processes suggests that disorder might depress collective efforts to solve local problems, while at the same time concern about such problems might stimulate privatistic, household-oriented efforts by people to protect themselves (Smith, 1987). In this view, we should find positive *and* negative effects of disorder, depending upon whether we are looking at individual or collective behavior. To explore this, we first look at whether disorder is associated with higher or lower levels of a community's capacity to exercise control, and whether it appears to encourage privatistic over collective action. And we chart the relationship between disorder and two measures of community solidarity—the extent to which neighbors are helpful to one another, and the frequency with which they cooperate informally to prevent crime in a "public-minded" way. These collective actions would seem to be particularly vulnerable to demoralization and distrust. Then we examine how frequently people pursue more "private-minded," household-focused crime-prevention efforts, and how those too may be affected by deterioration of the neighborhood environment.

Community Capacity and Collective Action. To judge the extent of collective efforts to deal with local problems, surveys assessed the extent of neighborhood solidarity in problem-solving, and mutual efforts to protect the community from crime. Solidarity in problem-solving was measured by asking respondents to characterize their neighborhoods as places where either "people help one another" or "people go their own way." Figure 4–1 illustrates the substantial negative (− .59) relationship between disorder and neighborhood solidarity in 22 areas where both were measured comparably. Where levels of disorder were high, respondents were more likely to report that people in their area tended to "go their own way." This negative relationship was significant, controlling at the same time for area poverty, stability, and racial composition. It does not provide any support for the proposition that there are tipping points somewhere along the disorder continuum, for the line formed by the neighborhoods in Figure 1 is fairly straight, and does not tilt one way or another.

The second measure of community capacity to exercise control referred more explicitly to crime-related problems. In 26 areas, respondents were also asked whether the last time they had gone away for a period of time, they had asked a neighbor to watch their home. Where levels of disorder were highest, fewer people reported engaging in cooperative informal crime prevention arrangements (the correlation was − .51). The negative relationship

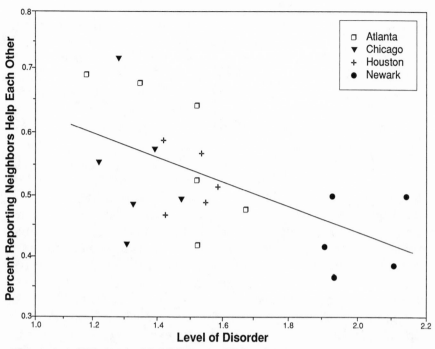

Figure 4–1 Helping by Neighbors and Disorder

between disorder and surveillance was linear; again there was no evidence of a tipping point. It was still significant, controlling for the effects of area crime (measured by the extent of robbery victimization), but it lost significance when the possible effects of area poverty, race, and stability were taken into account.

Not surprisingly, the two measures of community capacity were interrelated. In Britain, the extent to which people think their neighbors tend to help one another is strongly related to support for neighborhood-watch programs, even controlling for other factors (Hope, 1988). The same is true among our 40 neighborhoods—solidarity and informal surveillance were correlated + .82.

Privatistic Household Protection. The negative relationship between disorder and public cooperative action may be attributable to the atomizing, divisive nature of problems related to disorder. However, private defensively-oriented actions still may be sparked by concern about neighborhood disorder. High levels of disorder may lead people to withdraw from community life, but it may still encourage them to look out for themselves. Our measure of "privatistic" action comes from responses to questions concerning property marking. Marking an identifying number of one's household goods is one of the most widely-advocated and practiced forms of crime prevention. The popularity of property marking is attested to by the fact that every study examined here included questions about it. Across these 40 areas, an average of about 26 percent of respondents indicated they had marked at least some household property.

Across the 40 areas there was again a *negative* correlation (− .34) between prevention and disorder. This is illustrated in Figure A-4-1 in the appendix. As with cooperative surveillance, there was less household-oriented crime prevention where disorder was common. The relationship between property marking and disorder remained significant, controlling for the poverty, stability, and racial makeup of these communities. It was also significant controlling for the target of the program, the burglary victimization rate. The negative effect of disorder was almost twice as large as the remaining (positive) relationship between area burglary and property marking. Statistical tests looking for evidence of tipping points did not find any. The extent of property marking also was negatively related to several measures of crime that will be considered in detail, including ratings of neighborhood crime problems and the robbery rate. Even controlling for other important correlates of household crime-prevention efforts—including home ownership, which is very strong correlate of property marking—does not affect the negative relationship between crime and prevention behavior.

In sum, disorder may undermine in several ways the capacity of communities to preserve the conditions they value. Disorder may foster suspicion and distrust, undermine popular faith and commitment to the area, and discourage public and collective activities. Disorder may also undermine individual morale and the perceived efficacy of taking any positive action. Since there is little that individuals seem able to do about many forms of disorder, they may feel disheartened and frustrated, rather than motivated to do more, even to protect themselves. Events in these 40 neighborhoods support this "negative" view of disorder. There is no evidence that disorder creates a distinctive fortress mentality, but there also is no evidence here for the view that a little bit of disorder motivates people in positive directions.

DISORDER, CRIME, AND FEAR

As already noted, Wilson and Kelling proposed that disorder actually spawns more serious crime. They described a developmental sequence in which disorderly activity fosters theft and even more serious street crime and burglary. We have just seen evidence that supports part of their argument. They also think troublemakers are attracted into such areas because of the opportunities they offer for crime. This too is consistent with research reporting high correlations between area-level official crime statistics and disorder.

Here we examine the impact of disorder using two survey measures of the extent of area crime—the extent to which it is perceived to be a neighborhood problem, and the frequency with which residents were robbed. Ironically, the data from the 40 neighborhoods cannot shed a great deal of light on the details of the relationship between disorder and crime, for the measures all go together very strongly. With only 40 cases to untangle this web, the high correlation between measures of victimization, ratings of crime problems, and disorder make it difficult to tell whether they have either separate "causes" or separate "effects" at the area level.

Disorder and Common Crime. Figure 4–2 probes the relationship between disorder and crime, plotting the relationship between the robbery rate and neighborhood disorder. Victimization was measured by questioning survey respondents about whether or not they had been robbed in the past year.[1] As Figure 4–2 indicates, levels of crime were strongly related (+ .80) to levels of disorder in the 30 areas for which robbery was measured. We have already seen the strong link between disorder and poverty, instability, and the racial composition of these neighborhoods, and it will be no surprise that those factors are also strongly related to crime. To take into account the possibility that the relationship between disorder and crime is a spurious one (that the two appear to go together only because they share common causes), further analyses looked at the crime-disorder nexus while taking poverty, instability, and race into account. The crime-disorder connection was still highly significant, as documented in Table A-4-1. The correlation between *residual* values for robbery victimization and disorder, once the effects of poverty, stability, and racial composition had been removed statistically from each, was still high (+ .54);

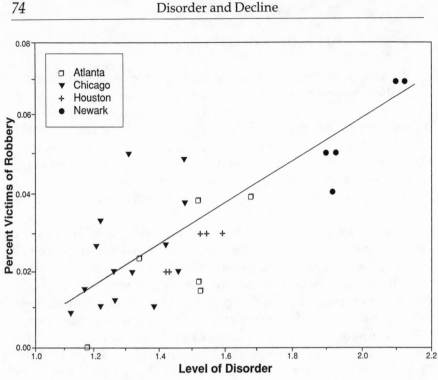

Figure 4–2 Robbery Victimization and Crime

ignoring these demographic factors, there still was quite a strong tendency for crime and disorder to "go together."

Another indicator of the magnitude of neighborhood crime problems is how bad people *think* the problems are. Comparable questions about local crime in 20 area surveys—questions asking about the extent of local problems with robbery, assault, and burglary—also document that disorder and crime problems go together in a substantial way. The strong link between disorder and an index of perceived crime problems (the two were correlated +.82) persisted when neighborhood stability, poverty, and racial composition were taken into account statistically. These results are also documented in Table A-4-1. In these areas, crime was by all measures higher in black, poor, and unstable areas; based on Table A-4-1, however, disorder was almost three times as influential as the strongest of the social factors, poverty. None of the social and economic correlates of crime problems was significant once disorder was taken into account, even if those factors were forced into the statistical analysis.

Exactly the same pattern appears if a measure of crime *trends* (not shown) is used instead. Perceptions that area crime has been on the increase are correlated + .52) with neighborhood disorder, and that relationship persists when many demographic factors are taken into account.

Does Disorder Cause Crime? The evidence suggests that poverty, instability, and the racial composition of neighborhoods are strongly linked to area crime, but a substantial portion of that linkage is through disorder: their link to area crime virtually disappears when disorder is brought into the picture. This too is consistent with Wilson and Kelling's original proposition, and further evidence that direct action against disorder could have substantial payoffs. Our data on urban neighborhoods are consistent with the causal diagram sketched in Figure 4–3, which can be tested. The statistical findings summarized there are based on data from 30 areas in which consistent questions about robbery victimization were included. In those areas, the effects of poverty, instability, and neighborhood racial composition were all about the same, as indicated by the path coefficients. There were no significant paths between those social and economic variables and neighborhood crime, except through disorder. Together, these factors explain 65 percent of the variance in robbery rates, with almost all of that being channeled through area disorder.[2]

These data support the proposition that disorder needs to be taken seriously in research on neighborhood crime, and that both directly and through crime it plays an important role in neighborhood decline. "Broken windows" do need to be repaired quickly.

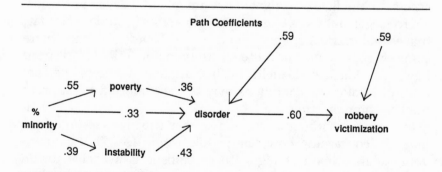

Path Coefficients

Note: Based on 30 areas with robbery victimization measures.

Figure 4–3 A Model of Disorder and Crime

Disorder and Fear of Crime. Levels of disorder are also related to fear. If "social control" is the development and enforcement of norms about public conduct, then visible evidence of anti-social behavior should seem to be a sure sign that the area is *out* of control. In their 1967 report to the Crime Commission, Albert Biderman and his colleagues reported:

> We have found that attitudes of citizens regarding crime are less affected by their past victimization experiences than by their ideas about what is going on in their community—fears about a weakening of social controls on which they feel their safety and the broader fabric of social life is ultimately dependent (Biderman et al., 1967: 160).

Dan Lewis and Greta Salem (1986) closely studied the thousands of pages of field notes that were the source of the quotations in Chapter 2, and concluded that people take disorder as a sign of the disintegration of the standards that guide local public behavior. Where disorder is common, area residents are continually confronted with obstreperous and unpredictable people, many of whom may seem hostile and potentially dangerous. People associated visible deterioration, gang graffiti, loitering teens and public drinkers, and other disorderly activities with a heightened risk of being victimized. Kenny's (1987) survey of New York City subway riders confirmed that those who feared for their safety also were likely to feel that drunks, loiterers, and public urination were problems on the train platforms and in the cars. Lewis and Salem also linked fear to peoples' perceptions that they could not control their lives. Neighborhoods with some political influence, and with access to public and private investment and development resources, generally have fewer problems with disorder. The fact that visual and experiential evidence of disorder is much more common than actual encounters with predatory criminals also led Lewis and Michael Maxfield (1980) to argue that citizens' perceptions of local crime conditions may be *more* affected by disorder than by common crime.

In the neighborhood surveys, fear was usually measured by a question concerning how safe people would feel "out alone in your neighborhood at night" (this statistic is available for 26 areas). Note that there is no reference to "crime" in the question, and presumably people's responses also took into account the types of racial harassment, threats by youths, and other neighborhood problems described earlier. Neighborhood levels of fear were correlated +.67 with disorder; where disorder was high, people did not feel safe.

The relationship between disorder and neighborhood safety also persisted when other factors affecting fear were taken into account. As Table A-4-2 indicates, disorder and fear of going out after dark still are very strongly linked when neighborhood stability, poverty, and racial composition are controlled for. This is true despite the fact that those factors also are correlated with fear. The link between disorder and fear is much stronger for the 26 neighborhoods than in Taylor, Schumaker, and Gottfredson's (1985) Baltimore study. There, physical decay and fear were not related once area, race, income, and home ownership were brought into the picture.

Disorder appears to be less influential when we take measures of area crime conditions into account. Not surprisingly, fear was more strongly correlated with crime (+.79 with the index and +.81 with victimization) than with area disorder problems (+.67). Studies of the relationship between crime and fear for neighborhoods (McPherson, 1978) or for cities (Krahn and Kennedy, 1985) also typically report correlations of +.60 or more between the two. When either of these crime measures are controlled for, the relationship between disorder and fear no longer is significant. On the other hand, this is also an unfair test of the disorder hypothesis. The disorder and crime indicators are so substantially intercorrelated that it would take a much larger sample of neighborhoods to untangle accurately their separate relationships with fear. Using a large national survey in Britain, Tim Hope and Mike Hough (1988) found that the relationships between disorder and fear of crime there is strong even when controlling for victimization levels and other features of community life.

DISORDER AND THE HOUSING MARKET

Disorder and crime play a critical role in urban ecology through their impact upon the number and mix of people moving into and out of neighborhoods. Selective emigration may be the most fundamental source of neighborhood change (Frey, 1980). As noted above, stable neighborhoods are places where about the same number of similar people move in as move out. Areas are stable

when the housing stock is continually renewed, and people can
sell and buy homes at appropriate prices. The following testimony
from Woodlawn illustrates what can happen when this stable pattern is upset:

> [Observer: I asked her how much Woodlawn changed.]
> When I first moved here, there were a lot of middle-class
> people here; my block was totally integrated; you know,
> blacks and whites got along fine and everything. There were
> a lot of lawyers and doctors and stuff who lived up in here,
> and students, and a lot of the blacks who moved in were
> middle class. But it seemed like overnight they started
> letting the poor into the area; people who just didn't care
> about the apartments or about the area one bit. And the
> neighborhood just changed overnight. Deterioration started
> occurring: abandonment, slum apartment buildings going
> up. Stony Island used to be just a nice shopping area, just
> beautiful. Most of the shops on one side of the street have
> been torn down. You can't even do your shopping in the
> area any more. . . . There's no more shows or movie theaters
> in the area; there used to be a drug store on 67th, but the
> drug store's gone. The first thing you know they stick up
> Chicken Shacks and Burger Kings, and they'll stick in a
> bunch of liquor stores. You know the area's going down
> when they stick in a bunch of liquor stores. It's really sad
> here now, 'cause I used to really love living in Woodlawn,
> but now you can't even walk down several streets by
> yourself. [Woodlawn, Chicago]

Many people will not want to remain in areas characterized by
disorder and crime, and fewer still will opt to move into them.
Measures of disorder and fear of crime are strongly related to
residential dissatisfaction and the desire to move to a safer place
(Kasl and Harburg, 1972; Droettboom et al., 1971), but studies of
actual moving—as opposed to residential dissatisfaction—document the realities of economics and race (Duncan and Newman,
1976). Middle-class, family-oriented, and white residents actually
move on, and their replacements are different. A comparison of
"movers" and "stayers" in the Chicago metropolitan area indicates that people who moved out of the central city were more
often affluent, highly educated, and intact families. This was despite the fact that blacks, unmarried adults, and the poor were far

more likely to be unhappy about their neighborhood. Those who moved out were "pulled" by the attractiveness of safe suburban locations as well as "pushed" by fear and other concerns (Skogan and Maxfield, 1981). Higher-income families and those with children are more likely than others to make moving decisions based on area crime rates (Katzman, 1980).

Some elderly and long-time residents may remain behind following this transitional period because they are unwilling to move, or cannot sell their homes for enough to buy another in a nicer neighborhood. They find themselves surrounded by unfamiliar people whom they did not choose to live with. Loneliness and lack of community attachment are significant sources of fear among the urban elderly, especially among older women (Silverman and Kennedy, 1985; Yin, 1980; Jaycox, 1978). An older woman living in Chicago's Wicker Park described her isolation this way:

> [Observer: I inquired about the neighborhood.] The older woman replied that she had lived here 13 years. The neighborhood had been real nice, but there had been a real change. Before, the houses and property were kept up and clean. She is renting a flat, and is contemplating moving because the area is getting bad. Many of her friends have left already, and she's planning to move near to them soon. She said that there's no money to be had for mortgages in this area, because the property is not cared for the way it used to be. If you tell a bank that it is the Wicker Park area you want to buy into, they'll refuse you credit. [Wicker Park, Chicago]

Demographic changes are very significant for the local housing market. If fewer or poorer people want to move in, real estate values decline. The market is dominated by "push" rather than "pull" factors. A soft demand for housing due to the undesirability of the area can be stimulated by cutting rents, slicing up older buildings into smaller apartments, and changing standards for tenant selection, but this further affects the mix of those moving in. Areas stigmatized by disorder are more likely to attract—and admit—individuals involved in crime and deviance (Stark, 1987). All of this was noted by a resident of Wicker Park:

> There's this landlord that's really been letting his building go. . . . He just stopped maintaining the building, and let it go. He stopped screening tenants, and they didn't have to

sign a lease any more, just put up the deposit. So we have got a lot of dope pushers and all sorts in there. So a lot of the old tenants moved out. Now there's only about half of the tenants left. And these guys are selling dope and bringing in gang members, and all sorts of stuff. Really tearing the place apart, knocking holes in walls and tearing out plumbing. The building is near ruined. [Wicker Park, Chicago]

Mounting levels of disorder and crime have a negative impact on the housing market. Statistical studies of the crime–property-value nexus typically find crime rates are so highly correlated with other physical and social determinants of property values that the independent effect of crime cannot be estimated very accurately (Frisbie, 1977). However, Taub, Taylor, and Dunham's (1984) survey of eight Chicago neighborhoods indicates that individual market evaluations and investment plans are affected by dissatisfaction with safety, by the perceived risk of victimization in the area, and by actual victimization. Crime affects the upkeep of the neighborhood; together, the two affect perceptions that the neighborhood is changing for the worse, and prompt residents to move away.

Here, the impact of disorder on residential commitment is measured in two ways. The first is a measure of neighborhood satisfaction; the second of moving intentions. (For a discussion of these measures, see Kennedy, 1984; Bach and Smith, 1977; Speare, 1974). Past research indicates that neighborhood satisfaction is undermined by disorder and crime. Hope and Hough (1988) found in Britain that indicators of disorder are strongly related to residential dissatisfaction and plans to move; and Taylor, Schumaker, and Gottfredson (1985) report that, in Baltimore, neighborhood "confidence" is negatively related to crime (− .49) and to observations of physical decay (− .58).

The surveys examined here included two questions which were combined to produce an index of neighborhood satisfaction; they asked whether respondents felt their neighborhood was a "real home" rather than "just a place to live," and how satisfied they felt with their area. In the areas for which both were available, responses to these two items were correlated .85, and the combined measure is available for all 40 neighborhoods. Figure 4–4 illustrates the relationship between satisfaction and disorder. The correlation between the two is − .64; in areas plagued by disorder, levels of satisfaction were lower. This relationship remained signif-

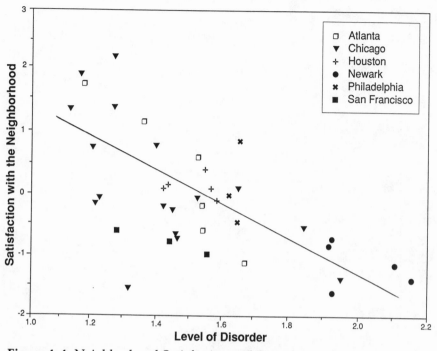

Figure 4-4 Neighborhood Satisfaction and Disorder

icant when area poverty, stability, and racial composition were controlled for.

In 30 areas, respondents were also asked about their intention to remain or to move from the neighborhood in the next one or two years. While moving intentions are not perfectly correlated with who actually leaves, they do serve as another indicator of the impact of disorder on the housing market. Figure 4-5 illustrates the link between moving intentions and disorder. The correlation between the two measures is − .40; however, Northeast Austin in Chicago clearly is a deviant case. Residents of Northeast Austin reported relatively low levels of disorder, but whites in the area perceived considerable pressure from blacks migrating into the neighborhood (for a description of Austin, *see* Goodwin, 1979). When this area is excluded, the correlation between disorder and moving intentions jumps to − .54. Controlling for area robbery victimization does not much affect the strength of the relationship, but poverty, stability, and racial composition did account for some of its apparent effect. This is in line with past research, which

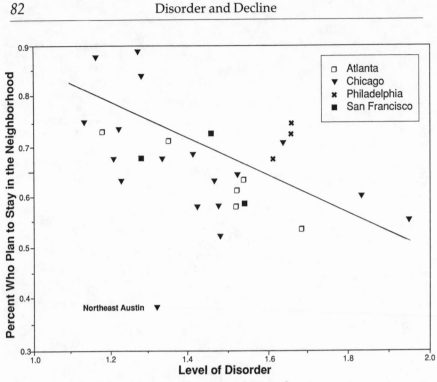

Figure 4–5 Residential Commitment and Disorder

indicates that moving intentions are greatly affected by marital status, home ownership, age, and dwelling unit type.

Some research suggests a nonlinear relationship between disorder and neighborhood commitment, affected by neighborhood social class. Physical and social disorder can be discomforting, and run counter to many people's expectations about proper conditions. However, they will vary in their tolerance of such situations. Taylor, Schumaker, and Gottfredson (1985) found that observational measures of physical deterioration had the greatest effect on neighborhood confidence in blue-collar areas of Baltimore, rather than in areas that were poor or in more well-to-do areas. They suggest that in wealthy areas instances of these problems may be ignored as atypical and non-threatening, and residents of poor areas have many other things to worry about. In moderate income areas of Baltimore, where market conditions for housing often are insecure, residents may be more sensitive to such barometers of decline. However, a test (not shown) for an interactive relationship between disorder and a desire to move—one that hypothesized that the two would be more strongly related in areas at the middle in terms of the poverty (and, separately, stability) measure—failed to support this proposition.

We have seen that disorder undermines neighborhood satisfaction and stimulates people to move. However, satisfaction is itself strongly related to moving intentions (and, in other research, to actual residential moves). In addition, both satisfaction and moving intentions are linked to levels of crime as well as disorder. Figure 4–6 shows how all these factors may be interrelated, and presents some estimates of the relative strength of each linkage.

Figure 4–6 posits that disorder and crime have both *direct* and *indirect effects* upon moving decisions—*direct*, by provoking personal fear and concern for the safety of family members, and *indirect*, through their impact upon satisfaction with the neighborhood. The importance of the satisfaction–moving path is apparent in Figure 4–6, but so is the strong linkage between disorder and satisfaction. Much of the effect of disorder on moving intentions may be indirect, through satisfaction, since its independent, direct-effect coefficient is relatively small even though the correlation between the two measures was −.54. To examine this possi-

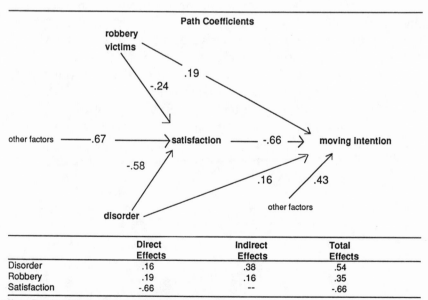

	Direct Effects	Indirect Effects	Total Effects
Disorder	.16	.38	.54
Robbery	.19	.16	.35
Satisfaction	-.66	--	-.66

Note: Data from 29 areas excluding Chicago-Northeast Austin.

Figure 4–6 Disorder, Crime, and Moving Intentions

bility, Figure 4-6 also presents summary estimates of both the direct and indirect effects of each of the three explanatory variables in the model. Disorder has a relatively large indirect effect via its impact on satisfaction, and its estimated "total" effect—while still less than that of satisfaction and *its* other determinants—looms large in shaping moving intentions.

THE IMPACT OF DISORDER

Here, we have tested three propositions about the impact of disorder on neighborhood stability and change. The first proposition involved the relationship between disorder and the capacity of communities to exercise control over local events and conditions. The neighborhood surveys suggest privatistic, household-oriented measures, as well as collective, community-oriented activities, were both undermined by area disorder. We also examined the relationship between disorder and area crime. Perceived crime problems, fear of crime, and actual victimization all were linked to social and physical disorder in the area. Those relationships were strong even when other important determinants of area crime were taken into account, suggesting that disorder could play a role in stimulating neighborhood crime. Finally, the neighborhood surveys suggest there is a strong direct and indirect link between area disorder and two of the factors that support stability in the housing market—residential satisfaction and commitment. These data probably underestimate the effects of disorder on neighborhood housing markets, since the stability of local markets is strongly affected by outsiders wanting to move *into* an area as well as by residents wishing to move out, and only area residents were interviewed. The stigma associated with high levels of visible disorder probably affects the perceptions and decisions of outsiders as well.

5

Policing Disorder

What can be done about disorder? Could police be involved in dealing with some of its important manifestations? Why are they not involved very extensively in problems of disorder? The last question is particularly interesting because police *were* responsible for dealing with many urban problems well into the twentieth century. Police conducted health inspections, cared for lost children, checked the oil supply in street lamps, monitored merchants' weights and measures, licensed street peddlers, tracked down smells emanating from tanneries, conducted city censuses, rounded up stray animals, enjoined people from raising pigs in their yards (Hartog, 1985), and maintained the sabbath. They were accessible at all hours of the day and night in small precinct station houses scattered throughout the city. Accounts of police departments before the turn of the century describe how, in the winter months, the homeless slept in large numbers in district station houses, and police soup kitchens fed the unemployed during periodic depressions. Police dealt with crises of all kinds: missing people, lost property, health emergencies, and accidents (Reiss, 1984; Monkkonen, 1981; Walker, 1977). Police were charged with maintaining the level of order appropriate to the situation in many facets of life. "Their objective was order, an inherently ambiguous term but a condition that people in a given community recognized when they saw it" (Moore and Kelling, 1983).

Police attention to many of these problems diminished over time, and this shift, encouraged by new technology and the emergence of new priorities, resulted in three major changes in how big-city police did their work. All of these changes affected their capacity to deal effectively with disorder.

The first change involved the centralization of police departments. This trend occurred partly in response to technological change. While crime control was the central function of big-city police by the end of the nineteenth century, many of the technological innovations shaping modern police organization emerged only in the twentieth. Residential telephones (widely available in big cities after about 1915) and two-way police car radios (first deployed at the end of the 1930s) blunted the impact of geography on police organization. The police no longer needed many station houses once they were motorized, and victims no longer walked to their precinct station or sought out a foot patrolman to register a complaint. Radio-dispatching shifted control of the routine activities of street officers to central headquarters. In the most technologically advanced departments, computers monitor the activity of the cars, know where they are, and quickly choose the closest vehicle available to respond to an incoming call.[1]

Other forms of police management were centralized as well. Beginning in the 1950s, a turn toward professionalism in policing put renewed emphasis (there had been waves of reform before) on instilling discipline in the ranks, controlling corruption, and limiting the influence of the political system on personnel and operating policies. This was accomplished in part by centralizing control of detectives and patrol officers working in sensitive areas (narcotics; gambling; vice; liquor inspections), and by using personnel rotation and large new districts (encompassing many political wards) as a tool to break the ties between police officers and politicians or criminals in their precincts.

The second change in policing was that departments *narrowed their focus*. A greater proportion of their time now is devoted to fighting what they define as serious crime. To be sure, they still spend a great deal of time resolving disputes, providing assistance in emergencies, and dealing with traffic problems. However, many of their earlier functions have devolved upon other municipal agencies, or have dropped from public responsibility entirely. There were a number of reasons for this. For one, by the late 1960s, adopting a "legalistic" style seemed a good way to stay out of trouble. The massive inner-city riots of the period frequently were sparked by abrasive confrontations between inner-city blacks and the police, and individual uprisings could often be traced to particular instances of curbstone justice. "Going by the book" and adopting a cool, bureaucratic demeanor while dealing with civilians was one way to defuse those tensions. Police were admonished to be evenhanded, to treat everyone with the same formal respect, and to stick to the rules. The success of the legalistic style is marked by the undoubted decline in the flagrant abuse of police power in black and poor neighborhoods over the past 20 years.

At the same time, changes in the legal system may have made it more difficult to respond "professionally" to many disorder problems. Several statutes, that were routinely used to justify rounding up people, did not survive court tests of their constitutionality. By the mid-1970s the police could no longer make "suspicion" arrests or freely pick up "vagrants," people "loitering" on street corners, and others they wanted to clear from the streets. Many statutes which were handy for rousting juveniles (as suspected runaways, or as curfew violators) also have disappeared from the books. In some areas local standards for making lawful arrests for street solicitation by prostitutes were very tightly drawn, leading to dramatic reductions in arrest totals; and, almost everywhere, public drunkenness is no longer a criminal offense. Departments focusing on "serious crime" generally do not want to deal with most of these problems, and have fewer clear standards to act on when pressed to do so.

Another factor leading to this emphasis on crime-fighting was, of course, a tremendous upsurge in the volume of crime reported to the police. It began in the mid-1960s. In U.S. cities with a population over 250,000, the number of recorded (Part I) offenses grew from fewer than 1 million in 1960 to 2.2. million in 1970, and to 3.8 million by 1980. Police budgets expanded in response, but not fast enough to catch up—the crimes-per-officer ratio almost doubled during each decade, from 10 to 19 during the 1960s, and from 19 to 34 between the beginning and the end of the 1970s.[2]

The third change in policing was that department managers sought *efficiency* in the delivery of their services. Centralized dispatching systems gave managers control over the activities of officers on the street, and over the statistical data generated from their reports. Modern administrators use activity measures and impose performance quotas to increase per-officer "output" and speed the crime-to-arrest process of their organization. They know how many minutes it takes to fill out each of the myriad forms that plague patrol officers, and approximately how many minutes of "service time" each kind of dispatch should take up. In their quest for efficiency, police departments even became the consumers of research. Police managers wanted to know how quickly they really needed to get to crime scenes; the effectiveness of saturation patrol tactics; how detectives could clear more cases; who their "supercops" were; what determined whether or not a felony charge would stick in court; and whether female officers or those patrolling in one-officer cars would be as aggressive yet as safe as their counterparts. Researchers often gave them unexpected answers (see Sherman, 1986; Skolnick and Bayley, 1986), and the suspicion cast by research on many "modern" police practices helped set the stage for the emergence of new ideas about policing in the 1980s.

One consequence of these changes in the organization and mission of big-city police was a dwindling interest in disorder. Other problems always seemed more pressing. This was in part because the way they are now organized and managed means the police are most "effective" (as they measure it) at responding to complaints about major crimes. As the volume of those complaints skyrocketed in the 1960s and mid-1970s, the commitment to respond to every emergency call as quickly as possible absorbed most of the police resources. In effect, not the top brass, but thousands of individual citizens dialing "911," set the day-to-day agenda for many police agencies. Departments had to meet these growing demands in the face of shrinking resources, for by the beginning of the 1980s many big-city departments were *smaller* than they were a decade earlier. With efficiency in mind, police managers adopted call-prioritizing schemes which guaranteed a rapid response to "man with a gun," "burglary in progress," and other emergencies, but put most complaints concerning disorder at the bottom of the stack. Many stoutly resisted providing services which were not "productive"—which did not give them wide-area coverage and speed their response time, or did not generate arrests. One early victim of productivity was foot patrol.

In addition, there are seemingly few rewards for either individual officers or departments to concern themselves with disorder. Homicide, robbery, and large-scale gang violence dominate the attention of the media. Virtually the only comparative and longitudinal data available by which the public can judge police success are yearly reports of the number of "Part I" crimes, and none of the incidents in that category measure disorder problems. Judges in clogged courtrooms often pay little attention to the kind of arrests that maintenance of order generates. Further, popular movements to decriminalize public drunkenness, and to trivialize the penalties applicable to minor cases of drug possession, suggest that vocal segments of the public do not support aggressive action against such misconduct. Police officers tend not to regard disorder arrests as a "good pinch." They have traditionally viewed themselves as strong and aggressive defenders of the public against the predations of vile and dangerous felons, while most disorder problems are a great deal more trivial. Sergeants smile at officers who make a robbery arrest, but those putting a drunk in the back of their car know there will just be vomit for them to clean up later.

The declining use of their formal authority to control disorder can be seen in the decline of arrests in the "big four" disorder categories: drunkenness, disorderly conduct, vagrancy, and suspicion. In 1960 there were 2.3 million of these arrests, and they constituted *52 percent* of all non-traffic arrests in the United States. In 1985 (when the population had grown considerably) there were only 1.4 million arrests in these categories, and they made up only *16* percent of the total (Federal Bureau of Investigation, yearly statistics). Both absolutely and relatively, the police appear to be paying less formal attention to major classes of disorder.

Motorized patrol, the continual shuffling of personnel from assignment to assignment, and their reaction to complaints also served to isolate the police from the communities they serve. They patrol in their cars, cut off from casual contact and informal communication with area residents. Because patrol officers get most of their assignments from the dispatcher, most people deal with the police only in crisis situations or when they are themselves under suspicion. Police do not hear any gossip. There are few opportunities for patrolling officers to hear about neighborhood problems, as opposed to tales of individual woe, or to develop rapport with the majority of area residents who have no occasion to call for their assistance. As Samuel Walker (1983) put it, "the police lost contact with 'ordinary' people and gained a great deal of contact with 'problem' people.

Community Policing

The problems caused by police estrangement from the communities they serve are now widely recognized. A new approach to police work, known as "Community Policing," promises to reverse many of those practices, and to repair the damage. It promises that police will be responsive to the expressed needs of the communities they serve. This is to be accomplished through organizational changes which open departments to public input concerning their priorities and procedures, coupling that with a broad, problem-solving orientation toward the issues which emerge from the process. Community Policing is currently the rage in Britain. It is that nation's major response to the racial violence which erupted there in the early 1980s (Brown and Iles, 1985). There is considerable interest in the United States as well, and elements of Community Policing are considered wherever departments attempt to innovate.

Community Policing does not focus exclusively on problems of disorder, but it is relevant because conditions of disorder could surface as a priority concern in many neighborhoods, and it might help the police do more about them. Once the public begins to play a role in defining what "important problems" are, and the police begin to define their problem-solving responsibilities more broadly, disorder will gain new attention. This was the case in Newark and Houston's Community Policing projects; they focused on such seemingly "soft" targets as fear of crime, neighborhood cohesion, social disorder, and physical decay, rather than on deterring major crimes. This emphasis was apparent both in the program-planning process and as the projects evolved in the field.

At this stage, Community Policing is not an operational "shopping list" of specific policing programs. Neither is it a particular tactical *product* to be adopted. Rather, it involves reforming organizational decision-making *processes*. It is at most a general set of guiding principles that might be implemented in a variety of ways, including those we have examined in detail. There is also a great deal of uncertainty about its practicality, and whether it reflects a too-optimistic or even a romantic view of what the public wants from its police, and the support they are willing to give them. It is also still an evolving concept. Academic thinking about Community Policing can be traced in books by legal scholar Herman Goldstein (1977) and sociologists Jerome Skolnick and David Bayley (1986) and Molly Weatheritt (1986); there are also important articles on the topic by criminologists Lawrence Sherman (1986) and George Kelling (1987). Together, they suggest that Community Policing is guided by the following principles:

1. *Community Policing assumes a commitment to broadly focused, problem-oriented policing.*

A key to Community Policing is a shift in orientation from "crime fighting" to "problem solving." During the post-1920 period, the police focused their attention on fewer matters. However, many of their non-constabulary functions were not picked up by other agencies. Lost from view were many problems—including most disorders—that no longer were defined as "police business." Community Policing takes a wider view of those responsibilities. Officers are encouraged to respond creatively to problems that come their way, or to refer people to public and private agencies that can help them. If they refer them to other agencies, they should follow up to make sure that something was actually done in response. This can even involve training officers in methods of identifying and analyzing problems. Police work traditionally consists of responding sequentially to individual events; in Newport, Virginia, however, and in other cities, officers are learning how to recognize *patterns* in incidents, converting them to "problems" and indicating something about their causes (Spelman and Eck, 1987).

2. *Community Policing relies upon organizational decentralization and a reorientation of patrol tactics to open informal, two-way channels of communication between police and citizens.*

Police departments are almost uniformly bureaucratic and hierarchical in organization. However, like many large organizations, police are learning that decentralization is often necessary, to allow flexibility in decision-making at the level at which the work is done. This involves granting police at the neighborhood level the decision-making power they need to function effectively. Police units need to discover and set their own goals, allocate and manage their own resources, and reward good work. Patrols need to be reorganized to provide opportunities for citizens to come into contact with police under nonstressful circumstances that encourage information to flow both to and from the organization. "The improvement of relationships with the police is the key objective of Community Policing" (Brown and Iles, 1985: 43). This justifies a great deal of foot patrol, which otherwise appears "unproductive" in terms of arrests or citations. Police also may find themselves attending PTA meetings, meeting with merchants' associations, and drinking coffee with block clubs, to facilitate this kind of interaction. Even traditionally-oriented officers can find some justification for this in the information and assistance that comes their way, and the trust that they develop in the community.

3. *Community Policing requires that police be responsive to citizen demands when they decide what local problems are, and set their priorities.*

In this view, effective policing demands responsiveness to civilian input concerning both the needs of members of the community and the best means by which the police can help in meeting them. This requires commitment and creativity on the part of participating officers. It also requires that a management structure be put in place that monitors requests for new kinds of service as well as the quality of the police response, to ensure that something happens. True effectiveness in responding to citizen input and actually solving problems, not just efficiency at pursuing the task, is crucial. This raises difficult management issues, for effectiveness is difficult to measure, and many of the abstract objectives of Community Policing are vague. However, they do emerge in concrete situations. The goals of Community Policing reflect theoretical notions about how the police can produce ''safety,'' but sergeants need well-defined, specific goals to pass along to their patrol officers (Southgate, 1985). This has led to renewed interest in how to measure police productivity, some of which is reflected in the evaluations reported here.

4. *Community Policing implies a commitment to helping neighborhoods help themselves, by serving as a catalyst for local organizing and education efforts.*

Commitment to Community Policing usually goes with the belief that police alone can neither create nor maintain safe communities. Rather, they need to help set in motion voluntary local efforts to prevent disorder and crime. In this role, the police are seen as valuable adjuncts to community crime-prevention programs. These include neighborhood watch, citizen patrols, and education programs stressing household target-hardening and the rapid reporting of crime. A common (but probably oversold) justification for diverting resources away from responding to 911 calls is that community-building will ultimately prevent problems from occurring in the first place (Trojanowicz, 1986; Morris and Heal,

1981). The police can assist in this process by lending support, continuity, and legitimacy to local organizing efforts.

Community Policing has been sold in many quarters as a new and hopefully more effective way to tackle both major crimes and antagonistic relationships between the police and racial minorities. However, it probably is *most* relevant to disorder. Problems of disorder now are not competing successfully for the attention of the police; presumably, a decentralized and responsive police organization would take note in places where such problems are high on the local agenda. Traditional police efforts do not have much impact on disorder problems, but Community Policing calls for different routines. Many types of disorder are not clearly unlawful, and require efforts by other municipal agencies, or even informal collective action; police can help bring such pressure to bear by encouraging community members to act on their own, and perhaps to be more vocal in their demands on public and private agencies.

The irony is that in certain respects Community Policing attempts to turn back the clock 70 years. Of course, it only *seems* to, for 70 years ago police were more frequently political, corrupt, lazy, and brutal. However, it does call for at least a partial reversal of all three of the changes in policing reviewed above—toward decentralization, a broadened focus, and an orientation toward effectiveness rather than efficiency.

Elements of Community Policing now are observable wherever police innovation is taking place. However, there is little systematic evidence that the premise of Community Policing—that officers can act in defense of community norms and preserve or restore order—is true. To examine this premise, two big-city police departments participated in an evaluation project supported by the federal government. They fielded programs designed to test the effectiveness of Community Policing in difficult urban settings. We will now examine those programs as well as their impact.

POLICING DISORDER IN HOUSTON AND NEWARK

The programs were tried out in Houston and Newark, in communities that are part of the 40-neighborhood survey. The two cities are extremely different. Houston is large, both in population and in physical size; Newark has only one-quarter the population. Houston is a sprawling, low-density, low-rise garden-apartment city laid out for easy access to freeway interchanges. The residents of Newark are packed together (380,000 people in about 19 square miles) in old wood-frame homes, apartments, and public-housing blocks set on narrow streets. In both cities the Chiefs of Police were avidly interested in the programs, and gave them a great deal of personal attention.

The programs were locally planned. In Newark, the planning process and its implementation was "top down"; that is, the command staff of the department and outside experts planned the program, which was then implemented by teams of rank-and-file patrol officers under the command of their sergeants and district commanders. In Houston, on the other hand, most elements of the program were designed by a group of patrol officers and a sergeant from the department's Planning Division; the same officers then took charge of individual projects, recruited helpers from the districts where the programs were to be run, and carried them out themselves. The Houston and Newark planners created somewhat different versions of "Community Policing." Houston's stressed local problem-solving, and granted the officers who were to do it a great deal of autonomy. Newark used its established management structure, and incorporated more traditional enforcement tactics into its programs. The relationship between the rhetoric of Community Policing and the mixed collection of projects actually fielded in the two cities seems somewhat vague. Talk about Community Policing had stressed its goals rather than how to achieve them, and the cities were left more or less on their own to figure out what Community Policing meant in practice.

The programs were evaluated by the Police Foundation, a Washington, D.C.–based research organization with a long-standing interest in police innovation.[3] To facilitate the evaluation, the program elements were implemented in different areas of the two cities, and one comparison area was set aside in each city to serve as a benchmark for the changes they were to bring about. The comparison areas were matched with program areas on several key demographic features. The evaluation involved two massive sets of interviews, observations of the programs in action, constant monitoring of events in the cities and in the police departments, interviews with the officers who participated, and the collection of large amounts of administrative data.

The programs (*see* Pate et al., 1986) were not explicitly aimed at crime prevention, although the planning task forces would have been happy to claim credit for that had it occurred. Rather, the programs and the evaluation were designed to test the hypothesis that the key elements of Community Policing—decentralization, police-citizen interaction, information-sharing, responsiveness to civilian input, and support for local self-help efforts—can have an impact upon neighborhood disorder and fear of crime. In addition, it was anticipated that, in the program areas, there would be an improvement in citizens' relationships with the police, and—if the programs were successful in reducing disorder and fear—there would also be citizen satisfaction with their residential environment.

COMMUNITY POLICING IN HOUSTON

The Houston planning task force focused upon two problems. The first was the lack of contact between citizens and the police. Houston's 1.8 million residents and 3,357 police officers were thinly spread over 565 square miles of city. There were constant complaints that people seldom saw the police. The average citizen had little opportunity to come into contact with police officers except under stressful circumstances—receiving a ticket, or calling the police after a crime had been committed. The task force felt that, because of the lack of communication between police and ordinary people, many officers had little understanding of the priorities and concerns of the people in their patrol areas. In return, residents seemed to feel that the police neither knew nor cared about them. The planners felt that this alienation led to public dissatisfaction with police services, and perhaps to fear of crime.

A second problem identified by the task force was the city's almost nonexistent neighborhood life. Houston has grown enormously in the past two decades; between 1970 and 1983 the city gained almost 500,000 new residents. By the end of the period described here the city's population was churning again following the collapse of prices in Texas' "Oil Patch." None of these factors facilitated the development of stable residential neighborhoods with a tradition of self-help; the task force thought that, more frequently, people did not know their neighbors at all, making it difficult for neighborhoods to respond to problems with disorder and crime.

The task force devised several new programs for Houston, including decentralized police offices; a new form of patrol that would increase their contact with ordinary citizens; and a team to organize communities to respond on their own to local problems.

The areas in which these programs would be tried out were drawn from a list of troubled neighborhoods that were racially and ethnically mixed, and were socially and demographically matched. Each had a population of about 3,500–5,000 persons. A political decision was made requiring that blacks, whites, and Hispanics be represented in all of the program areas, to ensure that no major contenders for power in the city could complain that they were being left out. District commanders and police crime analysts were asked to identify qualifying areas that were experiencing crime and disorder. The evaluation team visited all the recommended areas and, after more demographic and crime data had been gathered, a final conference picked the neighborhoods and the comparison area for use in the evaluation.

I.   The Community Station

The task force concluded that decentralizing control of some policing activities to small "Police-Community Stations" in storefronts could help close the gap between citizens and the police, and this was done in one of the program neighborhoods.* The task force located space in a small commercial building with adequate parking (a must in Houston). Station personnel took crime reports and gave and received information, and the office provided a place for people to meet with police. Station officers were freed from routine patrol. However, they did respond when residents of their area called the station directly for assistance. The office was to be their base of operations for getting acquainted with neighborhood residents and business people, identifying local problems and helping solve them, seeking ways of delivering better service to the area, and developing programs to draw the police and community closer together.

A central feature of the storefront office was that it was not

*A brief description of Houston's storefronts can be found in Bayley and Skolnick, 1986.

passive; people could walk in, and some activities took place there, but the staff quickly developed outreach programs that extended into the immediate neighborhood.* The programs included a series of community meetings, which were held monthly in a neighborhood church. The first attracted more than 100 residents; attendance in the seventh and eighth months averaged around 250. Officers discussed crime and other items of neighborhood interest and then presented guest speakers; during the evaluation period these included the Chief of Police, a judge, politicians, and bankers.

Station officers heard repeated complaints that a park in the center of the neighborhood had been taken over by rowdy youths; nearby residents were reluctant to use it. The police began patrolling the park regularly, and during the summer months they organized athletic events there. Residents returned to the area, and a vending machine, that had been removed after being vandalized repeatedly, was reinstalled at the park's swimming pool. Station officers also met regularly with neighborhood school administrators to discuss school problems, and cooperated with them by picking up truants and returning them to school. In addition, the station's staff fingerprinted young children whose parents brought them to the station. They later extended the identification program to a neighborhood hamburger shop in an effort to reach a larger segment of the community. Area residents also were invited to have their blood pressure taken at the station; one day each month a nurse or paramedic was available to take the readings. Finally, area churches and civic clubs were invited to select members to ride with officers on patrol.

On five occasions during the evaluation period the station staff distributed approximately 450 newsletters throughout the neighborhood. An additional 50–100 newsletters were picked up each month by visitors to the station. The newsletters advertised the station's programs and other community events, and reprinted hints about crime prevention.

The storefront provided a direct test of several aspects of Community Policing. It provided a great deal of management autonomy to the rank-and-file officers who staffed it, as well as flexibility in allocating their own time and effort. The officers responded by developing community-oriented programs that were virtually un-

---

*For more details about the activities at the storefront, see Wycoff and Skogan, 1986.

heard of in Houston's quite traditional department, and provided a variety of non-stressful contact points where police and citizens could meet. They tried to meet the planning task force's goal of establishing a visible police presence in the area and encouraging the development of a new sense of community identity in that part of the city.

II.   The Community Organizing Response Team

The Community Organizing Response Team (CORT) also addressed the limited sense of community which seems so characteristic of life in Houston. CORT attempted to create a community organization in a neighborhood where none existed. The team's immediate goal was to mobilize a group of residents who would work regularly with the police to define and help solve neighborhood problems. Its long-term goal was to foster the formation of a viable community organization, and leaving it eventually to its own devices.

To test the CORT concept, the task force selected an area to organize. The organizing effort involved becoming familiar with the area's problems; organizing meetings to introduce neighbors to one another, to familiarize them with the CORT program, and to identify potential community leaders; fostering the creation of a community organization, and using it as a mechanism for police and area residents to exchange information and views on how to tackle the area's problems; mobilizing the local business community in the effort; and promoting the program among patrol officers who regularly worked in the area.

The CORT team prepared for the task by visiting similar programs in Oakland and Contra Costa, California, and they were trained by a professional community organizer. As in all of Houston's experimental neighborhoods, CORT activities were monitored by an observer from the evaluation team.

The work began with a door-to-door survey of the target neighborhood. CORT members interviewed approximately 300 residents about problems that they felt merited police attention, and asked whether they might be willing to host meetings in their homes. The survey told them a great deal about the nature of area problems, and resulted in a few invitations to hold such meetings. The rather unusual experience of being surveyed in this way by uniformed police officers gave the program a great deal of initial visibility.

CORT members worked at selling the program to police at the district station house, for they needed the help of area officers to hold meetings, respond to problems, and sustain the program after they were gone. They spent a great deal of time at this, making speeches at roll-call, drinking coffee with fellow officers, and doing routine patrol in the area. Before the end of the evaluation period about ten other officers were involved in CORT in some way.

Thirteen neighborhood meetings were held, each attended by from 20 to 60 people. The CORT team optimistically had planned to hold 30 meetings, but found it *very* difficult to find people willing to open their homes to strangers, even those living in the immediate neighborhood. From the 13 meetings that were held, CORT members identified a group that met regularly with the district captain to discuss community problems and devise solutions involving both the police and residents. The group eventually held elections and formed committees, and by the end of the evaluation period had 60 official members.

The new group instituted a few programs: a "safe house" program marking places where children who needed help could go, a neighborhood beautification committee, a property-marking program, and a "ride along" program. The end of the evaluation period coincided with a day-long neighborhood clean-up campaign, and by that point the CORT team had for all practical purposes retired from the scene. The group's members had assumed full responsibility for organizing neighbor meetings and conducting their monthly sessions with the district commander.

During the evaluation period, newsletters were mailed monthly to residents who had been surveyed or who had taken part in an activity. The newsletters contained general news, crime prevention news, local stories, and information about past and coming CORT events.

In terms of Community Policing, the CORT program tested the ability of police departments to serve as catalysts in developing community mechanisms for self-help. Of all the programs discussed here, CORT took most seriously the idea that neighborhoods must organize in their own defense. The CORT officers were not seen as a permanent addition to the staff of the district they worked in; rather, their success would be measured by their ability to *leave* the area to its own devices.

Whatever successes CORT may have had, they were hard won.

The CORT staff succeeded in holding meetings and organizing a few activities, but it took a large investment of their time in a very small area of Houston to bring that off. They found the work frustrating and progress hard to see, for initially few residents shared their enthusiasm for the program. They had chosen to work in an area without any existing organizations at all, as opposed to one where there were active groups which, with some encouragement and support, might have focused on crime problems. It probably was harder than it should have been because the team came from outside the district, did not know anybody in the area or what the problems were, and had to spend a great deal of time selling the program to officers stationed in the district. A program involving officers who worked the beat regularly might have been easier to conduct. Finally, they did not have an office in the neighborhood. The Community Station program described earlier found it easier to do some organizing—without calling it that—out of their "home base," a storefront office which was clearly identified and (as the evaluation surveys documented) well known in the community.

III.   Citizen Contact Patrol

This program was to help Houston patrol officers become more familiar with the residents of their areas, learn about neighborhood problems, and devise methods to deal with those problems. Citizen Contact Patrol was to increase the number and quality of non-emergency contacts between the police and citizens, and to open two-way channels of communication between area residents and the police who served them.

To do this, officers in one of the program areas were freed from routine assignments outside the neighborhood. Further, as in many cities, Houston's computer-aided dispatch system matched squad cars to emergency calls based upon their availability and distance from the scene, without much regard to the area ("beat") to which they were formally assigned. For the Citizen Contact Patrol experiment, however, officers were given "beat integrity"—that is, they were not casually sent elsewhere, but were to remain active and on patrol in their own area. The officers responded to emergency calls originating in the neighborhood, whenever possible.

In other cities, what they did in their resulting "spare time" would have been called "directed foot patrol," but in Houston they drove rather than walked. The key element was door-to-door visits. Typically, officers would park on a block or in the parking lot of an apartment complex, and knock on doors. They introduced themselves to those who answered, explained the purpose of the contact, and inquired about neighborhood problems the police should know about. These were recorded on a small "citizen contact card," along with the name and address of the person being interviewed. The officers left personal business cards behind, noting that if there were further problems they could be contacted directly. In dense residential and commercial areas more characteristic of the Eastern and Great Lakes regions of the United States, people might approach a foot-patrol officer on the street; in Houston, the local equivalent is calling them on the phone. To guide further contacts, a record of their visits was kept at the program desk in the district station house. It also served as a mailing list for a newsletter tailored for the area, sent each month to those who had been contacted.

During the ten months of the program, officers tried to establish contact at 37 percent of the occupied housing units, and talked to 14 percent of the adult residents of the area. They also visited commercial establishments, and after 10 months about 45 percent of the merchants had been contacted. Because this was a small trial-program in just one area, it was carried out without an elaborate management structure. Only five officers (and their sick-leave substitutes) were involved on a continuous basis. An observer occasionally traveled with them, and was present for 40 home visits. She reported that they averaged 3–6 minutes in length, and that almost all were well received. The contact cards were monitored by the evaluators to ensure that visits were being made in all sections, and that representative groups of residents were being contacted.

What the contact team officers were then *supposed* to do was follow Wilson and Kelling's injunction "to protect what the neighborhood had defined was the appropriate public order" (1983: 13). This could involve using their authority to crack down on local troublemakers; referring people to city agencies for assistance; mobilizing those agencies on their own (for example, to tow away abandoned cars); or just providing residents with information. However, what the officers actually *did* in response to the prob-

lems they identified was not well monitored. About 60 percent of
the people they interviewed had something to complain about.
Conventional crimes were most frequently mentioned, but about
one-quarter of the residents mentioned a problem that might fall
into the disorder category, including disputes, environmental
problems, abandoned cars, and vandalism. The officers told the
evaluators about numerous actions they took in response to problems they identified, but their actions were not documented in
systematic fashion. (This was in sharp contrast to Newark's version of the program; there, a sergeant kept a careful watch on
problems, and saw to it that each was dealt with in some fashion.)
From the officers' point of view, they were very successful in
gathering a great deal of new information about crime and troublemakers in the area, and gained the trust of a number of informants
they expected to rely on in the future.

The Visibility of the Houston Programs

The programs in Houston (and Newark) were evaluated using a
quasi-experimental design. The areas were roughly matched on a
number of criteria, including crime and census data. Each program
was conducted in its own particular matched area, while one area
in each city was designated a "comparison area," and no new
policing programs were instituted there.

One task of the evaluation was to assess how visible Houston's
community policing programs were to area residents. To do this,
the program and comparison areas were surveyed before the onset
of the programs, and again after they had been in operation for 10
or 11 months. The samples were drawn randomly from a list of all
addresses in the areas. Personal interviews were conducted with
400–550 residents of each area. Included were panels of 200–275
persons who were interviewed on both occasions. Area residents
were asked about the programs beforehand, in order to measure
the extent of "background noise," or false recognition, such surveys always find; changes in the level of program visibility could
then be assessed afterward. The same questions were asked in the
comparison area, where no new police programs were instituted.
Apparent changes in "program visibility" in the area where there
was no program served as a benchmark of the effects of such
factors as radio and television coverage of the police.

Figure 5–1 depicts the results of the surveys. The highest level of recognition went (not unexpectedly, for it was an actual site and had its own big sign) to the storefront office. Before it opened, 3 percent of those interviewed in the program area, and 2 percent of those in the comparison area, claimed they knew of it. There was some media coverage of the office; and after it was in operation, 11 percent of those interviewed in the comparison area thought they were familiar with the office; in the program area it was 65 percent. In the other two areas, program officers made personal contact with a modest proportion of those interviewed. In the comparison area, a steady 3 percent of residents insisted before and after that they had received a door-to-door visit; about 12 percent of those surveyed in the Contact Patrol area recalled being visited, a figure closely matching the 14 percent contact estimate based on program records and census figures. In the CORT area, meeting attendance went from about 5 to 11 percent, and *awareness* that community meetings were being held (not shown in Figure 5–1) jumped from 16 to 32 percent after the program had been in operation for about ten months. CORT officers began their efforts by knocking on doors to conduct interviews, and this also showed up in these measures of program visibility; in terms of "home visits," they did as well as the Citizen Contact Patrol.

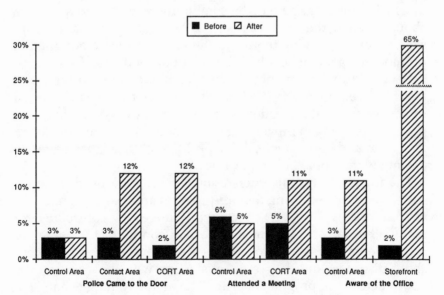

Figure 5–1 Awareness of Community Policing in Houston

The Impact of the Houston Programs

Methods for Assessing Program Impact. Disorder and fear were among the immediate targets of the program. Perceptions of the extent of *social disorder* were measured by combining responses to seven questions about "groups hanging around," panhandling, "people saying insulting things," truancy, public drinking, gang activity, and the "sale or use of drugs." Perceptions of *physical disorder* were probed by adding together responses to seven questions about problems caused by abandoned buildings, abandoned cars, vandalism of parked autos, dirty streets and sidewalks, residential vandalism, graffiti, and vacant lots filled with junk. In most areas of Houston and Newark responses to questions about disorder were two-factored, with social and physical dimensions. In addition, in Newark and the CORT area of Houston there were programs focusing specifially on physical disorder. As a result, separate indicators of physical and social disorder are employed in this chapter. *Fear of personal victimization* was measured by responses to four questions about worry about robbery and assault, fear of nearby places, and fear when out alone after dark. If they were effective, the programs could reduce levels of fear by reducing disorder, and by demonstrating to area residents that they had the active support of the police. *Satisfaction with the area* as a place in which to live was gauged by combining responses to questions about whether the area was getting better or worse, and about satisfaction with living there. All the programs were designed to promote the general health of the neighborhood, and if successful they could further cement residents' commitment to the area as a place to live. Finally, *satisfaction with police services* was measured by responses to six questions concerning "how good a job" the police were doing in preventing crime, helping victims, and keeping order, and how "polite," "helpful," and "fair" they were "in dealing with people" from the area.

The impact of the disorder reduction program on these measures was assessed using the pre-program and post-program survey interviews. Program effects were judged by controlling for many other factors. The most important control factors were the respondents' pre-program scores—their level of fear, concern about disorder, and degree of satisfaction with the area and the police before the programs began. The ability to judge change at the individual level was the biggest benefit of the repeated interviews, and those data are used here to assess program effectiveness. The statistical analyses also controlled for ten other factors that often affect fear and other attitudes: age, sex, race, income, education, marital status, home ownership, length of residence, dwelling type, and being older (here, over fifty). If differences remain between the comparison and program areas after controlling for pre-program measures and peoples' personal factors, they are evidence that the program had some effect. However, since this "quasi-experiment" used people living in two different areas as its program and comparison populations, it also is possible that *other events* in the areas affected the outcome measures. The observer monitored the areas, and reported that she found nothing else happening in the program areas that could have affected the results.

Program Impact in Houston. Table 5–1 summarizes the results of the before-and-after analysis. It indicates whether disorder, fear, and satisfaction went up or down significantly in each of the program areas. In Table 5–1, an "up" or "down" entry indicates that differences between the program and comparison areas were still significant; a " + " or " − " denotes the direction of a statistically insignificant effect.

Table 5–1 points to modest program successes. The projects were most successful at attacking disorder; in all cases, disorder went down, and five of the six comparisons were significant. The other measures all pointed in the right direction, and none of the programs seemed to have adverse effects on area residents. Neighborhood satisfaction, and satisfaction with police service, went up

Table 5–1 Program Outcomes in Houston

	Programs		
Outcome Measures	Citizen Contact Patrol	Storefront Office	Community Organization
Physical disorder	down	down	down
Social disorder	down	−	down
Fear of crime	−	down	−
Area satisfaction	up	+	up
Police performance	up	+	up
(N)	(475)	(401)	(388)

Note: "Up" and "down" indicate the signs of coefficients p<.05; "+" and "−" indicate relations more likely to occur by chance. Each column pairs a program area with Houston's comparison area. All analyses control for ten socioeconomic and demographic factors, and Wave1 levels of the outcome measures.

reliably in both the Citizen Contact and CORT areas. However, fear of crime went down significantly only in the storefront area. These welcome results were featured in the government's report on the program (Pate et al., 1985).

However, an important problem with the projects cannot be discerned in the evaluaiton results presented in Table 5-1. The program (and comparison) areas were chosen from communities in Houston housing blacks, whites, and Hispanics. This political choice, made so that all sections would be represented in the project, created an opportunity to examine the *generality* of the program effects identified above; that is, to see if everyone "got the message" (program visibility), and whether the programs had similar consequences for all groups.

The answer appears to have been "no" on both counts. There was evidence that only some people got the word, and that the programs helped only selected groups in these neighborhoods. In general, those at the bottom of the social ladder were not helped at all.

One part of the problem is documented in Table 5-2. It summarizes an analysis identifying special program effects reserved for subgroups. Where a "better" outcome is indicated, there was statistical evidence that group members were better off than their counterparts (e.g., less fearful, or more satisfied) after the program went into effect. Only two groups are described in Table 5-1, but other related social factors (such as length of residence and income) showed similar effects. Especially for the storefront and the

Table 5-2 Differential Program Effects for Subgroups

	Programs					
	Citizen Contact Patrol		Storefront Office		Community Organization	
Outcome Measures	whites	owners	whites	owners	whites	owners
Physical disorder				better	better	better
Social disorder			better	better	better	
Fear of crime			better		better	better
Area satisfaction	better	better	better	better		better
Police performance		better	better			

Note: The entries only report relations which were significant $p<.05$. The test was of the effect of being in a subgroup *and* living in the program area, controlling for pretest scores and the main effects of area and subgroup membership. Only residents of the program area are included in these analyses.

CORT program, the effects were generally confined to overlapping groups of whites and homeowners in the program areas.

The findings reported in Table 5–2 do not mean that things got worse for blacks, Hispanics, and renters, or that their assessments of police service went down. Scores for those groups simply remained the same. But in many instances the positive effects of the program were reserved for whites and homeowners, which was not welcome news to the evaluators.

WHAT HAPPENED IN HOUSTON?

Houston's three programs attained modest-to-high levels of visibility and contact with citizens, and they all scored some successes. Disorder of all kinds was down, and satisfaction with the area and police service was up. The evidence on fear of crime was mixed (only one of three downward shifts was significant), but none of the programs could be counted as a failure, as measured by these changes.

The darker side of these successes came to light in tests of the *generality* of the impact of the programs. Across a number of social indicators—most strongly in terms of race and class—those at the bottom of the local status ladder were severely underrepresented in terms of awareness and contact with the programs, and were unaffected by them. In short, the better-off got better off, and the disparity between area residents grew deeper.

The differences in program contacts and effects described here are not unusual. Often, it is the homeowning, long-term residents of a community who learn about and participate more easily in area-based programs. More evidence of this will come up when we discuss community organizations. Other social interventions have led to outcomes that differ by race and class. For example, the television program "Sesame Street" has more benefits for better-off children than for poor children. All do better after watching it, but the gap between those at the top and those at the bottom of the social spectrum also grows wider as a result (Cook et al., 1975).

The lack of positive effects for those at the bottom of the social ladder may be related to their more limited awareness of the programs. In many instances, blacks and renters were less familiar with the programs, and recalled fewer contacts with them. For example, the community station was recognized by 43 percent of blacks and 77 percent of whites; for renters and owners the comparable figures were 46 and 80 percent. Some other differences in program awareness and contact are illustrated in Figure 5–2. They show similar variations in program contact by race and affluence in all of Houston's program areas. Whites and homeowners were more likely to recall that the police came to their door, more likely to have been aware of community meetings, and more likely to have called or visited the storefront office (and all those differences are highly significant).

The differential in impact and program awareness documented in Table 5–2 and Figure 5–2 may be related to how the programs were run. The community station relied in part on established civic organizations to attract residents to station programs and to nominate candidates for ''ride-alongs.'' Neighborhood groups were used to organize the monthly community meetings. This approach appears to have worked well for members of these groups, but blacks and renters were less likely to be members of such organiza-

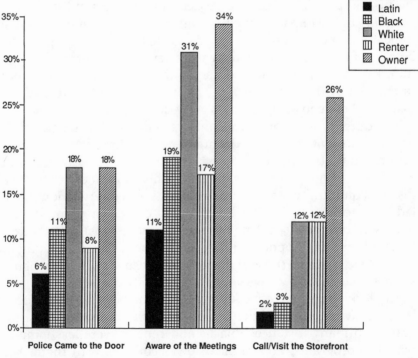

Figure 5–2 Race, Ownership, and Program Contact in Houston

tions. The CORT program held almost all of its meetings in that part of its target area that was dominated by owner-occupied single-family homes; the "problem" section of the neighborhood was where blacks were concentrated in rental buildings. In contrast, Citizen Contact Patrol featured police-initiated efforts that were monitored to ensure that all parts of the target area were canvassed. The officers conducting the door-to-door interviews could only talk to those who wanted to, but while the program also revealed race and ownership-related differences in contacts, it had fewer differential impacts.

These findings carry several significant messages. Merely making opportunities available for informal contact with the police, and participation in their programs (CORT and the storefront), was not enough. While the evidence is mixed, the program's impact seems to have spread more widely and equitably when it included an aggressive outreach effort (door-to-door contacts) that carried the program's message throughout the target area, and that did not depend on residents to come to the police.

The theoretical underpinnings of Community Policing may thus need to be reexamined. Albert Reiss (1971) suggested years ago that community-based policing may not be appropriate where communities are fragmented, and divided into competing groups along fundamental lines like race and class. The police are likely to get along best with the factions that share their outlook (Morris and Heal, 1981). The "local values" they represent are those of some of the community, but not all. In heterogeneous neighborhoods, some residents can easily become the *targets* of the programs, and are not likely to be happy about that. In the storefront area police got along best with organized segments of the community; for CORT it was homeowners in the nicer half of the neighborhood, who were worried about events in the poorer half. Equitable Community Policing may depend upon a degree of homogeneity and consensus that does not exist in many troubled neighborhoods.

CRACKING DOWN ON DISORDER IN NEWARK

The City of Newark also planned a series of special policing programs. Newark is a dense, deteriorating city ranking near the top on nearly every indicator of big-city problems. A planning task force representing the police, the Mayor's office, the courts, the

Board of Education, and the academic community devised several strategies to dealing with the situation. One of the problems they identified was disorder, and they drew up an inventory of measures to combat it.

These tactics were employed in many areas of the city, but the task force cooperated in a rigorous evaluation of the impact of the disorder-reduction effort; to do this, two versions of the program were implemented in different target areas, while in another comparison area no changes were made either in policing tactics or in the delivery of public services.

In one area the Newark police attempted to suppress social disorder using traditional police methods. These *Intensive Enforcement* tactics included foot patrol, special traffic enforcement, and cracking down on street disorder. The program was intended to demonstrate that the police controlled the streets of Newark and could exert their authority to discipline those they considered "out of line."* The crackdown was combined with a modest attack on physical disorder, through a clean-up campaign. This mix of activities was directly sparked by the hypothesis that both social and physical disorders lay at the heart of neighborhood decline.

In the other area, the Newark police fielded a *Community Policing* version of the program, employing tactics resembling those used in Houston. Police officers in this area conducted door-to-door visits as part of an intensive problem-solving effort; they also established a storefront office, and newsletters were widely distributed. These efforts were combined with intensive enforcement tactics, to produce a complex multi-program package. It was their heavy reliance on traditional enforcement tactics that differentiated both of Newark's programs from those in Houston.

In Newark, police officials and crime analysts identified potential project areas. They were all plagued by physical and social disorder, but at moderate levels that the task force thought might be "treatable" in the course of a year. This meant "moderate" for Newark; actually, these were 4 of the 6 most disorderly of all the 40 neighborhoods studied. An initial list of 34 areas of about 4,500 residents each was statistically screened to identify the most closely matching areas, and those were randomly assigned to the programs or as the comparison area. The residents were predominantly black and low-income.

*For a longer discussion of Newark's enforcement tactics, *see* Skolnick and Bayley, 1986.

I.   The Intensive Enforcement Program

Two separate but coordinated efforts were made to reduce the level of disorder in the Intensive Enforcement area of Newark. The first was designed to reduce the level of social disorder in the target area. The second focused upon physical disorder. Efforts to combat social disorder included:

Street "sweeps," to reduce loitering and disruptive behavior, drug sales, purse snatching, and street harassment. Many street corners along commercial strips in Newark were hangouts for bands of men who were perceived by the police to be "up to no good." In a sweep, groups of four or more persons "congregating to create a public hazard" (in the words of the state statute) were first warned by officers in a marked car, using a loudspeaker, that they were required to disperse. A few minutes later, vans and squad cars descended on the area to search and arrest those who failed to heed the warning. Newark's sweeps were very controversial, and of doubtful legality.

Foot patrol, to enforce laws and maintain order on sidewalks and street corners. On a typical evening, eight pairs of officers walked for one to four hours through residential areas as well as along the commercial strip running through the area. They were to establish contacts with passers-by, develop positive relationships with residents and merchants on their beat, and become familiar with area problems. They also were to disperse unruly groups, ticket illegally parked cars, and respond to requests for assistance.

Radar checks, to enforce traffic regulations. Radar units were set up on streets where citizens complained of problems with speeders, vehicles not stopping at signs, etc. Besides issuing summonses to violators, the officers checked the sobriety and credentials of the drivers, and whether the car had been reported stolen.

Bus checks, to enforce ordinances and maintain order aboard buses. This program was sparked by repeated complaints from riders about harassment, drinking, loud radios, and drug use on Newark's buses. Pairs of police officers boarded city buses passing through the target area, announced the purpose of the operation, and warned riders that those who were in violation of city ordinances would have to stop their activities or leave the bus. They then passed through the bus observing the passengers, ejecting some riders, and occasionally making an arrest.

Roadblocks, to identify drivers without proper licenses or under the influence of alcohol, to recover stolen vehicles, and to apprehend wanted offenders with outstanding arrest warrants. These operations were conducted in a formal manner and in accordance with guidelines drawn up by the department's legal staff. A clear standard—such as "every fifth motor vehicle will be stopped"— was employed in each operation, with the interval adjusted to meet traffic conditions. Police vehicles, reflective cones, and flares were used to designate paths through which cars flowed. Selected drivers were required to pull off the road. Their licenses, insurance cards, and vehicle registration certificates were inspected, and their status was checked by computer. Suspicious or seemingly intoxicated drivers were quizzed further, and summonses were issued or arrests made when appropriate.

At least some of the operations were conducted in the target area at least three times per week, at random times to minimize their predictability. Almost all were conducted between 4 P.M. and midnight by a special team of 24 officers who were trained for three days on the legal, tactical, and community-relations aspects of the program. Foot patrol was by far the largest component of the intervention package. In an average month the enforcement team issued 30 summonses, made 24 bus inspections (ejecting 7 persons), conducted 14 field interrogations, and arrested 8 people. In practice few complete street sweeps were conducted; after the first few, they were so widely recognized by local "street people" that groups disbanded quickly.

The second focus of the Newark program was physical deterioration. In the Intensive Enforcement area, two program components dealt with physical decay:

Intensification of city services. The city promised to speed up repair efforts, make structural improvements, improve garbage collection, and conduct clean-up programs in the target area. In the end, 16 of 20 locations identified as needing attention (mostly junk-filled vacant lots) were actually cleaned up.

Sentencing to the community. A legal mechanism was created to assign juveniles, who had been arrested for minor acts of delinquency and other petty offenses, to be sentenced (at their option) to perform supervised clean-up activities in the area. Their assignments were determined by a Juvenile Conference Committee representing area organizations and residents. The youths cut grass, gathered trash, and performed other tasks under the supervision of a police officer. A total of 113 hours of labor was contributed by this program, cleaning 5 of the 16 lots that were cleared up.

II. Community Policing

The Community Policing program package addressed several of the major causes of fear identified by the planning task force in Newark—lack of information on what to do about crime, a lack of communication between ordinary citizens and the police, and a high level of disorder in the city's neighborhoods. The test area happened to be in the most densely populated and crime-ridden part of Newark. There, enforcement tactics targeting social disorder were combined with a cleanup program, and with some of the community-oriented policing tactics being developed in Houston. The program components included:

Community Station. Newark opened a "Police Community Service Center" to help reduce the gap between the police and citizens. The storefront office was to handle "walk-in" customers who had questions concerning police-related matters, who needed information, or simply wanted to talk. Storefront officers distributed crime-prevention and property-marking information, took complaints about neighborhood problems for referral to other city and community agencies, and handled walk-in and telephone reports of crimes. One or two evenings a week, local groups—ranging from block organizations to a Boy Scout troop organized by the storefront officers—held meetings at the storefront. The office also served as a place for police officers to meet, fill out reports, and eat, which encouraged its use by officers in the vicinity.

Office records indicate that about 300 people visited the storefront each month. The office was staffed by a sergeant, two police officers and members of Newark's civilian auxiliary volunteer police group.

Citizen Contact Patrol. To help create positive contacts between police officers and citizens, the sergeant in charge of the service center assigned officers to knock on doors and fill out brief questionnaires. These visits were to elicit information about neighborhood problems, and the possible means of solving them. The officers were to encourage citizens to become involved in block-watch and other neighborhood groups, distribute crime-prevention information and the department's newsletter, and alert residents to the existence of the storefront office. A computer listing of all addresses in the area was used to monitor the progress of the home visits. The evaluation observer reported that a typical interview lasted seven to ten minutes. People were often puzzled at first as to why the police were at their door, but their confusion and wariness usually disappeared quickly. Many residents offered the officers coffee and invited them inside, seeking to talk at greater length.

Completed questionnaires were reviewed by the storefront sergeant. Problems could be dealt with by his neighborhood team, or by the group carrying out Intensive Enforcement tactics in the two Newark program areas, or they could be referred to other city agencies. The sergeant was responsible for seeing that steps were taken to address problems identified in the home visits, and that the citizens involved were informed about what action had been taken.

During the 10-month evaluation period, door-to-door interviews were completed at about 50 percent of the homes in the area. The most frequently mentioned problems were with juveniles, burglary, auto theft or vandalism, and personal crime (only 6 percent of the total). About 15 percent of the problems would be classified as disorders.

Neighborhood Police Newsletter. Between 1,000 and 1,500 newsletters tailored for this area were distributed each month to block and tenant associations, retail stores, apartment buildings, banks, grocery stores, and other locations. They were distributed by staff members of the community service center, by officers conducting directed police-citizen contacts, by auxiliary police, and by neighborhood volunteers.

Intensive Enforcement. A crackdown against street disorder was also carried out in this area by the same team of officers who carried out the enforcement program in the other area, and at about the same level of intensity. About 60 percent of their time was spent on foot patrol; the remainder was devoted to radar and bus operations, roadblocks, and street sweeps. Hundreds of tickets were given, and 62 people were ejected from buses passing through.

Neighborhood Clean-Up. Three of the six locations requiring clean-up were actually cleaned during the ten-month implementation period, and two abandoned buildings were demolished by the city.

Visibility of the Newark Programs

None of the special programs described above were conducted in the comparison neighborhood. However, several carried out in other areas of the city received some publicity. The roadblocks and bus checks involved vehicles passing through the program area and could have affected residents of other places. Although foot patrol had been cut back earlier for budgetary reasons, it had been used extensively in Newark for more than a decade, and was familiar to many residents. As a result, the evaluators expected that the programs would be ''visible'' even in the comparison area. This turned out to be so. In Figure 5-3, it is the *relative* increase in awareness of the programs in the program areas as opposed to the comparison area that should be used to assess their visibility.

As Figure 5-3 documents, the roadblocks thrown up in both program areas were especially visible, but the proportion of residents aware of the street sweeps went up distinctively (from 20 to 40 percent) only in the Community Policing area. Figure 5-3 also charts the percentage of respondents who recalled having seen the police in the past 24 hours. The police seemed to be especially visible after the onset of the program only in the Community Policing target area (which is labeled the ''multi-program'' area). Controlling for pre-program awareness measures and ten demographic factors, all of the measures were significantly higher in the Community Policing area. In the Enforcement area, awareness of roadblocks and street sweeps grew significantly, but general police visibility did not. The enforcement activities were carried out by the same team, for about the same number of hours, and using

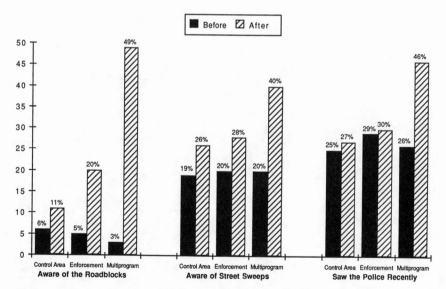

Figure 5–3 Awareness of Enforcement Tactics in Newark

the same mix of tactics in each area. But differences in program awareness between the enforcement-only and comparison areas were not as great. This was probably due to the visibility of the teams of officers making door-to-door visits, distributing newsletters, and working out of the storefront office.

Figure 5–4 documents the extent of popular awareness of Community Policing in Newark. The success of this aspect of the program in reaching residents is evident. While in the comparison area only a scattered few thought they had heard of a storefront office, said they had received a door-to-door visit, or claimed to have received crime-prevention information, the level of awareness of these activities in the Community Policing area was exceptional. More than 50 percent of those interviewed indicated that a police officer had come to their door, that they had received information, and had gotten a police newsletter (the last question was asked only in the post-program surveys). Fully 90 percent of the residents of the program area were aware of the storefront office, a figure so high that it would distort Figure 5–4 if it were graphed there. Other indicators of program visibility not included in Figure 5–4 were similarly impressive; for example, after the program, 13 percent of those interviewed in the comparison area reported seeing a foot patrol officer in their area; in the Intensive Enforcement area the

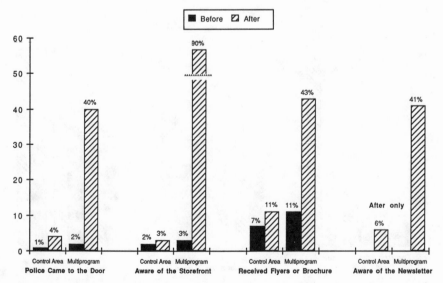

Figure 5–4 Awareness of Community Policing in Newark

comparable figure was 24 percent, and in the Community Policing area it was 63 percent. Only the youth-cleanup aspects of the programs (not shown) appear to have gone unnoticed in both areas.

Impact of the Newark Programs

Differences in the magnitude of public awareness of these programs were reflected in measures of how successful they were. Table 5–3 presents an analysis of program impact similar to that for Houston. Using the before-and-after panel surveys, it documents differences between those living in the program and comparison areas that appear to be the result of the two efforts.

The Intensive Enforcement program appears to have succeeded in reducing the level of social disorder problems in the area, its primary goal. Levels of physical disorder reported by area residents unaccountably seem to have *risen* after the program went into effect, but there is no reason to think this may have been caused by the cleanup effort. The program had no apparent effect on neighborhood satisfaction or fear of crime. On the other hand, the Community Policing package had a variety of effects. In that area, both social and physical disorder went down, fear of crime went down, neighborhood satisfaction went up, and residents were more satisfied with the quality of police service. Many of the projected effects of decentralization, of a problem-solving orientation, and of structured citizen input into policing, were apparent in that area of Newark.

Unlike the Houston projects, these programs showed little evi-

Table 5–3 Program Outcomes in Newark

	Programs	
Outcome Measures	Intensive Enforcement	Community Policing
Physical disorder	up	down
Social disorder	down	down
Fear of crime	–	down
Area satisfaction	–	up
Police performance	+	up
(N)	(493)	(525)

Note: "Up" and "down" indicate the signs of coefficients p<.05; "+" and "–" indicate relations more likely to occur by chance. Each column pairs a program area with Newark's comparison area. All analyses control for ten socioeconomic and demographic factors, and Wave 1 levels of the outcome measures.

dence of differential effects among subgroups. There also were only a few scattered subgroup differences in the extent of program visibility and contact in Newark, perhaps because these areas were racially homogeneous and more uniformly poor than those in Houston.

Monitoring Police Aggressiveness. Are the potential benefits of such enforcement and citizen involvement strategies likely to be negated by adverse popular reactions to the new police visibility and aggressiveness that they engender? Enthusiasm for closer police attention is not universally shared. In addition, the enforcement programs described above involved a wider-ranging exercise of police authority than was traditional in Newark's neighborhoods. The roadblocks, special traffic crackdowns, breaking up of streetcorner groups, and foot patrols down residential streets, brought the police into confrontational relationships with more people—and with people who might not think of themselves as criminals—than before. As a result, there was a "downside" risk to these programs—area residents might come to view the disorder-reduction teams as a new occupying army.

To monitor these potential consequences, the evaluation surveys included two questions directed at the perceived aggressiveness of police tactics. In both sets of interviews, respondents were asked if "police stopping too many people on the streets without good reason" and "police being too tough on people they stop" were problems in their area. Regression analyses like those in Table 5–3 revealed no evidence that those perceptions were affected by either version of Newark's program.

Effects of the Two Strategies. What were the comparative effects of enforcement and community programs in Newark? The Community Policing program included elements of each, and the Enforcement program featured a great deal of foot patrol in residential areas.[4] As a result, residents of each community were exposed to some elements of both programs, the effects of which may have been complementary or might have canceled each either out. The evaluation surveys can be used to contrast the effects of the two program elements on the neighborhood problems at which they were aimed. Table 5–4 shows the extent to which residents of Newark's two test areas came into contact with the programs. A measure of *contact with community policing* was constructed of responses to questions concerning whether respondents had seen a foot-patrol officer in their neighborhood, knew of the storefront office, had seen a police newsletter, or were visited by an officer assigned to citizen contact patrol. A measure of *awareness of intensive enforcement* was based on whether respondents knew about bus checks, roadblocks, and the street sweeps (very few of them recalled being personally caught up in them).

Table 5–4 reports the direction and significance of the correlation between these measures (taken from the second set of surveys) and program outcomes, controlling for first survey levels of outcomes and ten social and economic factors. The contact and awareness measures were weakly correlated (those who knew of one program tended to know about the other), so they both were included in the analysis at the same time.

Table 5–4 suggests that residents of the two Newark program areas who recalled having contact with Community Policing elements were affected in ways that were intended—they were less likely to see disorder problems, less fearful, more satisfied with their neighborhood, and more impressed with the performance of the police. Those who were aware of various elements of the Intensive Enforcement program also were more satisfied with their neighborhood, and (marginally) with the police in the second interview; however, they were also somewhat *more* fearful and *more* likely to perceive social and physical disorder problems in their area. The effects of recalled program-contact described here mirror some of those reported in Table 5–3, which indicated that levels of perceived physical disorder went up in the Intensive Enforcement program area. Those elements of the Newark pro-

Table 5–4 Effects of Program Contact in Newark

Outcome Measures	Combined Program Areas Only	
	Correlates of Various Types of Program Contact	
	Enforcement Contact	Community Policing Contact
Physical disorder	up	down
Social disorder	+	down
Fear of crime	+	down
Area satisfaction	up	up
Police performance	+	up
(N)	(499)	

Note: "Up" and "down" indicate the signs of coefficients p<.05; "+" and "–" indicate relations more likely to occur by chance. All analyses control for ten socioeconomic and demographic factors, and Wave 1 levels of the outcome measures.

gram may actually have been counterproductive. While signaling that the police were active in their area, those traditional, enforcement-oriented programs may have themselves been taken as "signs of crime."

WHAT HAPPENED IN NEWARK?

The Newark field experiment provides some support for the contention that direct police action to control disorder can help stem the process of urban decline. To test the hypothesis that they could, the Newark Police Department committed thousands of officer hours to a variety of enforcement tactics concentrated in each of two small areas of the city. In addition, other government agencies and the courts cooperated in cleaning up several unsightly locations. In one of the areas extensive efforts were made to get residents involved as well.

The *evaluation* indicates that the police can effectively reduce levels of social disorder by using Intensive Enforcement tactics. However, awareness of elements of the enforcement program was counterproductive in certain circumstances, and the foot-patrol components of the program may have been the positive force in the Intensive Enforcement area. Apparently, the Community Policing version of the program had more substantial consequences. That program was designed to increase the quantity and quality of contacts between police and citizens. The Citizen Contact effort gave police an opportunity to learn what residents thought the neighborhood's problems were, and what should be done about them. A large proportion of those interviewed remembered the police visit. The local Service Center provided a place for large numbers of area residents to drop in and register complaints, and the newsletter provided regular feedback concerning what the police were doing in the community. About 90 percent of area residents knew of the storefront office, and 40 percent were aware of the newsletter. Fewer of those who were reinterviewed in the Community Policing area rated social disorder or physical decay as "big problems"; they felt safer, and were more satisfied with their neighborhood and with the quality of police service there. Measures of individual awareness and contact with Community Policing activities in both areas were all significantly related to the desired program outcomes.

The flow of information fostered by the door-to-door visits and by the storefront office in that area may have improved the targeting of enforcement efforts, and may also have raised the visibility of those elements in the eyes of residents. An alternative explanation is that what really made the difference was the sheer visibility of the police as they walked the streets, staffed the storefront, and made informal contacts with residents. This could be the case if there were indeed some "reassurance factor" in those experiences, for activities in the Community Policing area seem to have made a big difference in the level of police visibility. For example, in the comparison area, 30 percent of respondents both before and after said they had seen a police officer in the previous 24 hours. In the Intensive Enforcement area (where most operations were conducted after dark, on arterial streets and commercial strips and not on residential blocks) the comparable before-and-after figures were 26 and 27 percent. However, in the Community Policing area the police were much more visible; the same percentage went from 26 to 46 percent. On the other hand, it is hard to conceive of Community Policing that does not routinely increase police visibility to ordinary citizens; it should probably be considered as part of the program package rather than as an alternative explanation for its apparent effectiveness.

Why did the Community Policing program enjoy some success, while Intensive Enforcement tactics by themselves failed to affect residents' perceptions of most neighborhood conditions? It might be argued that Intensive Enforcement did not accomplish very much because the sample sizes or the reliabilities of the measures employed were too small to document a real program effect. However, the survey samples and measurement reliabilities were similar in all areas of Newark (and Houston), arguing against this type of error as an explanation for a "no effect" finding. The programs also might have been vulnerable to the charge that the target areas were too small for changes there to have an impact on the lives of residents; however, the areas were virtually identical in size. Another explanation for the apparent failure of Intensive Enforcement could be the brevity or weakness of the program's implementation. However, with the exception of the citizen input into the Community Policing program, levels of implementation were very similar in the two areas. Hence, it was the structured community input provided by the storefront office, the door-to-door visits, and (perhaps; see Williams and Pate, 1987) the newsletters that made the difference.

Finally, the Intensive Enforcement program provided a kind of control for the "Hawthorne Effect." It was long ago noted in studies of working conditions in industrial settings that workers who were getting attention of some sort increased their productivity, almost regardless of the nature of that attention. One could hypothesize that in crime-ridden but resource-poor cities, *any* extra attention by the police will be appreciated, and that this will spread at least temporary goodwill over whatever they choose to do. But in Newark, special enforcement efforts that were not conducted along Community Policing lines affected only their direct target—social disorder—and had no ancillary benefits.

As police programs go, the Newark disorder control effort was substantial. To free up enough manpower to conduct the disorder reduction program, it was necessary to reassign administrative personnel to street duty, make staff schedule changes that arguably were in violation of the city's contract with the police union, and push the department's resources to the limit. It took extensive coordinating efforts to create the juvenile sentencing process that cleaned vacant lots, and a great deal of additional energy went into planning another, school-based, program that failed to materialize. It does not appear that a more intensive program *could* have been fielded in Newark; if so, this was a fair test of a *feasible* program for Newark, and perhaps for other cities that are short of resources.

Was disorder suppression a *wise* thing to do? Our evaluation cannot answer this question. It *could* document that residents of the Commuity Policing area in particular felt better about several aspects of their lives, and that residents of neither area seemed to feel the police exceeded their authority. Whether there were better things the police could have done with the considerable resources they invested in the project, or whether the city could have spent the money more wisely on some other, non-police activity, remain unanswered questions. As we saw in Houston, Community Policing does not have to be coupled with aggressive enforcement tactics to succeed. There is more than one community-oriented route to countering the forces behind neighborhood decline.

THE EFFECTIVENESS OF COMMUNITY POLICING

What can the police do about disorder? Here we examined how two cities planned and implemented their versions of Commuity Policing, to try to build bridges with their communities and reduce fear of crime. In Houston, a bottom-up planning process produced decentralized programs featuring considerable operating autonomy on the part of the small teams of officers who carried them out. The programs were modest, but showed consistently positive results. Newark's sole Community Policing program was more substantial; it involved more officers, and several elements of a Community Policing program were fielded in the target area. Compared to Houston's, it was much more visible—more than three times as many people in Newark recalled being visited in their home, one-third more knew about Newark's storefront office, and more knew about the police newsletter being circulated in the area. Newark's Community Policing program had more, and stronger, effects on area residents. In contrast, Newark's Intensive Enforcement program featured much less informal police-citizen contact, no large-scale problem-solving efforts by police, and no role for citizen input into enforcement priorities; it appears to have affected only its direct target, social disorder.

Despite these findings, and the widespread visibility of the Houston and Newark programs in the policing community, there is still a great deal of official resistance to the idea of Community Policing. It continues to be "inefficient" by many of the performance criteria employed by up-to-date police departments. The goals of Community Policing—information sharing; confidence building; self help—are seemingly "soft" and difficult to sell. Community Policing also runs counter to traditional police culture. Officers involved in it risk being classed with the "empty holster guys" in Community Relations and other peripheral parts of their departments. Many of the good reasons for centralizing departments and constantly rotating their personnel—in particular, to control corruption and break their ties with local politicians—are still valid. And neither has the burden of 911 calls for service been eased. Finally, decentralization of decision-making threatens the role of middle managers (lieutenants and captains) in the police hierarchy; they succeeded in killing earlier innovations (like Team Policing) which took away their power, and they may succeed again.

At the same time, Community Policing is not the same thing as community control of the police. Police officers and their supervisors make the decisions, and community input is not binding. The creation of mechanisms to ensure formal police accountability to the public has not been part of the current discussion surrounding

Community Policing. In this respect the debate about Community Policing differs from the community control debate of the 1960s; at that time, the Black Panther Party demanded that the public have a direct voice in hiring, disciplining, and firing officers, and in day-to-day management issues. The Black Panthers wanted to ensure that the police would reflect community priorities by making them *responsible* to the community, through political mechanisms that placed direct authority over them firmly outside the organization (Fogelson, 1977). Community Policing, by contrast, attempts to make police *responsive* to the community by restructuring authority within the organization.

Perhaps it was this police attempt to handle in an administrative manner decisions about what they should do, instead of democratizing the procedures, that contributed to one of the most striking findings of the Police Foundation's evaluation of these Community Policing programs—their unequal impact, and the great differences in program awareness and participation evidenced by different races and income groups in Houston's program areas. The police could work with whoever they felt most comfortable, and conveniently avoid conflict over what they should be doing, and to whom. They were not forced in any structured way to confront conflicting views of their activity, and in the end what they did seemed to have been irrelevant to the lives of many in the community.

Finally, the evaluations of policing programs in Houston and Newark also could not answer whether attacking disorder in this fashion was the wisest thing to do. Were there better things the police could have done with resources they invested in the project, or could the cities have spent their money more wisely on non-police activities? To probe these questions would involve fielding a variety of larger and much more expensive field experiments to test the costs and benefits of alternative strategies. Nothing like this has ever been done, but the next chapter does consider one alternative to formal policing: that of helping communities police themselves.

6

Community Organizations and Disorder

Can communities confront disorder on their own? In the 1970s and 1980s, there has been increased interest in the role that voluntary community efforts can play in dealing with local problems. Earlier in the 1960s, "more social programs" and "more police" seemed the obvious answers to urban decay and its attendant problems, but by the late 1970s municipal and federal fiscal crises made those solutions less viable, and a great deal of research had accumulated indicating they were not necessarily the best ideas. The emergence at about this time of community approaches to crime prevention presented a rationale for experimenting with off-budget approaches to local problem-solving. The community approach emphasizes collaboration between government agencies and neighborhood organizations. It also assumes that voluntary local efforts must support official action if order is to be preserved within realistic budgetary limits and without sacrificing our civil liberties.

The community approach assumes that disorder and crime (the two are almost always lumped together) reflect the dissipation of the forces that traditionally held urban neighborhoods together. In the past, many city residents were poor and illiterate, housing was crowded and conditions unsavory, wages were low, and cyclical unemployment levels were often extreme. However, levels of social disorder often remained low because the traditional agents of neighborhood social control were strong: families, parish churches, schools, the bonds of ethnic solidarity, and conservative values. Disorder problems are worse now because those forces have lost their hold.

The perhaps too simple idea is that, since mounting disorder and crime reflect the declining strength of informal social controls in urban neighborhoods, efforts to reinvigorate those informal controls may succeed in reversing the trend. While there might be other mechanisms for doing this (for example, by attacking unemployment and family breakdown, and upgrading the quality of schools) organizing communities to recapture the past has emerged as our newest hope for reshaping urban neighborhoods.

After a decade or more of focusing on crime and disorder problems, surveys point to modest national levels of participation in these efforts. In 1981, 12 percent of American adults claimed membership in a neighborhood group or organization that was involved in crime prevention (O'Keefe and Mendelsohn, 1984). A national survey conducted in 1984 found that 7 percent of adults had joined a neighborhood-watch group, one of the most common forms of collective activity (Whitaker, 1986). Organized participation (but not individual or household preventive measures, which are more uniformly adopted) is about twice as high in central cities as in non-metropolitan areas.

Here we explore the role that community organizations might play in the control of neighborhood disorder by examining the expectations of its proponents and reviewing some research on how things work in practice, followed by descriptions of organizing efforts in Chicago and Minneapolis which tested whether these efforts can be transplanted to new areas.

CURES FOR DISORDER: THE THEORY

There are really two steps in the process by which local groups can affect levels of neighborhood disorder. Both steps must work if group efforts are to make a long-term difference. The first step involves identifying "root solutions" for disorder problems; groups must identify the mechanisms that will suppress social disorder and reverse the process of physical decay. As we shall see, this is not necessarily the same thing as attacking their "root causes." Theories about solutions for disorder and crime problems take two forms: roughly, social and political. Social approaches stress the importance of communal forces within neighborhood exerting pressure to conform to an approved standard of behavior. They typically focus on developing neighborliness, watchfulness, a sense of territorial responsibility, and norms about public conduct. Political approaches point to key decisions by public and private organizations that provide leverage points for concerted action. Groups pursuing political strategies typically focus on the lending policies of local banks, on municipal land use and economic development policies, and on decisions in Housing Court about building abandonment and disrepair.

The second step involves identifying how organized efforts can set those social and political solutions in motion, and keep them moving over the long haul. Can local groups actually affect the factors that stimulate or retard disorder, and do so with practical levels of effort and within reasonable periods of time? We must pay particular attention to assumptions about how organizations can help rearrange neighborhood social processes. Their efforts typically involve the formation of block clubs, neighborhood patrols, and programs for teenagers. Social strategies have a great deal of romantic appeal, for they promise to bring village-like harmony to twentieth century city neighborhoods. However, they involve interpersonal relationships that are powerfully affected by other factors, including the family organization of the community, the age of residents, and the area's physical layout. The ease with which these interventions can be mounted is greatly determined by the social and economic stability of an area, and its homogeneity of class and race (Skogan, 1987). Political action, on the other hand, reflects an organization's analysis of its political position. Groups must identify the forces and actors inside and outside the community that lie at the heart of their problems, forces that they think they can successfully counter; thereby they must develop a political agenda. This assumes that urban neighborhoods are an effective locus for action—that regional and national macroeconomic forces and large-scale demographic shifts at the metropolitan area level can be countered effectively at the small-area level. As we shall see, this is more likely to happen in some areas than in others.

The key social factor shaping a community's capacity to control disorder is its *intervention capacity*. A great deal of evidence (summarized by Goodstein and Shotland, 1980; Shotland and Goodstein, 1984; and Greenberg, Rohe, and Williams, 1985) points to the importance of the territorial perceptions of neighborhood residents, and their willingness to intervene in events when necessary. Intervention in local events is a two-step process: area residents must be alert to untoward persons and activities, and they must be willing either to call the police or to challenge those who are up to no good. To do this effectively, they must know when and where to watch, and recognize what is or is not suspicious at that time and place (Mayhew, 1981). In stable neighborhoods, where area residents are familiar with one another, exchange information, share a solid sense of community, and define the block or the neighborhood as territory for which they feel responsible this capacity is a rather ordinary aspect of social life. But it is undermined in neighborhoods that have entered the cycle of decline, and evidence suggests that the commitment of individuals to "defending" their immediate turf is much reduced by the destabilizing forces of urbanization.

Community organizations have developed strategies to foster both watching and acting. Block-watch groups are intended to build the familiarity and exchange of information needed to make this work—who lives where; when they will be away; who the troublemakers are. For example, block-watch organizers stress the importance of setting up and maintaining phone networks so neighbors can contact one another if need be. At the extreme, neighborhood patrols may be mounted to watch and act aggressively. Information campaigns are aimed at enhancing people's sense of efficacy in taking action against disorder and crime, spreading the message that they can make a difference. Community meetings typically involve discussions of local problems; through this, organizers hope to identify the common interests of participants, emphasize their interdependence, and generate enthusiasm for intervention.

The second set of "root solutions" are political and economic rather than social in nature. They place much more emphasis on dealing with forces outside the neighborhood that impact upon local conditions. Strategies in this category include efforts to use building inspections, and housing court, as levers for resisting residential blight, keeping large old homes from being cut up into rooming houses through enforcement of zoning regulations, and seizing or demolishing abandoned buildings. Community groups interested in housing renewal (as most are) also keep a keen eye on the investment patterns of local banks and savings and loans associations, to ensure that they make reasonable purchase or rehabilitation loans in their areas. They battle "panic peddling" and blockbusting techniques by which real-estate operators reap enormous profits trading on fear of crime and racial change. They monitor land-use policies, resisting attempts to locate (for example) community-based drug or mental health treatment centers in their area, or new public housing. They also search for ways to reinvigorate the local employment market through government programs that leverage private investments likely to produce jobs for their constituents. Most root solutions involve property and land use, and take on a political cast when decisions are closely held by politicians and large corporate actors. These are fundamental to the political economy of American urban areas, and underlie the distribution of many forms of disorder.

CURES FOR DISORDER: THE PROGRAM(S)

The community approach stresses (a) identifying root solutions to problems (broadly characterized here as "political" and "social"), and then (b) mounting and sustaining programs to translate those solutions into action. The programs include several different tactics. They range from narrow, technical approaches to prevention to broader, social-reform strategies for reshaping communities. Some efforts involve collective action (these activities are carried out by groups), while others call for individual initiative, but can be encouraged and facilitated by groups. Some programs aim at *defusing the threat of neighborhood problems*. For example, groups offer escorts for senior citizens on shopping days, and produce and distribute newsletters identifying actions that individuals can take to make themselves feel more secure at home and on the street. Other programs focus on *collective surveillance* and on mobilizing the police. Groups organize neighbors to watch over the neighborhood and one another's homes, to be alert for suspicious people and for unsettling or disorderly circumstances, and to call the police promptly. Thoroughgoing surveillance programs can involve organized civilian patrols. Organizations also push for the *sanctioning of offenders*, through crime-tip hotlines that identify troublemakers, and by court-watch programs that attempt to ensure they get tough treatment from judges. Finally, organizations mount programs aimed at *attacking the social origins* of disorder and crime; what these causes are perceived to be varies from place to place, but the programs frequently involve recreational activities for youths, anti-drug and anti-gang efforts, and campaigns to clean up neighborhood parks and vacant lots, and to foster youth employment.

Where Are Organizations Active? Systematic studies of the distribution of anti-crime organizations across neighborhoods indicate that they are least common where they appear to be most needed —in low-income, heterogeneous, deteriorated, high-turnover, higher-crime areas. Community organizations are more frequently encountered in better-off neighborhoods.

Actually, it may be that the relationship between the number of local voluntary associations and indicators of social and economic stability is *curvilinear* (Podolefsky and DuBow, 1979). Aside from church activities, organizational life is at its nadir in poor, crime-ridden areas.[1] Residents typically are deeply suspicious of one another, report only a weak sense of community, perceive they have low levels of personal influence on neighborhood events, and feel that it is their neighbors, not "outsiders," whom they must watch with care (Greenberg, 1983; Greenberg, Rohe, and Williams, 1985; Garofalo and McLeod, 1986). As we saw earlier, crime-prevention activities which require frequent contact and cooperation among neighbors are less likely to be found in poor areas, and in areas where there are high levels of disorder.

Local organizations are also less frequently encountered in the most stable and tightly-knit (usually white, working-class) areas. There, informal networks take the place of formal channels of communication. Residents know one another, and frequently are linked by church and family to many others in the immediate neighborhood. Life in these areas can resemble an "urban village." This is not necessarily to their advantage. In modern society, tight-knit, cohesive neighborhoods, like those uncovered by sociologist Herbert Gans (1962) in his study of ethnic neighborhoods in Boston, can persist only in isolated nooks and crannies of the city, and are measured in size by blocks rather than square miles. Within a small area residents may still be able to identify "strangers," and quasi-vigilante activity may help preserve their isolation, but they remain very vulnerable to larger political and social forces.

It is the moderately cohesive areas that appear to need participation in more formally organized voluntary associations, and that do indeed support them. They may be the most typical urban neighborhoods. They are stable working-class and middle-class areas. Relatively prosperous and homeowning families live there, but they have few strong local social and familial ties. In the absence of close ties, residents require some mechanism to bring them together to deal with local problems. They may succeed, because they are familiar with using organizations for instrumental problem-solving (Crenson, 1983). Of course, their advantage is not complete; the poor are also capable of organizing. There is considerable variation in the extent of organization within categories of neighborhoods, and not all middle-class communities are capable of responding collectively to external threats (Henig, 1982). However, their head start in the quest for neighborhood advantage is clear.

Successful neighborhood organizations also are more common in homogeneous areas. Neighborhoods featuring a mix of life-styles may need organizations in order to identify their residents' common interests, but more frequently they do not seem to have any organization that meets that need. Anthropologist Aaron Podolefsky (1983: 136) noted the problem in an ethnically and economically heterogeneous area, Wicker Park in Chicago:

> While many community organizations and social service groups can be found in Wicker Park, there is no single cohesive organization with which the entire community can identify. Community groups are either almost exclusively white or almost exclusively Latino. None is composed of an ethnic mixture which replicates the population of the neighborhood. The concerns to which the white and Latino groups address themselves are frequently different (Podolefsky, 1983: 136).

Wicker Park was rated the third most disorderly of the 40 neighborhoods studied, and the worst in Chicago, but community-wide efforts to battle decay were almost impossible to organize. In heterogeneous areas, or those that like Wicker Park are undergoing transition, middle-class residents often unite against ''bad elements'' in their own community, and their organizations—and thus the residents' opportunities for participation—remain small and exclusionary. The advantage of economic, racial, and culturally homogeneous areas is that residents share a definition of what their problems are and who is responsible for them. They share similar experiences and objective life conditions, and the same broad conception of their public and private responsibilities (Henig, 1982). The empirical evidence (summarized in Rosenbaum, 1987) is that in homogeneous areas residents exercise more informal control, are more likely to intervene when they see problems, feel more positively about their neighbors and personally responsible for events and conditions in the area, and are more active in crime-prevention programs.

In multicultural areas, by contrast, there often are conflicting views of both the causes of local problems and what should be done about them. Where neighborhoods are divided by race and class, concern about disorder and crime can be an expression of conflict between groups. Watching for "suspicious people" easily becomes defined as watching for people of particular races and aggressively monitoring the circumstances under which different races come into contact. Robert Yin and his colleagues (1976) found that civilian patrols were most common in racially mixed areas of cities. Groups in these areas, rather than drawing the community together, may selectively recruit members on the basis of their values and backgrounds, and their efforts—including "crime prevention"—may be divisive rather than integrative (Emmons, 1979; Rosenbaum, 1987).

Gentrifying neighborhoods provide a case study of the process at work. In gentrifying areas, early comers and real-estate developers organize to promote the area and establish a middle-class environment. New residents use neighborhood redevelopment strategies to push up housing values and rents to levels which longer-term residents cannot afford. In these areas, "one group's solution is likely to become another group's problem" (Lewis and Salem, 1986: 90). Part of the redevelpment push involves attacking undesirable land use, including rooming houses and single-room-occupancy hotels. The newcomers often form patrols or block-watch groups (McDonald, 1986; Taub, Taylor, and Dunham, 1984), and attempt to use their political influence to persuade the police to act against "undesirables" (Bottoms and Wiles, 1986). In a study of Washington, D.C., Jeffery Henig of George Washington University (1984) found block-by-block differences in neighborhood-watch formation and participation that mirrored the spread of gentrification. Participation levels were higher and organized efforts more sustained on blocks with more homeowners, fewer blacks, fewer children, and fewer elderly residents.

Who Participates? Participation in community organizations is a form of "constrained volunteerism" (Emmons, 1979). That is, the extent and nature of organized activity in their neighborhood defines to a large extent the alternatives open to those who live there. Ordinary people participate by affiliating with existing groups, that have their own agenda and may or may not be interested in disorder problems. The local distribution of groups of various persuasions therefore defines the opportunities for individual participation in that area (Stinchcombe 1968). Who participates, and in what, depends on what opportunities are available, and neighborhoods differ in the opportunities they present.

Surveys suggest that individual participants in local voluntary associations are more likely to be better-off, married, more educated, have children, own homes, and be longer-term residents of their community (Greenberg, Rohe, and Williams, 1985). Involvement in anti-crime groups appears to be due to the same factors that stimulate other kinds of involvement in neighborhood affairs. Those factors are, above all, indicators of socioeconomic status and class-linked attitudes concerning personal and political efficacy, the extent of political information, and civic-mindedness (Lavrakas, 1985; Greenberg et al., 1984; Verba and Nie, 1972). In a national survey, Carol Whitaker (1986) of the Bureau of Justice Statistics found that, among those aware that groups were active in their area, participants in neighborhood-watch were more likely to be better-off homeowners. In a study involving 10 of the 40 neighborhoods examined here, Aaron Podolefsky and Fred DuBow (1981) also found that families with children and those who planned to remain in their neighborhood were more likely to report involvement in anti-crime groups. Where people know that community organizations are at work, general participation levels run between 10 and 20 percent, and participation of some sort in crime-linked groups runs at between 7 and 20 percent (Greenberg, Rohe, and Williams, 1985).

It appears that neighborhood as well as individual factors work along the same lines. Whitaker's national study confirms other research on the distribution of *opportunities* to participate in anti-crime efforts; in that survey, better-off, homeowning families were more aware of the possibility of participating in anti-crime groups. A study that examined the joint influence of *both* individual and neighborhood factors on participation found that area-level characteristics were at least as important as personal ones. Controlling for individual factors, program awareness and participation still were higher in racially homogeneous, higher-status areas (Bennett, Fisher, and Lavrakas, 1986). Survey studies of intervention behaviors, or (more often) self-reported predispositions to intervene, also point in the same direction—intervention is less frequent in central cities, in poor and heterogeneous communities, and in highly disorganized areas.*

Research has found few unique factors that directly drive people to join organizations involved in anti-crime activities. Participation is a function of opportunity, while what the groups are doing is a function of leadership and group decision-making. Where such an alternative is available, some people participate in local voluntary associations. Joiners participate in what their group chooses to do. The level of participation in organized efforts against crime thus stems mostly from the degree of success of the local organizations that happen to pursue these issues. This explains why programs organized on the premise that people join groups "because of crime" (for example, because they are driven by fear) usually lose momentum.

This suggests that individual decisions to participate in efforts against disorder will not be critical to the survival of disorder-prevention initiatives. Rather, the critical factor will be decisions by *organizations* to add disorder to their agenda, and to keep it there. Participation levels will be high in areas where those organizations are successful and attract members. Most successful organizations have complex agendas, and people join them for a variety of diffuse reasons revolving around their stake in the community and their citizenly instincts. It is when these groups tackle disorder that this form of participation will peak. As a result, there is a great deal of interest in some quarters in manipulating the agendas of successful local organizations.

What Are the Effects on Participants? One way in which organizations try to control disorder and crime is by initiating and supporting activities that will enhance residents' feelings of efficacy about

*Greenberg, Rohe, and Williams, 1985; Hackler et al., 1974; Boggs, 1971; Maccoby et al., 1958.

individual and collective action, as well as increase their sense of personal responsibility for taking these actions. Organizers hope to stimulate attempts to regulate anti-social behavior in the neighborhood by enhancing the residents' feelings of territoriality and willingness to intervene in suspicious circumstances, and they hope to facilitate neighboring, social interaction, and mutual helpfulness to enhance solidarity and build commitment to the community. These ideas are as old as the Chicago School of Sociology. They assume (and this is supported by a great deal of evidence) that qualities such as efficacy, responsibility, territoriality, and commitment are undermined by the destabilizing forces of urbanization. In this view, the way to put trouble-ridden communities right is to organize them. Since disorder and delinquency are themselves evidence of social disorganization, organizing forces can defeat them as well.

Research on the linkages between organizing efforts and these social processes suggest that community crime-control theory contains a nugget of wisdom, but may also point in some wrong directions. Surveys typically find that participants in community organizations are more likely than nonparticipants to take protective measures.* They are also more likely to report being predisposed to intervene (Rosenbaum, Lewis, and Grant, 1985; Lavrakas and Herz, 1982). Political scientist Anne Schneider (1986) found that, controlling for a host of demographic and victimization measures, attendance at local crime-prevention meetings was correlated with more frequent watchfulness, asking neighbors for assistance, intervening in suspicious circumstances, and taking personal and household crime-prevention measures.

There is less evidence that organizing efforts have much effect on nonparticipants, those who did not personally attend meetings. This is very important, for informal control can work only when a large proportion of area residents can be counted on to watch and act; there should probably be many more of these (no one knows what the threshold figure is) than can be counted on to join organizations or show up at meetings. A quasi-experimental evaluation of several organizing efforts in Chicago concluded there were no "rub-off" effects on nonparticipants (Rosenbaum, Lewis, and Grant, 1985). Another, more modest, one-time study

*Lavrakas, 1981; Skogan and Maxfield, 1981; Pennell, 1978; Schneider and Schneider, 1977.

of 43 blocks in New York City concluded that there were general effects on participation, individual protection, and informal social activity (Perkins et al., 1986). However, activists are self-starters with many distinctive attributes, and block groups form more readily where trust and informal social activity are already high (Unger and Wandersman, 1983). Because individual activists or active blocks usually differ from their quiescent neighbors in many ways other than their level of participation, we should pay more attention to the findings of two-wave comparison-area evaluation strategies like those described in the last chapter and this one.

Individual efficacy and responsibility may be enhanced by what goes on when people do succeed in getting together. Organizers lead discussions of local problems, try to identify the common interests of the participants, emphasize their interdependence, and drum up support for the organization's political agenda. They also stress the efficacy of specific actions, such as target hardening, property marking, and setting up telephone networks so neighbors can contact one another (Cook and Roehl, 1982; Podolefsky and DuBow, 1981; McPherson and Silloway, 1980). Some descriptive reports of those meetings (e.g., Lewis, Grant, and Rosenbaum, 1985) reveal there can be a great deal of confusion, uncertainty of purpose, and poor leadership at them, and a great deal of frustration with the process among people who have few meeting skills and no familiarity with Roberts' Rules of Order. The effects of all this are not clear. In a review of many research reports and his own work on community organizations, Dennis Rosenbaum (1987) concluded that such meetings may magnify perceptions of area problems, stimulate fear, exaggerate the individual racial concerns of participants, and lead them to feel more helpless as a result of attending.

Thus, neighborly activities may not be the best approach for community organizing efforts. The assumption may be correct that these rather ordinary aspects of social life are "the precursors of social control" (Fisher, 1977). However, it may be difficult to launch practical programs that encourage them. The reality is that levels of active participation in neighborhood associations usually are so low that those individuals classified by researchers as being "active" in groups typically attend just one or a few meetings, and often are only peripherally involved in group programs (Podolefsky and DuBow, 1981; Rosenbaum, Lewis, and Grant, 1985). Merely attending a few meetings or receiving a newsletter cannot change behaviors that are rooted in people's lifestyles and household organization. Moreover, there is only a very tenuous link between the frequency of these behaviors and levels of area disorder (Skogan, 1987). Neighboring activities in particular activate very subtle social processes; they exert control by reinforcing certain norms about appropriate public behavior and by teaching new residents how to behave; their sanction is gossip, social exclusion, and embarrassment. Research does not suggest that theories emphasizing the role of social processes in the informal control of disorder will steer organizing efforts in the right direction.

TWO EXPERIMENTS IN ORGANIZING

The "transplant" hypothesis is that community organization activities can be implanted in neighborhoods where they do not now exist (Rosenbaum, 1987). Transplant efforts have been pursued along two lines. The first involves identifying existing organizations and encouraging them to make a greater commitment to the prevention of disorder and crime. The money behind this comes from private foundations, real-estate developers, private or not-for-profit institutions, and the federal government. The funding agencies do this in the hope of grafting the local organization's visibility, legitimacy, leadership, and membership on their own agenda for solving urban problems. An alternative strategy is to encourage the formation of organizations in communities where viable opportunities for participation in anti-crime activities do not appear to exist. This is a far riskier approach, albeit one more likely to help poor communities that lack an infrastructure of successful organizations.

The Ford Programs

In 1982, the Ford Foundation paid ten community organizations in Chicago a total of about $550,000 to organize new block-watch groups and other crime prevention efforts. They were not amateurs; the groups were all long-established and staffed by professionals. Most had already experimented with crime prevention, with support from the now-defunct federal Urban Crime Prevention Program. They were awarded the Ford money so that they could hire new staff to expand their grass-roots organizing efforts.

They worked with the guidance of a citywide organization that monitored their expenditures and activities. Four of the groups were selected for a full-blown evaluation of the impact of their organizing efforts. They were chosen because they were the largest and most professional of the groups, and seemed the most likely to succeed. The evaluation also was sponsored by the Ford Foundation, and was conducted by Dan Lewis, Jane Grant, and Dennis Rosenbaum at Northwestern University.[2]

The four organizations which were evaluated developed somewhat different programs. The umbrella agency monitoring their activities encouraged them to devote a considerable amount of effort to organizing block-watch groups. This involved leafletting, door-to-door canvassing, sponsoring block meetings and educational workshops, and holding leadership training sessions. Other elements of their programs varied from place to place, as did their success in implementing them.

The Ford program billed itself as a "community crime-prevention" effort. However, a close examination of what most of the groups did most of the time indicates that it just as fairly could be dubbed a "disorder reduction" project:

> The *Northwest Neighborhood Federation* traditionally was involved with housing, and during the evaluation period they continued to promote housing rehabilitation and monitor building-code violations, building abandonment, unscrupulous real-estate practices, and mortgage redlining. They agitated for the cleanup of dangerous dump sites in their area. They gathered local crime statistics and attempted to identify local "hot spots" for intensive police attention. They also gathered information for the police on local drug trafficking and gang activity, and formed special crime-prevention committees to plan other activities in the future. In addition, the Federation was the most successful of the groups at organizing and maintaining block-watch groups.

> The *Northeast Austin Organization* organized neighborhood patrols which coordinated their activities via citizens' band radios (until they were stolen). They also organized recreational and job-counselling programs for area youths, held workshops on drug abuse, burglary prevention, and self-defense, posted signs marking the area, and tried to close down an adult bookstore in the area. They sponsored a

victim/ witness advocacy program and agitated for improved city services. Theirs was a racially changing neighborhood, and many of NAO's activities focused on disinvestment— mortgage and insurance redlining, building deterioration, inattentiveness by absentee landlords, and real-estate sales practices. NAO's goal was to stabilize the racial balance of the community and "preserve the quality of life" of area residents. It ranked second in the number of block-watch groups it formed.

The *Back of the Yards Council* sponsored a number of different activities, befitting its status as a large and powerful community organization. In addition to organizing some new block-watch groups (it ranked third in this respect), it also deputized a network of block representatives who were to organize "phone trees" linking their neighbors. Security inspections were arranged for area businesses, and a youth-counselling program was set up. The organization's staff met with the police to encourage them to be responsive to local complaints. During the evaluation period the Council also helped close down two taverns whose customers were disrupting nearby residential areas. Its other programs focused on delinquency prevention and treatment, senior citizens, parks, schools, commercial development, building maintenance and code enforcement, and towing abandoned cars.

The *Edgewater Community Council* did the least. Its block-watch program was virtually nonexistent, although large numbers of people did turn out for meetings in one area plagued by a rash of burglaries. Its other activities emphasized arson prevention, property marking, lakefront development, youth recreation, and problems with video arcades, massage parlors, street prostitution, and liquor stores in the area. It was very involved in housing rehabilitation and building code enforcement in the worst part of its service area, and at least one staff member was concerned about what to do with visibly disturbed people who had been placed in halfway houses in the community when the state released many patients from its mental hospitals.

Given the traditional concern of community organizations with zoning, housing, and local investment, it was inevitable that many of these groups would focus on disorder reduction. Problems in the physical disorder category generally are those they were already organized to combat. As a practical matter, those problems may also appear a bit more tractable than common crime. It is almost an article of faith among organizers that crime is a no-win issue, and few would be willing to bet their organization's survival on its capacity to focus exclusively on crime, much less on its ability to succeed in doing anything about it. Most criminals are a furtive, almost invisible enemy; crime is an atomizing force; and victories are difficult to point to, or sustain next year. Community organizations actually may be more effective at controlling social and physical disorder than at controlling crime, no matter what they choose to dub their activities. For example, stable zones of visible social disorder (such as street prostitution, "shooting galleries," or bad bars) can provide a rallying point for area residents and can be forced to the attention of the police.

The Evaluation. The evaluation of the Ford-financed programs resembled those conducted in Newark and Houston, described above. Surveys of neighborhood residents were conducted before the new programs were put into effect, and again one year later. As in the evaluation of policing programs, the repeated interviews allow us to control for the perceptions and behaviors of respondents living in the target areas before the programs got off the ground. Matched comparison areas were also surveyed, to monitor general trends in similar areas of the city that might otherwise be taken for effects of the programs.

An important feature of the evaluation is that it was designed to examine both the anticipated *outcomes* of the programs and the *linkages* that in theory should have (a) been affected by the program, and in turn (b) should have affected levels of disorder in the program areas. Measures of the perceived extent of social and physical disorder could be constructed that would be almost identical to those employed in the previous chapter on the police. In addition, the surveys were designed to gauge the extent of program awareness and participation, and the level of cooperation, intervention behavior, and prevention efforts reported by community residents.

Impact on Participation. To assess the impact of the Ford programs on opportunities for local participation, respondents were asked if they were aware of, and had participated in, either "neighborhood crime-prevention meetings" or "a block-watch program on your block" during the past year. If the leafletting, canvassing, block-watch meetings and other workshops or forums sponsored by these organizations did translate into generally higher levels of awareness and participation, the surveys conducted at step 2 should reveal distinctively higher levels of activism in the program areas. Of course, those surveyed were aware of and reported participating in similar activities in the comparison area as well, for activities resembling those fielded under the auspices of the Ford Foundation are an every-day feature of big-city life. Did the Ford efforts add to the total? Both awareness and participation were somewhat higher in the program areas than in the comparison neighborhoods even before the program began, despite some success in matching them demographically. Also, both the program and comparison areas demonstrated increased awareness and participation over the next two years. This illustrates the importance of employing pre-tests and comparison areas in the evaluation. The evaluation could still reveal that there were significantly greater percentage changes in the program areas. Participation in community organizations went from 12 to 16 percent in the program areas, and from 8 to 10 percent in the comparison areas. There were parallel changes in awareness that those activities were going on.

The statistical analyses summarized in Table 6–1 are more revealing; they take into account pre-program levels of participation and awareness, and eight other demographic differences between

Table 6–1 Program Impact on Awareness and Participation

| | Program Effects Controlling for Pre-Program Measures and Eight Other Factors | | |
	Awareness of Programs	Participation in Programs	N
All Programs	up	up	1026
Northwest Neighborhood	+	+	386
Northeast Austin	+	+	199
Back of the Yards	up	up	179
Edgewater Council	up	up	262

Note: Significant effects are described as "up" and "down;" insignificant effects are described as "+" and "–". The multivariate controls include pre-program levels of the linkage variables, plus age, sex, income, education, home ownership, marital status, race, and length of residence. Each program area is contrasted to a matched comparison area which was also surveyed at both points in time.

residents of the two areas, to see if there were significant differences between the program and comparison areas after two years of organizing. This is done separately for each target neighborhood. If the programs were universally successful, all the entries in Table 6-1 would read "up," indicating that levels of program awareness and participation had gone up significantly in the program areas. For the four areas as a whole, and for two of the four individually, there were significantly higher levels of both program awareness and participation when those other differences were taken into account, and they at least went up (but not significantly, which is indicated by a "+") in the remaining areas. In sum, these data point to the modest but real effects of the programs on opportunities for participation in two of these Chicago neighborhoods.

An analysis of *who* participated reveals that these Chicago neighorhoods resemble others. In the program areas, where widespread efforts were made to contact residents and inform them of what was going on, program awareness was significantly higher among higher-income, homeowning, more educated, long-term residents; actual participation was higher among homeowners and the more well-to-do. For example, 38 percent of renters and 68 percent of homeowners were aware of the programs; in terms of participation, the comparable figures were 6 and 22 percent (these findings are not displayed). As in many places (including Houston, as we saw earlier), it appears that where expanded opportunities for participation were made available, those who were already better off were more likely to take advantage of them.

Impact on Linkages. Did the programs affect important social *linkage* factors that they were to activate, and that in turn were to reduce levels of neighborhood disorder? The original proposal presented to the Ford Foundation stressed that an important goal of the program was to increase community cohesion, and organizers and theorists alike stress the potential that organizations have for enhancing neighborhood interaction, building shared norms, fostering community attachment, and enhancing an area's capacity for intervention. Four propositions about the linkages could be tested using the Ford evaluation data:

1. the programs should increase local social interaction and mutual solidarity;
2. the programs should enhance people's feelings of efficacy about individual and collective action;

3. the programs should stimulate action to regulate events in the neighborhood by enhancing residents' willingness to intervene in suspicious circumstances;

4. the programs should encourage residents to take positive steps to prevent disorder and crime.

The extent of neighborhood *social interaction* was measured by combining responses to three questions about knowing neighbors, visiting neighbors' homes, and chatting with people on the street. *Solidarity* was measured by responses to four questions about neighbors helping out, neighbors working together, feeling a part of the neighborhood, and liking living there. These two measures were used to test Proposition One. The perceived "helpfulness" of each of six common kinds of crime-prevention tactics were combined to measure how respondents perceived the *efficacy of prevention efforts*. This was used to test Proposition Two. *Intervention* in local events was measured by counting the number of times respondents reported taking some action on a list of neighborhood problems. The problems included "garbage and litter on the streets," "vandalism," "teenagers hanging out," and other forms of social and physical disorder. Finally, *prevention* efforts were assessed by whether or not respondents had installed special locks or window bars, marked their property, and had a home security inspection. These measures were used to test Propositions Three and Four.

Table 6–2 summarizes the effects of the programs on those linkage measures. If the programs were universal successes, all the entries in Table 6–2 would read "up"; however, insignificant find-

Table 6–2 Program Impact on Linkages

	Program Effects Controlling for Pre-Program Measures and Eight Other Factors				
	All Areas	NoWest Neighb.	NoEast Austin	Back of the Yards	Edgewater
Interaction	–	+	down	–	–
Solidarity	down	–	down	down	+
Efficacy	+	+	–	up	+
Intervention	+	–	+	up	–
Prevention	+	+	+	–	+

Note: Significant effects are described as "up" and "down;" insignificant effects are described as "+" and "–". The multivariate controls include pre-program levels of the linkage variables, plus age, sex, income, education, home ownership, marital status, race, and length of residence. Each program area is contrasted to a matched comparison area which was also surveyed at both points in time.

ings (shown as "+"s and "−"s) predominate, and most of the significant differences are in the *wrong* direction. Nowhere did neighborhood solidarity go up or social interaction increase, and any success in increasing residents' sense that what they could do was efficacious, or in increasing their self-reported activism, was confined to Back-of-the-Yards. In brief, none of this suggests that the programs had any impressive effects on day-to-day activity in these Chicago neighborhoods.

In the chapter on policing we saw how the Houston and Newark programs had different effects on different kinds of peple. That possibility was also examined here, but there was no clear pattern of differential effects in community organizing efforts in Chicago. Higher-income residents of the program neighborhoods were somewhat more likely to feel that they could take effective steps to prevent crime, but at the same time they were less likely than others to act in response to specific neighborhood problems. Even though differences in levels of program awareness and participation were linked to social and economic factors, there seem to be no major social groups within these programs areas who were especially helped (or hurt) by the programs. The Ford Foundation programs simply had little effect on the factors underlying social theories of disorder control.

Impact on Disorder. Table 6–3 examines the impact of the Ford programs on disorder and fear. *Social disorder* was measured by responses to questions about "teens hanging out," insults by passers-by, gang activity, and drug use. *Physical disorder* was measured by answers to questions about vandalism, abandoned build-

Table 6–3 Program Impact on Disorder and Fear

	Program Effects Controlling for Pre-Program Measures and Eight Other Factors				
	All Areas	NoWest Neighb.	NoEast Austin	Back of the Yards	Edgewater
Social disorders	+	−	up	up	−
Physical disorders	−	−	up	+	−
Fear of Crime	up	up	up	up	−

Note: Significant effects are described as "up" and "down;" insignificant effects are described as "+" and "−". The multivariate controls include pre-program levels of the linkage variables, plus age, sex, income, education, home ownership, marital status, race, and length of residence. Each program area is contrasted to a matched comparison area which was also surveyed at both points in time.

ings, and problems with refuse handling. In these areas, problems of vandalism clustered together with other physical rather than social disorder problems. *Fear of crime* was indexed by responses to questions about neighborhood safety and concern about being assaulted and robbed in the area.

In light of the programs' apparent failure to affect people's perceptions and behaviors, the results to no one's surprise are equally gloomy. If the programs were a complete success, all of the entries in Table 6–3 would read "down." However, all of the significant differences between the program and comparison areas were in the wrong direction, pointing toward *higher* levels of social and physical disorder in areas served by the groups being evaluated. The most consistent finding was that fear of crime went *up* overall, and this happened in three of the four areas. Some of the insignificant area differences documented in Table 6–3 also point in an unexpected direction. This was also true of the program's only apparent differential impact—long-term residents were *more* likely to think that social and physical disorder were "big problems" after the program than before; the perceptions of short-termers did not change.

Organizing in Minneapolis

The preceding section examined the success of an attempt at encouraging new efforts by existing local organizations to reduce crime and disorder, and indicated how difficult that can be. It should be a great deal more difficult to transplant collective anticrime groups to poorer, high-crime areas plagued by fear and other severe social problems. To organize such areas it is important that incentives be distributed early to participants, with vigorous support by the police (Garofalo and McLeod, 1986). Someone has to make hundreds of door-to-door contacts, distribute flyers, identify and train block captains, organize meetings, and find some way to get people to attend them. Paid staff appear to be crucial to sustain the level of participation of local voluntary associations of all types, particularly in such areas (Garofalo and McLeod, 1986; Greenberg, Rohe, and Williams, 1985; Taub, Taylor, and Dunham, 1984).

A transplant experiment of this type took place in Minneapolis in the early 1980s. The program is described in more detail in a report by Tony Pate, Marlys McPherson, and Glenn Silloway (1987), published by the Police Foundation. In brief, professional organizers working for the city attempted to organize neighborhoods around crime issues "from the ground up". Their efforts were carefully monitored by an evaluation team from the Police Foundation in Washington, D.C. The program involved all of the grass-roots organizing efforts described above. The Minneapolis project in effect created an attractive new opportunity for participation by neighborhood residents. A distinctive feature of the evaluation is that it directly examined the relationship between this increased opportunity to participate and how people reacted to it. The results were not encouraging.

The object of the program was to create block clubs. Early in the program, professional organizers tried to work through local leaders by training them to organize the clubs; later, they went on the streets to do grass-roots organizing themselves. The program was structured so that there was continuous organizing in each area. If it was not successful, the organizers tried harder, devoted more staff time to the area, and increased the intensity with which households were bombarded with pleas to come to meetings. What residents were to *do* at and after those meetings was left up to them. The leaders and organizers encouraged them to pursue a fairly narrow, "crime-prevention" approach to their block's problems; they stressed security consciousness, meeting your neighbors, and setting up phone networks.

The evaluation of the project followed now-familiar lines. Seven different areas of the city were identified as ripe for organizing. Each was divided into three matched subareas about 21 square blocks in size; one subarea was the target of the city's organizing efforts, in another these efforts were supplemented by the assignment of a uniformed police officer to assist the block group to be formed, and one was set aside as a comparison area. The true randomization of areas set this evaluation apart from those in Houston and Chicago, where areas were selected for the program, and matching comparison areas were chosen separately later. As in the other evaluations, before-and-after surveys were conducted to gauge each program's impact on perceived neighborhood conditions, citizen's attitudes, and their behaviors. Because groups first had to be formed, then given an opportunity to affect neighborhood conditions, the program ran for two years before the follow-up evaluation survey was conducted.

A unique feature of this organizing experiment was its "cop-on-the-block" component. Police officers were to be assigned to assist block clubs in their efforts, to lend them legitimacy and technical support. This was to be done in a random half of the target areas. However, cop-on-the-block proved to be a logistical failure. As in many cities, Minneapolis police officers rotate between the day and night shifts every few months, so it was not possible to assign an officer permanently to assist an organization; it also proved impossible for the city to free up enough police to attend meetings during busy evening shifts (Silloway and McPherson, 1985).

Impact on Participation. From the outset, the evaluators planned to examine the relationship between the *effort* extended by organizers and leaders and the *response* to that effort by neighborhood residents. Effort was measured by such things as the frequency with which leaders were trained and meetings were called; the response was measured by the number of people who showed up and the percentage of households in each area that could be classified as organized.

The effort was real. The professional organizing staff invested about 25 hours of on-street work in each target block; this does not take into account their planning and administrative efforts, or the training of block leaders, which would add about 10 hours to this figure, or activities by the block leaders themselves. *Every* household in the program areas was contacted an average of 4 times. A full 85 percent of households received an invitation to a scheduled block-organizing meeting. In areas where local leaders could not turn out participants, the organizers conducted "blitz" campaigns to back their efforts. People did turn out in substantial numbers in some places, but not in others, and there was not much response on about 30 percent of the target blocks. Only 17 percent of all blocks fully met the project's goal of having a trained leader and holding one meeting in each of the two years of the program.

The evaluation confirmed the power of the matching and true random assignment procedure employed in this research; there was a close match between the two sets of areas in the preprogram surveys. As in Chicago, involvement in crime prevention went up in both areas during the two-year implementation period, but it went up much more in the program neighborhoods. Both recalled-awareness and (especially) recalled-participation were *much* higher in these program areas than in comparable areas of Chicago. In the program areas, awareness that organizing was going on went from 37 to 77 percent, and participation in those activities went from 11 to 38 percent. As can be seen in Table 6–4, comparable changes in the comparison areas were much smaller. These differences were significant in multivariate analyses that controlled for pre-program levels of awareness and participation, and for a host of demographic characteristics.

Now the familiar irony. As in Chicago (and Houston), higher-income, homeowning, long-term residents of single-family homes were more likely than others to learn about the opportunities for participation provided by the program, and the same group—with the addition of whites—were more likely than their counterparts to take advantage of them. Block-level records on participation in meetings indicated that people turned out in substantial numbers only in the better-off areas. The lack of any early response by residents of poor and minority areas led organizers to increase their efforts there, but participation remained slight. Because the program continued to push where there was no early success, overall turnout in the end was *inversely* related to program effort. Even though program effort was greatest in poorer, black, and higher-crime areas, attendance at meetings was highest in white and middle-to-upper-income areas where crime problems were not substantial. Better-off areas were organized with the least effort.

To redouble the irony, those middle-class successes then faded. The initial block meetings in better-off areas were well attended, but at the end of the evaluation period they were not particularly likely to have been followed up with any other efforts. The evaluation team attended a number of those meetings, and speculates that the difficulty was there were no real problems to be dealt with in those areas, or at least no problems that block clubs could deal with. There was hopeful news in the finding that the few Minneapolis groups that *did* persist were in poorer, minority neighbor-

Table 6–4 Program Impact on Participation

	Two Waves of Surveys for All Areas					
	Awareness of Programs			Participation in Programs		
	Wave 1	Wave 2	(N1-N2)	Wave 1	Wave 2	(N1-N2)
Program areas	37	77	(783-496)	11	38	(792-502)
Control areas	39	48	(402-259)	11	17	(403-257)

Note: Recalculated from Tables 6.1 and 6.3 in Pate, McPherson, and Silloway, 1987.

hoods with real problems. They were, however, painfully few in number.

Impact on Outcomes. The before-and-after evaluation surveys revealed that the Minneapolis programs were extremely visible. There were large increases in the percentage of program-area residents who had heard of the program, and impressive increases in the proportion who reported participating in some way. But the programs appear to have had no discernible impact on neighborhood processes or problems. There was no evidence of any program impact on such factors as residents' watchfulness, or reporting to the police. After two years, residents of the program area did not differ in any significant way on measures of perceived social disorder, physical deterioration, crime problems, and fear of crime. As in Chicago, in most cases the statistically insignificant changes were in the wrong direction, accruing to the disadvantage of residents.

WHAT HAPPENED IN CHICAGO AND MINNEAPOLIS?

The Chicago and Minneapolis organizing experiments were two of the most carefully evaluated efforts to attack local disorder and crime by organizing block-watch groups and encouraging household and community prevention efforts. Both had a great deal of visibility, and generated levels of participation that seem substantial. However, both programs failed to affect neighborhood problems, and failed to affect the processes by which they were to have done so. These failures—especially in light of their success at gaining visibility and involvement—raise important questions about the viability of community approaches to disorder and crime control.

Were they bad programs? Could their apparent failure be attributed to the fact that they were poorly designed, badly implemented, or missed their target? If this is true, they could not have set in motion the forces required to reduce levels of disorder and crime, but another—better—program might have done so.

The answer, of course, is a judgment call. In both cities the programs were in the hands of experienced professional organizers. In Chicago, they were designed and fielded by long-established community organizations with a track record of success. The Minneapolis organizers made extensive, documented efforts to rally area residents. Their efforts were widely visible and generated impressive levels of initial program participation. In the view of the evaluators, "[T]he program was implemented energetically and appropriately, ruling out program failure as a possible explanation for the failure to achieve results" (Pate, McPherson, and Silloway, 1987: 7–13). The Minneapolis program's biggest flaw was probably that what the block clubs were to *do* was left in their own—largely untutored—hands.

The Minneapolis experience parallels the findings of research on participation reviewed earlier in this chapter. Voluntary participation cannot easily be initiated in poorer, higher-crime areas. Studies of organizations find they arise and are disproportionately concentrated in the homogeneous, better-off areas of cities. Better-off city residents more frequently know of opportunities to participate, and are more likely to participate when they have the opportunity. Attempts to transplant organized anti-crime efforts are more likely to get off the ground in better-off target areas. This does not mean that it's impossible to organize areas that are in need, but that it is not possible to do so "easily." Governments must find relatively simple and direct mechanisms for effectuating social change, if they are to engineer that change across many areas, among many kinds of people, using relatively blunt policy instruments.

It may be that "more" of a program, or a "longer" program, *could* have succeeded in organizing and sustaining anti-crime efforts in worse-off areas. As criminologist Dennis Rosenbaum (1987) points out, *any* evidence of program failure is liable to that countercharge. However, the effort involved in the Chicago and Minneapolis programs was substantial enough to raise another question—*can* reasonable, affordable organizing efforts affect day-to-day life in city neighborhoods like these?

The logistical problems that torpedoed Minneapolis' cop-on-the-block component of the program seem simple in retrospect, but that does not mean they would now be easy to solve. Minneapolis could not get the police involved in their program, and in Chicago the Ford projects chose not to involve them in their social strategies, so neither of these programs sheds any further light on the hard question of the role of the police in commuity crime-prevention. Several observers have noted that crime-focused groups start up and persist more easily when they operate in conjunction with the police (Garofalo and McLeod, 1986; Yin,

1986). Criminologists James Garofalo and Maureen McLeod (1986) conducted a questionnaire study of 550 neighborhood-watch programs across the country. They found that only 6 percent had not received help from the police, who provided them with training, information, technical support, and equipment. The police can also lend visibility and apparent legitimacy to organizing efforts, which can be important in neighborhoods starting out with lower levels of mutual trust. We have seen that Houston's effort to use police to organize a community and spawn a viable group concerned with disorder and crime appears to have been a substantial success. Unfortunately, police-community cooperation is more difficult to secure in poor and minority neighborhoods in which those relationships often are strained, and the first impulse of organizers in those areas will not be to attempt to borrow legitimacy from the police.

Was the underlying premise wrong? Is it hypothetically possible that reasonable, affordable programs can work in this way? Are day-to-day interaction, intervention, and prevention efforts powerful enough to reverse the course of neighborhoods that have slipped into the cycle of decline?

Even if extensive organizing efforts are mounted, it is not clear that they will have their intended effect. The Minneapolis and Chicago projects described here found that professional and well-financed organizing campaigns increased target area residents' awareness of opportunities to participate, and stimulated participation in (some) organized activities. However, in neither case (and both projects involved several target areas and programs) was there any evidence of the hypothesized *effects* of these efforts. These findings raise the issue of whether "program failure" or a more fundamental "theory failure" was at work in the two cities. It may be the former—that the programs were too weak, that their "dosage" levels were too low, or that they were not correctly targeted at neighborhood problems. However, in both these cases there was a documented program of some magnitude, and it was reflected in impressive survey measures of awareness and participation.

An alternative explanation is that the root solutions which the organizers pursued may have been wrong, or misdirected in terms of what they presumed could be accomplished with realistic levels of local organizing. Past research and the Chicago evaluation presented here both suggest that a focus on *social* solutions may be misguided. There was no evidence of area-level effects on the attitudes and behaviors they intended to improve, and they may in fact have spread concern and enhanced levels of fear. Fear of crime went *up* in virtually every area of Chicago after the programs had been at work. There is no good evidence that the effects of participation "rub off" on (more numerous) nonparticipants, and more that most people find it easier to be a free rider and reap any benefits of local activism without becoming involved themselves. To attempt to tackle neighborhood disorder by rekindling local friendship networks, seeking solidarity, and encouraging informal intervention is to define a solution that is difficult to implement effectively.

It is also possible that there *were* real effects of these programs, but that the evaluations were inadequate to discern them. There is a long list of standard problems with evaluations in the criminal justice field (cf. Lurigio and Rosenbaum 1987), some of which are applicable to the Chicago and Minneapolis evaluations. The major problems of relevance here include:

> (1) *There might be problems with the program and comparison areas—they might be "unmatched," "self-selecting," or competing events could have occurred there.*

The evaluations could have been threatened by some of these problems. The Minneapolis areas were selected as being "ripe" for organizing; then they were matched, and each matched group of three was randomly divided into program and comparison groups. In Chicago, the program areas were selected by the Ford Foundation and its local umbrella organization; the evaluators could only pick the comparison areas. In both cities the evaluators had an idea of what was going on in their program areas, but did not closely monitor events in the comparison areas. However, in both cities respondents from the comparison areas did not come from just one neighborhood, but from a variety of places; in Chicago, small comparison samples were interviewed in each of *several* scattered areas which matched each program area, while in Minneappolis 21 different comparison areas were combined in the analysis.

As a result, the biggest problem here was probably self-selection. In Chicago, self-selection could account for the unexpectedly high level of pre-Ford participation and awareness in the program areas there. The apparently negative effects of the programs in Chicago *may* have been because the areas chosen for treatment were "on the brink" of a downward trend, while the demographically-matched comparison areas were not.

(2) The evaluation surveys might not have been large enough to detect modest program effects.

None of the Chicago panel surveys were as large as those employed in Houston and Newark, and none of the individual target areas in Minneapolis could be analyzed separately (the evaluation surveys were designed from the outset simply to be pooled into large program and comparison samples). However, the pooled multivariate analyses for Chicago (Tables 6–1 to 6–3) and the Minneapolis evaluation were based on large samples of respondents, and there was no relationship between the size of the evaluation surveys and the significance (or not) of the findings.

(3) The evaluation findings may have been threatened by panel attrition.

None of these evaluations had substantial problems with people refusing to be reinterviewed. However, as is frequently the case in longitudinal time studies of not-so-nice neighborhoods, a number of people *moved out* and could not be reinterviewed. In order to account for this, both the Minneapolis and Chicago evaluations (and those in Houston and Newark) conducted supplemental interviews to represent new residents. All the analyses were duplicated using both the respondents who were interviewed twice and the new data which represented all the residents of the areas at Step 2. The panel data are better suited for measuring true individual-level change, and a few more findings were significant (often in the wrong direction) when those interviews were analyzed, but in the main both sets of data pointed to the same gloomy conclusions.

(4) The evaluations might have employed poor or inappropriate measures of linkages and outcomes, and the data analysis may have been insensitive to the real effects of the programs.

In this regard, these evaluations were better than many. All of the linkage and outcome measures were based on several questions and had acceptable reliabilities. The measures probably were weakest at tapping informal social behavior (for example, visiting or talking with neighbors), for it is difficult to get people to recall with any accuracy the frequency with which they actually perform routine, low-salience, almost habitual acts. As a result, it may be that these evaluations, because of measurement error, are biased against finding any program effects of that type. All of the analyses were controlled for pretest scores and individual demographic characteristics, and their panel design was best suited for making efficient inferences about individual change.

In summary, each of these evaluations had its individual flaws. Those flaws *may* have shrouded what were in fact successful attempts to set in motion neighborhood processes that reduced the level of disorder. However, not all of the evaluations shared the same flaws, yet they came to the same conclusions. Further, the Houston and Newark evaluations reported in the previous chapter shared most of these flaws in varying degree, yet many of those programs appear to have scored some successes. In Chicago and Minneapolis, community organizing probably did not work the way it was assumed it would.

Finally, were these programs still *political* victories? As the evaluators point out, there is more than one level at which the organizations involved could count these programs as successes or failures. For example, in Chicago they succeeded in getting the money, they were able to hire more full-time staff members, they could sport the imprimatur of the Ford Foundation, and through the project they were linked in a city-wide movement with other large and successful organizations. Staff members of the organization hired by Ford to provide technical assistance to the neighborhood groups in Chicago "spun off" their own organization, which now operates independently and receives public and private contracts to do crime-prevention work. In Minneapolis, the city agency running the program was able to hire more staff; in bureaucratic circles this is no small victory. The two Chicago organizations that were the most decentralized, membership-based, and participatory in style succeeded in enhancing their recognition and "presence" in the community, expanding their network of block clubs, and activating new local leaders. All of the groups in Chicago used the opportunity to make more (and often successful) demands on the police and other city agencies for support and services. In short, in Chicago they were able to exert some political as well as social pressure in seeking solutions to their problems.

In this case these organizations clearly were not outstandingly successful at meeting their proximate social goals, for none of the community factors or disorder problems they aimed at changed substantially. This is important; as the evaluators point out:

> The groups we studied all took as their mandate the exercise of control over the local areas; by that, we mean they sought to shape the nature of the community in terms of the activities that took place and how their turf was used. Community organizations seek to shape the character of the area they purport to represent (Lewis, Grant, and Rosenbaum, 1987: 1–8).

There was also no evidence that the groups in Chicago had any special success with "political" strategies that could be attributed to their participation in the Ford program. In Minneapolis, the city employees who conducted the program stuck to narrowly defined "technical" solutions to crime problems, and could not encourage political action, for fear of running afoul of the City Council. However, organizations also have "maintenance" needs—they must recruit and maintain members and generate resources to pay their staff and reward their members. It is difficult to judge how great their victories were on this front, and that probably varied by how large and successful each organization or agency was before the Ford Foundation came along. However, their success at meeting their maintenance needs through this program may have made up somewhat for their apparent failure to make a dent in the problems on which they focused.

CONCLUSIONS

During the 1970s and early 1980s, the community approach to local problem-solving developed a diverse constituency. It attracted the attention of politicians, who found various reasons for supporting it. It emphasized volunteerism and had smaller budgetary implications than most alternatives for dealing with crime and disorder-related problems, and it diverted attention from what some thought to be their root causes—poverty, illiteracy, and racism. This suited conservatives. On the other hand, it promised to support organizing efforts in poor neighborhoods and to provide money for established community organizations—which suited many liberals. The community approach also attracted the attention of researchers. During a period of growing public militancy with respect to crime, it offered an alternative to hiring more police, which researchers generally did not think would work. Researchers were skeptical that affordable increases in traditional policing would have many positive effects on neighborhood problems. In addition, the concurrent political exhaustion of rehabilitation as the ideal for dealing with individual offenders also had created an intellectual vacuum, one that was easily filled by the notion of empowering people to solve their own problems. Finally, community-based programs attracted the attention of public and private agencies with money. During the 1970s, a succession of federal agencies stepped forward to support organizing efforts around crime problems, and in the early 1980s the Ford Foundation put private support behind them as well. During the same period, federal research agencies sponsored studies of many aspects of this new approach to crime prevention, which further fueled the interest of the research community.

Here we reviewed some of the results of this research. The attempts to create new opportunities for participation in Minneapolis, and to manipulate the agendas of successful local organizations in Chicago, provided a test of the "transplant" hypothesis. They also tested the conclusions of earlier research concerning the relationship between community organizations and disorder, conclusions based upon studies of "naturally occurring" groups. Together, these two streams of evidence suggested some sobering conclusions.

They are sobering because troubled communities *need* organizations, notwithstanding all the difficulties involved in forming and sustaining them. Serious neighborhood problem-solving admits to few avenues for autonomous action. However, social change at the end of the twentieth century is working in the opposite direction. Most of the demographic correlates of opportunities for participation, and levels of actual participation (income, ownership, education, family status, length of residence), show a trend in the wrong direction in cities. Demographic projections of these factors predict declining activism in the future. To a certain extent, theories that stress the importance of resurrecting informal social control reflect nostalgia for a village life that is long gone from cities, and which certainly will not look like life there in the twenty-first century.

However, the practical dynamics of neighborhood organizing may also work to the positive *disadvantage* of the poor. Group

formation succeeds more easily in better-off and white neighborhoods. They focus on housing, and want to freeze the current race
and class distribution of desirable real estate. Residents of those
areas find it much easier to work in conjunction with the police,
and their programs frequently can function autonomously and
without external funding. Better-off areas are more often ''self-
starters.'' Foundations or agencies that provide assistance to
neighborhoods that organize to ask for it, or which try to assist
neighborhoods and only pursue those efforts in places that seem
responsive, will also contribute to class and race-based inequities.
It appears that the government and foundation funds that are
available for community mobilization efforts are now usually
scooped up by a few aggressive and already well-organized neighborhoods, while most languish without support (Henig, 1982). To
the extent to which the organizations can actually make a difference with regard to disorder and crime, the differential distribution of opportunities to participate has further implications for the
quality of life in city neighborhoods. Relying upon voluntary local
organizations to deal with disorder and crime places poorer communities at a disadvantage relative to middle-class areas.

7

Dealing with Disorder

What have we learned about disorder? Are there any other promising strategies in the wings that might contribute to combating urban decline?

Before discussing public policies concerning disorder, it is important to be explicit about the general social and legal context of American policy problems, for it affects what can be done about many social problems. These are the contexts of *diversity*, of *rights*, and of *limits*. They have a great deal to do with the seeming ineffectiveness of American public policy: the implicit conclusion that "nothing works" pervading policy analysis reflects in part the constraints imposed by these contexts.

The context of diversity describes the social and political milieu within which public policies concerning disorder must be crafted. Americans are divided by class, race, region, religion, and immediate environment. There is a great deal of local variation in how we think and behave, and consensus is hard to achieve. Attempts to regulate behaviors, or to tell people how they ought to feel about local issues (that they should clean up their yards, or that pornographic movie houses should be free to open nearby) can encounter stiff resistance when they run against the grain of local custom. In a heterogeneous society like ours, public policy often cannot rely on any implicit consensus of values to legitimate official intervention (Glazer, 1988). As we saw in chapter 3, there is a substantial consensus concerning the kinds of disorders considered here, but it is obvious that not everyone is going along.

The ability of groups or communities to resist the imposition of "universal" rules is enhanced by the nation's political structure. The American system of federalism, coupled with the devolution to municipalities of control over the police, and of such planning tools as zoning and land-use regulation, encourages and protects both diversity and innovation. Someone will run for office somewhere in opposition to almost any policy. Authority is dispersed and countervailing and if anything, things are moving further in this direction toward the end of the twentieth century. In a recent book on policy-making, Nathan Glazer (1988) makes a persuasive case that trends toward decentralization, deinstitutionalization, and a growing reliance on privatization and the market will counter other, older trends in urban, industrial societies toward centralization and uniformity.

The context of rights reinforces this diversity. Not only is political power dispersed, it is also limited. Large segments of people's lives are largely immune from official regulation. It is hard to stop people from "doing their own thing" if they do not *want* to stop, difficult to tell fiercely independent shopping-bag ladies what to do or where they should go, and seemingly impossible to make them go away. The authority of street-level bureaucrats like the police is severely limited when violations of the criminal code are not plainly in view. It can be difficult for them to act lawfully, and easy for them to make a mistake that someone may challenge. Some disorders clearly fall within their mandate, but others are difficult for the police to do much about without restructuring their job. Community organizations must rely upon even more subtle sources of legitimacy, for they cannot tell anyone what to do. We have seen how difficult it is for neighborhood residents to exercise control over events taking place in parks; neither can they keep people from walking or driving through their area.

The fact that diverse behaviors can claim legitimacy, coupled with the limited power of the state, implies that public policies aimed at disorder need to focus on securing voluntary compliance. In a diverse society, neither the police nor neighborhood activists can assume that their views about appropriate levels of order will automatically be accepted as authoritative, or even that they will get much in the way of deference when they speak out. When it comes to a great deal of disorder, police and community organizations are just additional interest groups jockeying for attention. Order is more likely to be negotiated than imposed. For order to emerge in troubled areas, we need to devise ways of restructuring the risks and rewards associated with various behaviors, in ways that favor compliance.

The final context for policy formulation is that of limits. This is partly a question of resources, which are scarce. It will be difficult to mobilize support for policies aimed at disorder reduction if they cost very much. There are many pressing problems on the American agenda, and when resource can be freed, disorder may not be an obvious target. For example, Community Policing is labor-intensive, and thus is very expensive; it is not clear that many departments would put their resources there by choice. Houston and Newark assigned many more officers into their field tests than they could possibly afford on a day-to-day basis. It is also hard to measure the output of Community Policing, so its accomplishments will not be there to be counted when police managers look at "the stats." The task of policing disorder competes with other personnel needs, including the need for rapid-response teams and visible motorized patrol, and it must battle for attention with conventional kinds of drug-enforcement efforts. It is difficult to make out a case for investing resources in Community Policing in a political environment dominated by concern about crack.

The idea of limits is important in an even more fundamental sense. Most public policies have to focus on the proximate causes of the problems they address, not on their ultimate origins. Chapter 6 advanced the idea that there are "root solutions" for problems that may differ from their "root causes," in order to distinguish what community organizations can realistically hope to achieve. Root causes are mostly beyond their reach, and in a liberal democratic society they frequently are beyond the purview of government as well. This chapter considers some relatively expensive and "fundamental" solutions to disorder problems, but even they are still more than a step away from the attitudes and values that reinforce or undermine order. However, there may still be a great deal of merit in interim, practical solutions to particular problems. It may be of interest to researchers why people litter, but most would probably agree that the question of how to make them stop can be pursued without getting into a deep analysis of their motivations.[1] Policy analysts have to focus on the conditions they want to bring into being, and think of ways of encouraging behavior consonant with those conditions. It is also probably best to pursue multiple strategies at the same time, for most significant problems have multiple, overlapping causes. This is probably nowhere more true than in the case of neighborhood disorder.

POLICING DISORDER

New ideas are circulating concerning proper priorities for policing disorder. As we have seen, Community Policing involves commitment to a broadly focused, problem-oriented view of the police mandate. It relies upon organizational decentralization and a reorientation of patrol tactics to open informal, two-way channels of communication between police and citizens. This decentralization involves moving to the neighborhood level the locus of decision-making about what the police will do, and sharing it with the community. Community Policing requires that police be responsive to citizen demands when they decide what the local problems are and set their priorities, and implies a commitment to helping neighborhoods help themselves, by serving as a catalyst for local organizing and education efforts. Once these elements of policing are in place, and the public begins to play a role in defining what "important problems" are, it is likely that disorder will gain their attention.

This decentralization and information-gathering is a direct police response to diversity. It emphasizes working with communities to help them get where they want to go. Community Policing also is clearly predicated on the understanding that order is usually negotiated rather than enforced. It emphasizes practical solutions to everyday problems; police are the most realistic and least romantic people imaginable, and they are instinctively skeptical of solutions that do not appear closely linked to problems. However, Chapter 5 also suggested that there is potential conflict between Community Policing and the diversity, rights, and limits that characterize the policy environment.

Community Policing, as implemented in Houston and Newark, showed some success at responding to neighborhood disorder. All of the programs (particularly those in Houston) involved organizational decentralization, and placed considerable responsibility for problem-solving in the hands of officers on the street. The Community Policing teams in both cities found distinct ways of reaching out for community input and support—through foot patrol, by walking door-to-door, distributing newsletters, holding meetings, allying themselves with local organizations, and opening highly visible and approachable neighborhood offices. In almost every instance, disorder went down and satisfaction with the area and with the police went up. The Community Policing projects achieved a surprising level of visibility. The more traditional Intensive Enforcement effort mounted in Newark had fewer measurable benefits, but social disorder—a special focus of many of the enforcement efforts—went down there as well.

The evaluations suggest some caveats to the notion that Community Policing is a cure-all, however. In particular, they raise two issues concerning the exercise of police power in defense of public order. They question the limits of direct, aggressive police action against "disorderly" people, and they raise the question of whose order is being defended.

The Limits to Policing Disorder. The police always walk a tightrope in maintaining order. Their problems are threefold, and the solutions to them are not all in their hands. Can legislatures write constitutional statutes concerning disorderly behavior? The contexts of rights and of limited government, and how they shape our ability to respond to disorder, are most apparent at this point. In the past, state criminal codes provided numerous grounds for lawful police maintenance of order; they defined (with varying operational clarity) disorderly conduct, breach of peace, vagrancy, suspicion, loitering, panhandling, public intoxication, and soliciting for prostitution. However, it has proven difficult to sustain the constitutionality of these statutes. Order-maintenance statutes have been voided because of the vagueness of their terminology, or for being overly broad and thus proscribing some constitutionally protected conduct, and for violating the equal protection clause of the Constitution by calling upon the police to act without having real probable cause to think a crime has been committed (Markowitz, 1977). To arrest someone for "repeatedly beckoning"—presumably a prostitute flagging down a customer—runs afoul of all of those standards (Murray, 1979). However, statutes aimed at disorder often cannot rest solely upon behavior to define the condition they seek to protect. Ordinances regarding disturbing the peace have prohibited using profane language "within the presence of children," or "causing a crowd to collect," in an effort to differentiate disorderly speech from dirty talk. Anti-loitering laws forbade "lounging in a public place," as well as being "unable to give a satisfactory account" of one's self. Begging is "loitering with intent to solicit.'' The difficulty is that disorder frequently involves more than behavior; the location and circumstances of the activity in question, its intent, and how others react to it, all must somehow be included in defining what is unlawful.

The second issue *is* in the hands of the police, and that is how to use their discretion to maintain order in a lawful manner. They have a great deal of leeway in how to act to contain disorder, for the rules for these cases always will be ambiguous. Patrol officers enforce them in the field, out from under the eye of their immediate supervisors. In these cases there typically is no victim or complainant around to keep an eye on what they do. They are relatively unconstrained in their ability to use these statutes to harass or punish people they dislike, or to settle past accounts. As James Q. Wilson (1968) points out, police also choose what to do in an environment that is frequently hostile and emotionally charged, and while dealing with people who may challenge their authority to act. Under these circumstances, instances of excessive use of force or brutality by the police are doubtless more common. Finally, officers are free to act upon their prejudices or stereotypes in virtually unchecked fashion when *they* are the upholders of order who must be satisfied. How to constrain the discretion of patrol officers is the most important and enduring issue in police management, and it is one that is magnified when control of disorder is at issue.

The third limit to policing disorder is imposed by other elements of the criminal justice system. Pressed as they are with seemingly more important cases, it is difficult to sustain the interest of judges and prosecutors in cases that arise from disorder arrests. In a lawful society, arrests lead to prosecution; if they do not, then they are simply a form of extra-legal harassment of people through the repeated inconvenience and fear of the police that they engender. If prosecutors do not prosecute, nor judges take disorder cases seriously, there are grounds for taking action against the police for pursuing them. For example, in 1983 a federal judge ordered the City of Chicago to erase more than 800,000 arrests for disorderly conduct from the record, finding that they were unconstitutional because there had been no intention to prosecute those who had been arrested. Many of the arrests were generated by special tactical units doing aggressive disorder enforcement in and around public housing projects. Relying on the police to control disorder ultimately means relying on the rest of the criminal justice system to follow through as well.

The street sweeps and roadblocks in Newark's Intensive Enforcement area tested the limits of lawful police order maintenance. They were concerted efforts to reestablish faltering police authority over the streets in deteriorating parts of the city. The sweeps were aimed at bands of males (mostly young) who gathered there; police flooded target areas with police cars and vans, made announcements to "move on," and searched and arrested those who did not. After observing them in action, Jerome Skolnick and David Bayley (1986: 199) noted:

> If such a sweep is legal, it is only marginally so. No lawyer committed to traditional constitutional conceptions of Fourth Amendment rights of citizen privacy would regard the sweeps as anything but unlawful. Statutes forbidding loitering are unconstitutional, and the [loudspeaker] "warning" is an evasive device intended to afford the police an arguably legal position. . . . [T]he police have no legal "probable cause," no reason to believe that a crime has been or is about to be committed, and thus should have no right to search.

Of the roadblocks that the Newark police threw up in the Intensive Enforcement area, Skolnick and Bayley observed:

> To many citizens—and judges—they represent an unreasonable invasion of privacy, a heavy-handed assertion of authority by police against citizens driving cars, about whom there is not even a shred of reasonable suspicion of illegal activity (p. 201).

If disorder *is* causally connected with crime there might be much to be gained from focusing more efforts upon it. Sociologists Robert Sampson and Jacqueline Cohen (1988) conducted a statistical study to discover whether or not police who act aggressively toward disorder (measured by the number of disorderly conduct and drunk-driving arrests they make per police officer each year) can reduce burglary and robbery rates. They concluded that visible police involvement in controlling disorder had a deterrent impact on the commission of other crimes. They did not consider the additional possibility—suggested in Chapter 4—that there also may be a direct causal link between disorder and crime. Such a link would multiply the effects on crime rates of police efforts to maintain order.

Besides the legal concerns, there is another reason for retreating from aggressive order maintenance—the abrasive impact this kind of policing can have on the residents of poor, inner-city neighborhoods. Even if they are conducted in strictly legal fashion, aggressive tactics such as saturating areas with police, stopping cars frequently, conducting extensive field interrogations and searches, and bursting into apartments suspected of harboring gambling or drugs, can undermine police-community relations in black and Hispanic neighborhoods. The police will inevitably err on the side of employing their distinctive advantage on the streets—their capacity to use coercive, and even fatal, force. While Community Policing emphasizes the need to negotiate solutions to problems, police have the power to impose (perhaps short-term) nonnegotiable settlements, and will do so. However, tactics like these triggered riots in American cities during the 1960s and in Britain in the 1980s (Sherman, 1983; 1986; Baldwin and Kinsey, 1982). Since unimaginative and mechanistic enforcement of ''the law'' can create more problems than it solves, a balance must be maintained between the tranquility that police can hope to impose on a community, and the disturbance they may create while doing so. As Lawrence Sherman (1983) notes, ''less law may produce more order.''

Of course, there are many elements of the Community Policing package that do *not* involve aggressive policing of social disorder. In their role as problem-solvers, police can assist community residents in securing municipal services; they can also support local crime-prevention efforts, and provide technical and moral support to community organizations. They have traditionally conducted special programs for youths. Officers working out of the Community Station in Houston worked with schools in a truancy-prevention effort, and Newark police sponsored a youth recreation program. Through foot patrol and other high visibility tactics that provide a noticeable police presence in the community, police can act to support the legitimate use of threatened public places, including parks and transit stops. Finally, many disorders do not call for aggressive policing, or even for an arrest. Telling people to ''knock it off,'' or to ''go home and sober up'' may often be more appropriate. All of these efforts are part of Community Policing as well.

Policing Heterogeneous Communities. The Houston programs also questioned the ability of the police to deal evenhandedly with disorder in response to ''community demand'' and in concert with community groups. Wilson and Kelling, and many others, have suggested that police take the initiative in acting against disorder, in response to what they dub "communal needs." They admitted that many of these needs would not be found in the criminal code, but rather would reflect what "the neighborhood had decided was the appropriate level of public order." They thought that in the past, when police acted more aggressively to assert their authority on behalf of the community, "the objective was order, an inherently ambiguous term, but a condition that people in a given community recognized when they saw it."

However, advocates of Community Policing need to spell out clearly just how the police can come to know what a neighborhood wants in the way of order. We saw some evidence of how this can go sour, in the outcomes of the Community Policing projects in Houston—there was a clear tendency for whites and homeowners (a surrogate measure of class) to enjoy the benefits of the programs, and for blacks and renters to be unaffected by them. These unequal outcomes were paralleled by substantial race and class discrepancies in peoples' knowledge of the programs, and contact with them. In their day-to-day activities, officers involved in those programs faithfully served some residents of the program areas, but their efforts were irrelevant to the lives of the remainder.

In retrospect, the reasons seem clear. Policing by consent may be an unrealistic goal in places where communities are fragmented, and divided into competing groups by race, class, and lifestyle. The diversity poses serious challenges to some of the assumptions behind Community Policing. If, instead of trying to find common interests in this diversity, the police deal mainly with elements of their own choosing, they will appear to be taking sides. The police will get along best with those who share their outlook, and the "local values" they represent will be those of some in the community, but not all. In Houston, whites and homeowners were more likely to participate in the community organizations that the program officers worked with. Blacks and renters could easily become the targets of policing where homeowners lived in the nicer parts of the neighborhood. The Houston experience reinforces the concern of critics who question how interests are represented in police policy-making, in their decisions about resource allocations, and in the drafting of departmental regulations.

Police autonomy has been so strong that there has not been much debate about this issue in the United States since the 1960s. There has been more discussion in Britain over the role of local consultative committees and "lay visitors" in shaping district policing policies; however, little is known about how they actually work. The British have also discussed how the *police* could be represented on local planning committees concerned with housing, recreation, and health problems, reflecting the broad focus of problem-solving by police (Reiner 1985). The problem is how to turn consultation into representation, which has the advantage of cloaking the process with symbols of legitimacy. This would be one of the benefits if locally elected representatives to consultative bodies represented the interests of the community in policing. Americans in general accept the consequences of electoral contests even where they disagree with the views of the winners, because they believe that is a fair way of making decisions (Lind and Tyler, 1988). Otherwise, equitable Community Policing efforts may only be possible when there is a degree of homogeneity and consensus that does not exist in many troubled neighborhoods. If the police are only accountable internally to their superiors, they will not garner the advantages of this form of procedural consensus-building, one that has proven so successful in the political arena.

COMMUNITY INSTITUTIONS

During the past decade, there also has been a great deal of interest in remobilizing communities to deal with disorder in collective fashion. Since mounting disorder seems to mirror the declining strength of informal social control in communities caught in the cycle of decline, efforts to reinvigorate those informal processes might succeed in reversing the trend. However, the difficulties involved in actually organizing communities to cope with disorder problems are monumental. It is hard to get organizations going in poor areas; they may act upon faulty assumptions about the locus of the problems; and there is evidence that the theory of community crime-prevention on which many are based is erroneous.

Community organizing tactics are aimed at improving the residents' awareness of opportunities to participate in local problem-solving, and to stimulate actual participation in these activities. However, little organized community participation exists in neighborhoods plagued by disorder. Area disorder discourages neighborhood social activity, informal cooperative action, trust in one's neighbors, participation in local activities, and even self-help. The apparently destructive impact of disorder on community institutions impairs the capacity of residents of problem-ridden neighborhoods to solve their own problems. Problem-solving mechanisms that rely upon self-initiated citizen action require community institutions that foster interaction and cooperation. Where community solidarity is so low that there are no viable mechanisms for solving problems informally, or where they do not embrace all major local groups, conflict may undercut the social and economic forces underlying neighborhood stability.

One of the greatest problems is that it is difficult to organize low-income, heterogeneous, deteriorating, high-turnover, disorderly neighborhoods. For community organizers, the American context of diversity is a fundamental part of the problems they face. Earlier we saw how difficult it was even for professional organizers to make much headway under such conditions. Voluntary problem-solving organizations are more frequently found in homogeneous, better-off areas. For example, awareness of neighborhood-watch programs is just as high in surburan areas as in central cities (Whitaker, 1986). In Minneapolis, attempts to transplant organized anti-crime efforts were more likely to succeed in the nicer parts of town. Whether they are self-initiated or fostered by outside agencies, the more an area needs these programs, the less likely it is to have them. This was true in Minneapolis even though organizing *efforts* were directed disproportionately toward areas in need.

An approach to neighborhood problem-solving that relies upon informal social-control mechanisms also assumes that, to a large extent, it is the ordinary residents of the area who are "the problem." This may often be the case. Surveys indicate that about one-third of city residents *think* that people from their neighborhood are at least partly responsible for area crime (Hindelang et al., 1978). They may be appropriate targets of gossip and watchful stares, and if they are young their parents may be shamed into action, but problems generated by outsiders are another story. People passing through the community, and even area businesses that generate litter or attract a boisterous clientele, may fall beyond the reach of informal mechanisms for controlling disorder. Informal controls also will not do much about the drug market. Rumors of drug use and sales were common in our study neighborhoods, and they were highly related to poverty (for example, the correlation between area unemployment and drug problems was +.80). The drug business is awash with money and conducted by violent people. Drug enforcement teeters between alternative tactics to control drug trafficking, focusing one year on higher-level whole-sale suppliers and the next on street dealers; however, both strat-egies make use of the tight organization, expertise, and coercive power of the police. Community organizations have none of these resources. The same shortcomings limit their capacity to control modern youth gangs. These days they are rarely led by "youths," and many are large, armed, and violent (Klein and Maxson, 1989). Their internal economy is built on drugs and extortion, and they are not to be dealt with lightly. Informal efforts to control these types of neighborhood problems may be too diffuse to have much impact.

It may also be that the theory upon which disorder and crime-prevention programs are based is faulty. Many of them (especially those favored by governments and foundations) have focused on enhancing the capacity of communities to intervene, to extend the net of informal social control. However, we have seen how difficult it is to engineer changes in subtle aspects of social relationships.

The intellectual appeal of the informal control approach to neighborhood problem-solving is world-wide. Social approaches to crime control, neighborhood-watch schemes, and situational crime-prevention programs that emphasize surveillance and inter-vention are being organized throughout Britain (Hope and Shaw, 1988). And the hypothesis that there are self-help cures for com-munity ills was clearly articulated by two researchers, in a discus-sion of neighborhood-watch programs in Australia:

> The most important element of community
> crime-prevention appears to be to bring about social
> interaction, whereby residents of the community maintain a
> degree of familiarity with each other. Such interaction and
> familiarity should, in theory at least, make it possible to
> detect strangers in the community. And finally,
> crime-prevention theory suggests that such interactions may
> lead to a cohesive neighborhood. The basic philosophy of
> community crime-prevention is that social interaction and
> citizen familiarity can play an important role in preventing,
> detecting, and reporting criminal behavior (Mukherjee and
> Wilson, 1987: 2)

We have seen, however, how difficult it is to make changes in people's daily routines, which are shaped by diverse economic, social, and physical factors, including their age and the physical layout of area sidewalks and streets. Even in neighborhoods where organized efforts to mobilize residents were highly visible, there were no changes in the intervening mechanisms—including interaction, solidarity, and intervention—that in turn were supposed to reduce disorder and crime.

Where community institutions are strong and inclusive, gossip, social exclusion, negotiation, and even mediation by trusted figures might be able to resolve at least some disorder problems. The difficulty is that fewer and fewer places resemble urban villages, and American society near the end of the twentieth century does not have that much capacity for local problem-solving. William Felstiner (1974) argued that the ways in which societies resolve disputes are related to their social organization. The social organization of the United States (one of his "technologically complex, rich societies") is characterized by unstable nuclear families, very weak extended-family networks, and frequent residential mobility and job changes. Neighborhoods are not the emotional or economic locus for much of this activity. In this kind of society, "friends are not necessarily neighbors and neighbors are not necessarily friends." This can also be said of their enemies. Americans are more dependent on the large bureaucracies that regulate their health and welfare, education, employment, and retirement. These features of life lead Americans to rely on formal mechanisms for settling disputes, and on formal social-control institutions for protection—ways of making and imposing decisions that are backed by the coercive power of the state.

The police have this coercive power, which is why they are a seemingly attractive resource to involve in reducing disorder. In the case of drugs, neither investigations of "Mr. Big" nor wars against street dealers are likely to be effective without the police. Their support may be crucial for the success of community organizations as well. This was suggested by James Garofalo and Maureen McLeod (1986), who found that almost all of the enduring neighborhood-watch organizations they studied enjoyed the active support of local police. Police provided these groups with information, training, technical support, and equipment. Police can also lend visibility, continuity, and legitimacy to initial efforts to organize communities; we saw in Houston's CORT program that they can do so with surprising effectiveness. A fundamental tenet of Community Policing is its commitment to "helping neighborhoods help themseves" by serving as a catalyst for local organizing and educational efforts.

The problem for American cities is that residents of poor and minority neighborhoods with serious disorder problems often have antagonistic relationships with the police. They regard the police as another of their problems, frequently perceiving them to be arrogant, brutal, racist, and corrupt. Groups representing these neighborhoods will not automatically look to the police for legitimacy and guidance; rather, they are likely to be involved in monitoring police misconduct and pressing for greater political accountability. In poor neighborhoods, community groups can make progress only by extracting resources from the outside; thus, they are much less likely than groups in better-off areas to accept a narrow, technical view of crime prevention, or to see it as a high-priority solution for the problems facing their constituents. Groups in these areas are more likely to point with alarm to "the causes of crime" in their area, and press for jobs, better housing, and health care; yet more intensive policing in areas they represent, instead of helping solve any fundamental problems, might seem more likely to generate new complaints about harassment, indiscriminate searches, and conflicts between police and area youths.

THE POLITICAL ECONOMY OF DISORDER

The strong link between disorder and the economic and social makeup of communities examined here also cannot be ignored. Referring to causal factors such as the economic and social makeup of a community makes many policy analysts more than a little nervous. These factors often prove to be stubbornly intractable targets; they call for more "fundamental" (read that "expensive and long-term") solutions to community problems than either policing or organizing efforts. However, such efforts, if they were to get off the ground, they are also more likely to succeed at empowering people to be orderly. By some reckonings, community development efforts are still not "root solutions" to disorder—which is rooted in capitalism, racism, and the emerging role of the United States in the international division of labor. However, such efforts have possibilities.

Disorderly communities are poor and unstable. Chapter 3 indicated that one of the strongest correlates of disorder was area poverty. The correlation between disorder and unemployment was +.84; on the other hand, communities with many high-school graduates enjoyed lower levels of disorder (the correlation was −.53). The importance of other social and economic factors was also apparent in these data. Housing arrangements appear to be important, for the extent of owner-occupied housing also was linked to lower levels of disorder.

Well-off neighborhoods seemed able to overcome other liabilities. For example, Figure 3–2 turned up two notably deviant cases, places which were low on stability yet also low on disorder—Hyde Park and Lincoln Park, both in Chicago. Those two heavily gentrified areas were the second and eighth richest in this set of 40 communities. Hyde Park maintained high levels of order despite its continguity with one of the most disorder-prone areas of them all, Woodlawn. Its principal resource is the University of Chicago, whose huge investment in the area has forced it to pay attention to the surrounding neighborhood. The University has invested millions of its own dollars, and leveraged millions more in federal urban renewal grants, to acquire and demolish blighted buildings and level nearby taverns. The University actively participates in the real-estate market by purchasing marginal or deteriorating buildings in the vicinity and making low-cost mortgage loans to its faculty. It operates fleets of buses that safely whisk students and employees around the campus and downtown (Taub, Taylor, and Dunham, 1984). Disorder reflects the inability of communities to mobilize these resources to deal with urban woes. The distribution of disorder thus mirrors the larger pattern of structured inequality that makes inner-city neighborhoods vulnerable to all manner of threats to the health and safety of their residents.

Why dub this a problem with an area's "political" economy? Because many features of life in city neighborhoods are shaped in important ways by essentially political decisions. These decisions are made by governments and large institutional actors like banks, insurance and utility companies, and real-estate developers. The causes of disorder problems as well as their solution lie in part in what these powerful players decide to do. Many neighborhoods plagued by disorder have lost out as a result of past politics, and because they are overwhelmingly poor their redemption will depend to some degree on their capacity to extract resources from the wider community, through future politics.

Clearly, much of the condition and composition of urban neighborhoods reflects the sum of thousands of individual, market-driven consumer decisions by people choosing to move here or there, and to invest or disinvest in this or that piece of property. Those decisions are in turn shaped by the skill, cash-flow, lifestyle preferences, family organization, and fears and prejudices of people seeking suitable employment and housing. The character of the existing housing stock and the locational advantages of particular neighborhoods count for a great deal as well. Owners of small businesses lining the arterial streets that surround residential neighborhoods read those factors carefully as well, to adapt to market conditions. Sociological studies remind us that local government in the United States have only limited ability to exercise much control over market forces. For example, sociologist Harvey Molotch's (1972) study of the housing market of one of our neighborhoods, Chicago's South Shore, found that once residents started making decisions about moving or staying, concerted action by the city, community organizations, and major developers could not significantly delay racial transition in the area. In an attempt to maintain neighborhood stability, they set up housing referral committees to strategically distribute blacks and whites who were looking for a place to live. They also organized renovation and beautification efforts, redrew attendance boundaries to increase the number of white children in the local school, and secured the cooperation of the police in maintaining high-visibility patrols and cracking down on gangs in the area. In the face of all this effort, blacks quickly replaced whites, buildings were subdivided and undermaintained, area property values stagnated, and the crime rate soared.

While many aspects of the configuration of communities reflect these types of consumer decisions, some closely held institutional decisions and practices affect levels of local disorder as well. These are the province of government and private corporate actors. They include investment decisions, national and local housing and transportation policies, real-estate sales practices, and the construction and demolition activities of local governments.

The two key investments are in job creation and housing. Most of the neighborhoods examined here were located in cities that faced a precipitous decline in the availability of stable, well-paying industrial-sector jobs during the 1970s and 1980s. For example, Chicago lost 50 percent of its manufacturing jobs (250,000 of them) between 1970 and 1985. Comparable new jobs in these metropolitan areas were largely confined to the suburbs, beyond the reach of less well-off inner-city workers. New downtown jobs in Chicago, Philadelphia, San Francisco, and Newark lay in the transactional sectors of the economy—banking, insurance, corporate front-office operations, and government. These positions generally call for more formal education and technical skill than typically can be found in disorder-plagued communities; at best they spawn a demand for lower-paid service-sector personnel—janitors, guards, cashiers, and food service workers. These limited opportunities were clear to one Woodlawn resident:

> I can't see any future in Woodlawn, at least not for myself. I
> can't see staying down here because it's a dead end. . . .
> It's a dead end because you can't find no jobs down here;
> you have to go outside the neighborhood to find a job. You
> look up and down 63d street and most of the stores that are
> up in here are boarded up or gone or burned up. So there's
> really no future here. There's no job opportunities for young
> people. All we do is sit around or lay around on the streets
> everyday doing nothing. You ought to see them, its all they
> do is get high, play basketball, walk around doing nothing.
> [Woodlawn, Chicago]

The suburban sprawl around these cities (the exception is Houston, whose vast boundaries encompass most development in the area) is a reflection of the urban political economy. This sprawl was made possible by freeways, which provided handy connections between bedroom suburbs and downtown, and by an interstate highway system that make it convenient to locate new office buildings, manufacturing, and assembly plants near interchanges on the edges of metropolitan areas. Movement out of the city after World War II was financed to a signficant extent by federally-insured FHA mortgages, and encouraged by federal tax policies favoring home ownership. The location of much of this new growth in the South and West was stimulated by corporate searches for lower-wage, non-union workers; by tax abatement deals by state and local governments with modest regulatory ambitions; and by a pattern of federal defense expenditures that generally favored these regions over the North and East.

Back in the frost-belt cities, investment in housing as well as in the creation of new jobs faltered. Institutional decisions about the viability of neighborhoods are an important factor shaping local real-estate markets. A refusal by banks and insurance companies to make reasonable housing loans, or to issue policies in certain neighborhoods, effectively condemns them to decline (Bradford and Rubinowitz, 1975; Urban-Suburban Investment Study Group, 1975). This practice is called "redlining," to conjure up the image of a greedy banker slashing a red line around a doomed community. Disinvestment decisions are "a sign for all that the neighborhood is 'going.' Powerful and influential interests have lost faith in it, and that stands as a warning to any home-seekers or commercial investors to look elsewhere" (Goodwin, 1979). This is a self-fulfilling prophecy. Without mortgage money, home sellers cannot find buyers, and those who want to stay cannot secure rehabilitation loans. This quickly leads to deflating real-estate values, and increased vulnerability to either panic sales or abandonment. The importance of rehabilitation loans to property owners living close to the margin is illustrated by this report from Wicker Park:

> They just have everything invested in their house. And sometimes they can't even get insurance or loans for their property. Especially loans. I know one Puerto Rican lady who lives near here who had her old boiler break down. She went all over to find out how much it would cost to get it fixed, and the cheapest she could get it fixed for was $2,000. Well, where is she going to get it? No one will lend her the money or anything, and there's no heat in the winter. Now she thinks she will probably have to abandon the building and lose it to the city, because she can't get any heat in the winter and you can't live in it like that. [Wicker Park, Chicago]

There are federal and state regulations against formal redlining, but its informal manifestations are more difficult to document. A "cautious evaluation" of the soundness of a neighborhood can have the same effect. It is disinvestment, not gentrification, which threatens poorer neighborhoods. In many cities, representatives of long-time residents of gentrifying communities are battling this new investment and rising real-estate values, arguing that it drives up rents and displaces their constituents. In many cities, however, much more housing has been left to rot, or put to the torch for insurance money, or knocked down by the city. In the aggregate, relatively few household moves are forced by rising property values, and gentrification has affected a relatively small fraction of the housing market (albeit one prominently featured in the media). Investment is not the principal threat to the availability of housing for the poor in America's inner cities.

In addition to private-sector decisions, the residential quality of neighborhoods can be eroded by land-use decisions by local governments. The freeway networks driven through the hearts of many American cities in the 1950s greatly reduced the desirability of surrounding neighborhoods. Typically, the highways were channeled through low income, minority neighborhoods where land was cheaper and local resistance to destruction could more easily by overcome. This forced area residents into other neighborhoods, a consequence not appreciated by those already living there (Altschuler, 1965). In the 1960s and 1970s, federally financed urban-renewal programs mainly displaced low-income blacks, and destroyed rather than rebuilt residential districts close to downtowns. Demolition and new construction is generally favored over rehabilitation by development coalitions of real-estate combines, banks, corporate investors, contractors, and their allies in city hall. Their planning and construction activities create artificial neighborhoods that cannot easily recapture the stability of the areas they replaced (Bursik, 1986).

Various policies have been advocated to change the consequences of these decisions. Supporters of "linked-development" schemes press city governments to require that developers invest in low-income housing elsewhere in the city as the price of being allowed to build downtown. Urban enterprise zones could offer tax-abatement incentives and infrastructure support (new sewers and streets) to enhance the attractiveness of inner-city locations for businesses. Industrial parks and business "incubators" push the concept one step further, supplying the buildings in which start-up companies can locate. These attempts to hold on to old jobs and to encourage inner-city job creation reflect the fact that the changing economic face of metroplitan areas has severely limited access to jobs by inner-city residents.

There have also been attempts to deal with short-term sources of neighborhood destabilization. One strategy for coping with some of the potentially destabilizing consequences of neighborhood change is "home equity insurance." Illinois has established a self-financing insurance fund which underwrites the general market value of homes. Neighborhoods opt into the program through a petition by residents; those who live in insured areas pay a supplemental tax in return for the option of selling their home to the fund for its assessed value. Equity insurance is designed to protect homeowners against local, short-lived gyrations in the value of residential property; these shifts are often associated with prospective racial transition. Equity insurance is designed to stabilize property values, bolster the confidence of homeowners, and alleviate fears of resegregation in areas undergoing moderate levels of racial transition (Lyons, McCourt, and Nyden, 1986).

Equity programs could go hand-in-hand with other efforts to stabilize communities. Many municipalities have challenged real-estate sales practices. Efforts in this area include measures to discourage "panic peddling," a process by which unscrupulous real-estate agents reap enormous profits trading on fear. By stirring up concern about crime and racial change, panic peddlers frighten white residents into selling their homes at reduced prices; then the homes are resold at inflated prices to blacks and Hispanics desperate for better and safer housing, a practice known as "block busting."

Impending changes in federal housing policy could also have a dramatic impact on local housing markets. One such program is a voucher approach to providing subsidized housing for the poor. The United States is no longer constructing large blocks of publicly managed housing; one policy to stimulate the growth of affordable alternative housing is to provide the poor with cash-equivalent vouchers that can be used to pay part of their rent. This would presumably stimulate the market for lower-cost housing throughout the metropolitan area, making it profitable for landlords to maintain, upgrade, and even build low-income units. Because they would still have to compete for tenant's vouchers, much of this new housing would presumably be attractively managed as well. As an alternative measure, some cities have secured federal funds to develop scatter-site, low-rise public housing. This typically involves purchasing smaller run-down buildings and contracting with private, nonprofit organizations to rehabilitate and manage the properties.

In sum, it should be clear that many factors that appear to engender disorder or may counter its spread are shaped by conscious decisions by persons in power. These decisions reflect the interests of banks, real-estate developers, employers, government agencies, and others playing for large economic and political stakes. None of these decisions are irreversible, although they obviously may be motivated by still larger economic and demographic forces. The closely held nature of these decisions has not been lost on community organizations that have tackled redlining, blockbusting, land use, and economic development issues. They highlight the larger—but often invisible—political context in which disorder problems are set. To the extent to which disorder is driven by these decisions, it can be seen as a manifestation of the American urban political economy.

"DESIGNING OUT" DISORDER

Environmental design (ED) strategies provide "soft" solutions to disorder problems. The ED approach involves arranging social and physical constraints which "naturally" control public activity; these foreclose opportunities for disorderly behavior and create opportunities for socially constructive behavior. The solutions are "soft" because they do not involve coercion; people are allowed to make choices about their behavior. ED strategies manipulate the environment within which those choices are made, to assure that people generally will choose to act in a socially desirable way. They can also be relatively cheap, and can work well in diverse environments. ED stategies rely on creative thinking and advance planning; they call for thoughtful consideration of how day-to-day routine activities can be structured to minimize the extent of disorder.

For example, the ED solution to littering problems is to give value to refuse. This can be done by regulation, by paying a bounty, or by providing tax incentives for dealing with it. Many states have at least considered imposing significant deposits on bottles and cans to encourage their return, a regulation strategy. In recent years this has been reinforced by the increased market value of aluminum cans, which has created incentives for people to pick them up for recycling. A municipal recycling policy that would pay a bounty for about-to-be-abandoned cars would work in the same way; it would give such hulks a turn-in value, and probably would not be more expensive than dealing with complaints concerning abandoned cars and then eventually towing them from the streets. Private and municipal recyling centers and resale shops for used goods and furniture, run for a combination of public-spirited and

entrepreneurial reasons, also provide alternative outlets for potential refuse.

There are two ED approaches to controlling vandalism, both of
which involve physical design. The first approach to "designing
out" vandalism emphasizes the use of *damage-resistant materials* in
the construction of private and (especially) public facilities.
Shatter-proof plastic replaces glass; hard-to-mar and easy-to-clean
ceramic surfaces cover high-risk locations such as transit stops,
school buildings, and sports stadiums. New York City's new subway cars are clad in easy-to-clean stainless steel. The second approach to vandalism control stresses designing *surveillance* into
high-risk places, opening them to supervision. For example, subway information booths in the Washington, DC, subway system
overlook the platforms, which in turn are designed to provide few
places to lurk. There are few surfaces to mar, for at many stations
the ceiling soars far overhead and cannot be reached from the
platform. The ED approach uses existing supervisors of at-risk
spaces—bus drivers, parking lot attendants, shop owners, caretakers—to monitor public behavior near where they work. Research
in Britain indicates that there is less vandalism on buses that have
conductors rather than just drivers, and less vandalism on the first
floors of two-decker trams, in both cases because of the higher
levels of surveillance and control (Mayhew, 1981; Clarke, 1980).
ED recommends positioning pay telephones and vending machines within view of clerks or attendants, even if they are en-
gaged in other tasks.

These principles also extend to residential environments. About
30 percent of all housing in Britain is publicly owned, so government is greatly interested in ways to control disorder in lower-
income, family oriented housing estates. Barry Poyner (1982) presents a long list of options which seem to work, including efforts to
break up large areas into smaller and more manageable sub-
communities that can be supervised by residents. To this end, he
recommends closing off streets; putting limits to pedestrian access
to areas that seem excessively "public" and thus no one's turf;
arranging windows to overlook playgrounds and other public
spaces, and hiring resident caretakers.

At the extreme, disorder can be managed by completely privat-
izing residential areas. This can already by seen in what William H.
Whyte (1988) dubs "megastructures"; they merge apartments,
recreation areas, health clubs, shopping, services, and parking lots

under one roof, and sometimes have their own parks, trees, boat docks, and jogging paths. Often, no children are allowed. Life in megastrutures is free from litter, traffic, harassment, crime, and fear. These facilities remove residents' lives from the public domain, barricading away disorder for the benefit of those who can afford the protection (Felson, 1987). There are obvious social costs to this, including the class segregation it entails, but megastructures certainly accord with a growing reliance on privatization and the market to provide what were previously perceived to be public benefits, including safety.

ED strategies are underappreciated, and have not been widely studied. Even short of complete privatization, they have the potential to maintain order in unobtrusive and uncoercive ways. Manipulating the physical and social features of environments that are at risk, in order to limit opportunities for disorder and discourage its opportunistic participants, often calls for creativity rather than for significantly greater expense.

A related strategy for dealing with some forms of disorder is zoning. Designed to limit diversity, it has an honorable legal pedigree. Cities have a long tradition of excluding from residential neighborhoods activities that threaten to adversely affect the quality of life. Economic activities deemed too unhealthy or unseemly—even simply being too smelly—have long been banned from the parts of town where people live in substantial numbers. Cities also isolate activities that pose an undue risk of fire, or attract too much traffic.

Now there is interest in segregating disorder, for similar reasons and using similar legal tactics. Zoning is being used to drive massage parlors, "modeling studios," bath houses, and sexually oriented bookstores and theaters into isolated areas of cities, away from residential neighborhoods. In 1986, the U.S. Supreme Court upheld the constitutionality of a municipal zoning ordinance prohibiting such activities within 1,000 feet of any residence, church, park, or school (*City of Renton* v. *Playtime Theaters*, 1986). This effectively barred adult theaters and bookstores from 95 percent of the community. In 1988, the Supreme Court also upheld a Cook County, Illinois, ordinance restricting adult bookstores to areas zoned for industrial rather than residential or commercial use. Perhaps the best-known areas which have been officially zoned for disorder are "The Block" in Baltimore and "The Combat Zone" in Boston. The latter is a two-block area that in 1975 was chosen as a suitable site for sexually-oriented establishments that were prohibited elsewhere in the city.[2] A decade earlier, the court upheld a Detroit ordinance that required the dispersal of adult theaters, pawnshops, pool halls, and shoeshine parlors (*Young* v. *American Mini Theaters*, 1976). In Detroit, these establishments could neither be near residential areas nor within 1,000 feet of each other, in line with the argument that the sheer concentration of such activities contributed to their deleterious impact.

It was important that neither the Renton nor the Young case was defined as involving obscenity. In both instances the cities argued they were acting to check neighborhood deterioration, to protect (other) small businesses, prevent crime, and enhance the quality of life in residential communities. The court accepted this line of argument, thus avoiding the "strict scrutiny" of the ordinances that would have been demanded if they had been classed as potential assaults on freedom of speech. Rather, these establishments were treated as "abateable nuisances" that could be dealt with like any other "obnoxious" land use (cf. Giokaris, 1987). In Illinois, on the other hand, the state Supreme Court ruled that the legislature cannot use nuisance laws to close adult bookstores even if they have been convicted of selling obscene material, because that might prevent the sale of magazines that are protected by the Constitution. The Illinois statute, however, also authorized establishments to be closed if they had been used in connection with kidnapping, prostitution, gambling, and a long list of other common crimes. Those grounds remain on the books.

It is unlikely that the United States will use zoning tactics to control public prostitution. Other nations do it this way; for example, prostitution is legal in Germany, but public solicitation for the purpose of prostitution is legally (and also in practice) confined to designated areas. In the United States, on the other hand, explicit zoning would require legalizing the trade, and few politicians would be found in the forefront of that movement. It also continues to be difficult to draft sexual-conduct statutes that do not violate the rights to due process, equal protection, and freedom of speech and association. Often the inconvenience of arrest is the only penalty for streetwalking; a study of the handling of prostitution cases in 16 cities concluded that up to 90 percent of arrests in this category escape judicial sanction (Pearl, 1987). In many places we have quasi-decriminalized prostitution through an ad hoc set of arrangements that informally recognize its role in the economy of the convention business, while keeping it out of neighborhoods whose complaints can be heard downtown.

CARE AND TREATMENT

Some disorder problems are a direct outgrowth of the failure of governments to deliver on two important policy innovations of the 1970s—the decriminalization of public intoxication and the deinstitutionalization of the mentally ill. Both were laudable attempts to approach old problems with new and intellectually stimulating solutions. In the case of public intoxication, the problem was that criminal sanctions (typically, being locked overnight in the drunk tank) were demonstrably ineffective at dealing with this lifestyle; the solution was to move public drunks from police lockups to therapeutic detoxification centers. This converted them from a criminal justice problem to a public health concern. In the case of mental illness, the solution to the mounting cost of warehousing seemingly incurable yet non-dangerous patients was to move them from the stultifying confines of hospital wards into community-based residential-care units where they could learn to function in normal society. Many individuals who would have been hospitalized are now classed as outpatients. Because of new restrictions on involuntary commitment, and the absence of any place to put them anyway, this means they are out for good.

The problem is that society did not deliver the alternative treatments. "Under-staffed and ill-prepared clinics lost track of patients, failed to offer jobs and housing, and ultimately consigned many to shadowy lives on the streets or in seedy boardinghouses" (*New York Times,* September 4, 1988). Not enough detoxification facilities were constructed, and removing public intoxication from the purview of the criminal law eliminated most incentives for police officers to pick up any but the most pitiful cases and carry them away to safety. Detoxification centers frequently refuse to admit chronic inebriates, as well as those who are combative or might be dangerous. The patients who were moved out of mental hospitals too frequently were dumped on a fee-per-head basis into substandard housing, and were left undersupervised by untrained staff. Such staff do not provide adequate psychiatric care, and too often provide precious little care of any sort. The right of outpatients to refuse treatment further complicates the situation

(Teplin, 1983). Nicer neighborhoods have successfully resisted the opening of community treatment facilities (as they now resist shelters for the homeless), so commuity-care patients often find themselves adrift in "normal" milieus that in fact are unsavory and sometimes dangerous.

Both groups are casualties of public policies of the 1970s. To an unknown (but undoubtedly substantial) extent those policies have contributed to the public drinking, panhandling, trespassing, garbage scrounging, and street fighting that plague some neighborhoods.

Decriminalization and deinstitutionalization also are related in complex ways to an issue of the 1980s, homelessness. There is perhaps no topic about which social researchers are more divided than the extent of alcoholism and mental illness among the homeless. One view is that homelessness is a simple economic problem—people are homeless because they have no jobs or cannot make enough to pay for shelter, and because the stock of affordable housing is rapidly being depleted by urban renewal, gentrification, and abandonment. They have been thrown out by their landlords and have exhausted the patience of their relatives and friends. A large proportion of them are families; in Chicago, perhaps 40 percent of shelter residents are women and their children. Another view is that a large fraction of the apparently homeless are in one way or another crazed, and are to one degree or another responsible for their own fate. These views (and some in-between positions) have different implications for what is to be done with regard to those defined in some fashion (this is itself a divisive issue) as homeless.

The disorder problems attributable to street people usually involve the crazed fraction, however large or small it may be. They are the most visible residents of the street, and draw the complaints of merchants, shoppers, and area residents. They live on hustles and scams. They dislike the regimentation of shelter life (curfews; fixed meal times), as well as crowded and unsafe conditions in flophouses. They avoid missions or detoxification centers, where submission to one form of treatment or another is a condition of admission. They present a difficult policing problem. The police can watch for criminal violations, but otherwise can only attempt to harass them into "moving along." They are fundamentally a social-service problem. Peter Finn (1988) describes a number of programs for street people; all involve some combination of detoxification units, shelters, and social work. In most jurisdictions the police have the authority to take the inebriates, the obviously disoriented, and those who appear ''dangerous to themselves'' or unable to guard themselves from harm, to these units without making an arrest. In the absence of any other ''health care delivery system'' for street people, the police usually are on the front line. However, it is difficult to get them to act. There are few organizational rewards for doing so, since they do not constitute a ''good pinch.'' Dealing at length with drunks and the mentally ill also runs counter to typical police disdain for doing ''social work'' rather than ''fighting crime'' (Bittner, 1967a); they rationalize that it diverts them from ''real'' police work. Finally, police perceive (frequently correctly) that the shelters they take people to are inadequate and ineffective—they are revolving doors that do not have a cure to deliver (Aaronson et al., 1984; Teplin, 1984).

While the problem may lie in the inadequacy of alternatives to institutionalization and criminalization, that does not mean the solutions are simple. It is not just a question of money, although that is the first issue that must be addressed. Delivering better care and treatment to street people will not be an easy task. Detoxification centers can only take in people who voluntarily submit themselves for treatment. The mentally ill are difficult to put back into hospitals, due to new restrictions on involuntary commitment in many jurisdictions; many of those hospitals are now closed, and there are few community-based programs to which they can now be admitted (Teplin, 1984). To be admitted they must be seriously delusional, and many disorderly people are not over that threshold. They also must be ''pure types''—i.e., free of complicating factors. It is easy for street people with complex problems to fall through the cracks of care systems. In Chicago, mental health centers will not take the mentally retarded, alcoholics, seemingly dangerous persons, or anyone with a criminal record. Detoxification centers shun chronic alcoholics and combative personalities. As sociologist Linda Teplin (1984) of Northwestern University notes, ''mental health programs found persons with alcohol problems to be disruptive to the patient milieu and often would not accept them for treatment. Conversely, the staff at detoxification facilities felt they were not equipped to deal with persons exhibiting signs of mental disorder and would turn away persons with such 'mixed' symptomatology.'' As a result, homeless street people with complicated mental, drug and alcohol problems were dealt with in the only fashion the care system allowed—they were arrested.

There is no "quick fix" for many of the forms of disorder that plague city neighborhoods. Solutions need to be carefully matched to the specific problems facing individual communities, and in many cases it will take a combination of approaches to make a significant difference in the lives of area residents. The organization and coercive power of the police will prove invaluable under some circumstances, but might be counterproductive in others. Local organizations can turn their efforts inward, to strengthen ties between community residents, and outward, to extract from power-holders the development resources they cannot generate internally. State power can be used creatively to contain some forms of disorder, and to reduce opportunities for others. Finally, it is important not to deal with the victims of failed public policies as if they are the enemies of order, but rather as a challenge to our capacity to maintain order by healing.

Methodological
Appendix

In this book we took a new look at the findings of five studies of disorder, crime, fear, and community decline. They all involved surveys of the residents of several urban neighborhoods, sometimes in more than one city. The surveys were conducted in six U.S cities between 1977 and 1983, and included 40 areas. It was possible to combine the findings of these studies because they shared a number of common survey questions and techniques. Beginning with the evaluation surveys conducted for the National Institute of Justice by Floyd Fowler and his associates (1979) at the University of Massachusetts, Boston, researchers investigating neighborhood crime problems have borrowed freely from one another's questionnaires, and usually have employed survey procedures that yield respondent samples of roughly comparable quality and size. Together, these surveys constitute a valuable "national" data base.

Despite their rough similarity, the process of drawing together the data from all of these studies involved a number of strategic and analytic decisions. No two studies were identical in methodology, and some used similar but frustratingly different wordings for their questions or response categories. Because they had differing goals, the surveys covered in varying depth the concepts of interest to us here. This appendix describes the sources of the data and how they were combined to produce the area indicators presented in this report. There also is a brief discussion of the analytic methods utilized for this study. A more detailed technical report is available from the National Criminal Justice Reference Service (Skogan, 1987b).

Survey Sources and Methods. Table A presents a brief summary of the studies and suggests a book or report in which further details about the surveys may be found.

All of the areas were in the nation's largest cities. They were selected for a variety of reasons—among them, because they were high or low-crime areas, because programs were about to be started in them, and because they were stable or undergoing racial transition. All seemed interesting to study, so this set of neighborhoods underrepresents the relatively stable, family-oriented, non-poor, run-of-the-mill places that make up most of America's urban areas. The collection of areas examined in detail are a far from random sample of neighborhoods; their strength is that they vary fairly widely on a number of theoretically important dimensions. A brief demographic profile of the areas is presented in Table B.

The study areas differ in the extent to which they would be considered neighborhoods by their residents. Boundaries for the ten areas included in the three-city study were defined on the basis of extensive ethnographic research, so the areas surveyed could resemble the cognitive maps respondents had of their neighborhoods. On the other hand, the survey simply asked them about "your neighborhood." The boundaries of the ten areas surveyed in Houston and Newark were based on census tracts, and tract boundaries were only slightly modified to take into account expressways, major arterial streets, and housing projects. However, those surveys were done in person, and respondents were given a sketch map of their tract and asked to think about the specified area as they answered the questions. It is hard to judge which was a better procedure.

The studies utilized a diverse mix of data-collection methods. Three were conducted by telephone, two used personal inter-

Table A Summary of Survey Studies

Study	City	Areas	Date of Collection	Major Citation
Houston	Houston	5	1983	Pate et al., 1985
Newark	Newark	5	1983	Pate et al., 1985
Chicago	Chicago	6	1983	Lewis et al., 1988
Chicago	Chicago	8	1979	Taub et al., 1985
Atlanta	Atlanta	6	1979	Greenberg et al., 1982
Three Cities	Chicago	4	1977	Skogan and Maxfield, 1981
	Philadelphia	3	1977	Skogan and Maxfield, 1981
	San Francisco	3	1977	Skogan and Maxfield, 1981

Table B The 40 Study Areas

Study and City	Unweighted Percent		Weighted for Estimation Percent Who Are:			
	Cases	Female	NonAnglo	Elderly	Renters	Unemp
Chicago 1983						
Northwest	395	58	3	46	34	5
Northside	194	57	14	42	38	4
Northeast Austin	191	54	31	36	27	2
Auburn-Gresham	245	58	96	28	13	9
Edgewater	255	54	20	27	55	2
Back-of-the-Yards	123	59	43	24	52	8
Newark, NJ						
Newark South-1	412	56	99	17	48	20
Newark South-2	347	59	98	20	43	13
Newark North	385	58	99	22	61	21
Newark West	418	58	95	11	44	16
Newark South-4	450	67	99	12	55	15
Houston						
Wood Bayou	518	52	72	3	71	11
Northline	406	52	40	13	34	8
Langwood	395	49	22	9	39	8
Golfcrest	543	53	60	13	56	11
Shady Acres	389	47	52	19	63	7
Chicago 1979						
Portage Park	395	70	4	25	25	1
Lincoln Park	433	63	22	7	74	3
Austin	395	71	82	8	55	3
Back-of-the-Yards	418	68	51	16	55	7
Beverly	401	70	15	19	11	1
Hyde Park-Kenwood	417	61	39	15	70	2
South Shore	441	67	94	10	69	3
East Side	410	66	12	25	21	0
Three City-Philadelphia						
West Philadelphia	450	73	86	17	40	17
South Philadelphia	449	69	21	14	31	16
Logan	201	52	61	9	34	15
Three City-Chicago						
Lincoln Park	450	59	23	7	78	9
Wicker Park	451	64	48	8	65	14
Woodlawn	200	68	96	18	83	16
Back-of-the-Yards	200	61	38	13	57	11
Three City-San Francisco						
Sunset	453	63	21	18	47	7
Visitacion Valley	448	67	53	15	33	9
The Mission	201	46	36	10	82	14
Atlanta						
Upper Virginia High	80	58	0	22	38	4
Lower Virginia High	83	60	9	10	73	7
Grove Park	86	57	95	16	49	5
Dixie Hills	93	66	98	25	36	2
Mechanicsville	87	58	98	21	74	8
Pittsburgh	93	62	98	29	66	3

views, and the five studies employed four different ways of selecting sample households. They all selected an adult (usually 19 years
of age and older) to interview in random fashion, from an initial
listing of everyone who lived in the household.

This report relies principally on neighborhood-level estimates of
the frequency of disorder and other variables. The estimates were
made from the individual-level survey data. To generate those
estimates, the original survey samples were weighted to better
reflect the population values of those variables.

First, all of the studies interviewed only one adult respondent
per sample household, regardless of its size. This underrepresents
persons living in households with two or more adults, in contrast
to single-person dwellings, so the data were weighted by the *number of eligible adults* in each responding household, when available.

Next, several of the surveys were conducted using random-
digit-dialing telephone techniques. This involves calling randomly
scrambled telephone numbers, and then screening respondents to
make sure they live in the area of interest. In this case, households
with more than one telephone number (or, for the Chicago 1983
study, households with more than one listed number) are more
likely than others to fall into the sample. So, respondents were
weighted to *equalize their probability of being selected* for study via
telephone. Residents of households selected at random from address lists (in Houston, Newark, and Atlanta) did not need to be
weighted in this fashion.

Finally, the surveys were weighted to *standardize the sex distribution* of the respondents. Almost all surveys overrepresent women,
who are more likely to be found at home regardless of sampling
technique. This can be seen in Table B, which presents the un-
weighted sex distribution for each neighborhood sample. In addition, females were deliberately over-sampled in selected areas for
the Three City study, which focused to a large extent on fear of
sexual assault. However, gender is *by far* the strongest individual-
level correlate of victimization, fear of crime, and individual crime-
related behaviors, so sex-distribution differences by neighborhood
could disguise other important, area-level contrasts. To counter
this, each area sample was weighted to standardize it at 53 percent
female, the Census Bureau's usual figure for the distribution of the
urban population in the nation as a whole.

The Disorder Measure. Three measures were constructed to indicate the area-level distribution of disorder. *Social Disorder* com-

bined values for questions about loitering, drugs, vandalism, gangs, public drinking and street harassment. *Physical Disorder* combined responses to questions concerning noise, abandoned buildings, litter, and trash. These measures were available for all 40 areas. Where questions about other forms of disorder were asked, they were highly correlated with these, but they were not included in enough neighborhood surveys to be combined in the indices. In Chapters 1 and 2, vandalism was counted as a form of physical disorder. However, analyses of responses to individual disorder questions frequently clustered vandalism with other social disorders, so it was included as one component of the social disorder index.

The two subscales were constructed by summing the component items that were available for each area and then dividing that sum by the number of available items. Thus the scale scores for each set of study areas could be made up of slightly different combinations of particular items, although the component items chosen for inclusion in the scales were available for most of the areas. Each subset of items was substantially intercorrelated; area ratings of social and physical disorders both were internally correlated an average of +.83. An earlier study suggested that physical and social disorders might be distinct dimensions with different consequences for neighborhoods (McPherson et al., 1983). Analyses of the individual surveys suggested that this distinction was a useful one in some areas, where responses to disorder questions broke into two clear clusters. However, at the area level the social and physical disorder measures were highly correlated, and for most purposes there are few differences between them. As a result, the two equally weighted subscales were added together to form a global disorder index. The summary disorder index averaged responses to the two, in effect equally weighting their contribution to the total score for each area.

Data Analysis Strategies. The bivariate and multivariate statistical analyses reported here utilized a conventional $p < .05$ level to determine what was "significant" to report. Because of the sometimes ambiguous causal ordering of many of the factors examined here, a conservative two-tailed test of statistical significance was employed throughout.

The small size of the neighborhood and project-level samples examined here raises the spectre that a few cases exerted excessive influence on the statistical findings. The first line of defense against this problem was illustrated in the book: all bivariate relationships were plotted and examined with care for both nonlinearity and the presence of extreme values. Measures which were "positively skewed" (i.e., that evidenced a few high values) were logged for statistical analysis; those that were negatively skewed were squared to normalize their distribution. One example is the disorder measure: it was slightly right-skewed, and therefore it was logged for statistical analysis. However, it was graphically presented in its original form.

Bivariate relationships also were screened for the influence of outliers using the "influence" measure in SYSTAT. It identifies cases that contribute disproportionately to the linear correlation between two measures.

The multivariate analyses included here demanded more complex treatment, for one cannot easily observe the joint distribution of three or more variables. Whenever multiple regression was used to control for "other" factors or to determine if two related variables each had an independent effect, a direct measure of the "leverage" of each case on the coefficients was calculated, as recommended by Velleman and Welsch (1981). If a case showed high leverage, the analysis was rerun excluding it. This is a more elegant version of the "jackknife test" procedure long employed in the examination of small data sets. Leverage analyses were conducted for each regression analysis reported in the book.

Table A-3-1 Neighborhood Social and Economic Factors

Measures	Principle Components Factor Analysis Factor Loadings	
	Stability	Poverty
Average length of residence	.862	.187
Average age of respondents	.836	.087
Percent single-family homes	.711	-.041
Percent rental dwellings	-.811	.250
Percent high school graduates	.123	-.710
Percent working full-time or part-time	.381	-.780
Percent incomes over $20,000	-.020	-.799
Percent unemployed	-.450	.532
Percent of total variance explained by factor	37.1	28.6

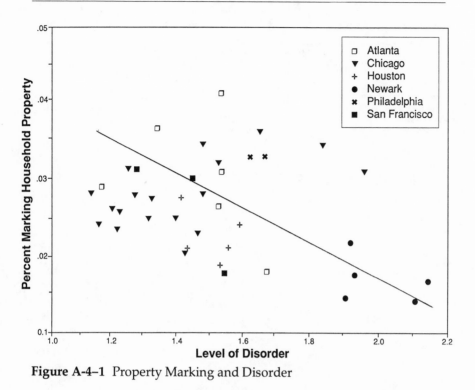

Figure A-4-1 Property Marking and Disorder

Table A-4-1 Socioeconomic Factors, Disorder, and Crime

Measure	Crime Problems		Robbery Victimization	
	Standardized Coefficient	Significance	Standardized Coefficient	Significance
Poverty Score	-.32	.08	.05	.78
Stability Score	-.01	.95	-.04	.82
Percent Minority	.14	.51	.23	.20
Disorder	.88	.002	.58	.008
R^2 (adj)		.65		.59
(N)		(20)		(30)

Note: Two-tailed significance tests are used in all analyses. The disorder measure is logged.

Table A-4-2 Socioeconomic Factors, Disorder, and Fear

| Measure | Neighborhood Fear at Night | |
	Standardized Coefficient	Significance
Poverty Score	-.40	.04
Stability Score	.01	.96
Percent Minority	.32	.10
Disorder	.66	.02
R^2 (adj)	.54	
(N)	(26)	

Note: The disorder measure is logged.

Notes

Chapter 3
The Extent of Disorder

1. Taylor et al.'s (1985) measure of disorder was a factor score loaded heavily on counts of physical dilapidation, but it also reflected some components of social disorder.

Chapter 4
The Impact of Disorder

1. Robbery victimization is used to index local levels of crime for several reasons: methodological research suggests it is reliably measured (cf. Skogan 1981); it tends to correspond better than many other victimization measures with comparable official crime statistics (Gove et al., 1985); aggregate city-level studies indicate it is linked to fear of crime (Skogan, 1977); and comparable measures of robbery victimization were included in 30 of the areas surveyed.

2. This differs from the findings reported by Taylor and Gottfredson (1986). They found a simple correlation of +.63 between area physical decay and crime rates, but when they controlled for social class this disorder-crime link disappeared. They took that as a challenge to the "disorder thesis," but it is not consistent with the findings reported here.

Chapter 5
Policing Disorder

1. Harring (1983) stresses the role of mechanical call-boxes in controlling dispatching as early as 1880. However, they probably were more useful as a device for keeping officers out of saloons and walking their rounds. Walker (1983) and others do not attach much importance to car radios, and focus more on the impact of motorized patrol.

2. Monkkonen (1981: 155) puts the shift toward a crime-control stance (which he dubbed "disengagement from everyday life") earlier than I do, arguing that it was completed by the 1920s. However, the time frame of his research lead him to ignore the effects of the big-city riots and increasing crime rates of the 1960s.

3. The Police Foundation's evaluation was conducted by Antony Pate, Mary Ann Wycoff, Sampson Annan, and Lawrence Sherman. It was supported by a grant from the National Institute of Justice. Everything reported in this chapter is primarily a product of their effort.

4. The evidence is mixed concerning the effects of foot patrol. It does not do much about crime, but appears to reduce fear and increase citizen confidence in the police, and it may stimulate greater cooperation with the police and with crime-prevention efforts. *See* Pate, 1986; Trojanowicz, 1986; Trojanowicz, 1983.

Chapter 6
Community Organizations and Disorder

1. Church-related activity is an exception to the rule that organizational life is more limited in poor neighborhoods. Frequently church activity is higher in poor and minority neighborhoods. There has been little mention of church-based anti-crime activity; however, parish churches were active in Saul Alinsky's original community-organizing efforts, and in many inner-city neighborhoods they are a significant political force.

2. The programs and the evaluation findings are described in Rosenbaum, Lewis, and Grant, 1986, and Lewis, Grant, and Rosenbaum, 1987. They kindly made their evaluation data available for reanalysis, but they bear no responsibility for the findings and interpretations presented here. The concepts and measures employed here were developed independently of theirs, and the data analysis was done somewhat differently. However, their conclusions and mine, which are drawn directly from the data, turned out to be about the same.

Chapter 7
Dealing with Disorder

1. William H. Whyte (1988) tried to understand the motivations of litterers, by observing thousands of people to see what they did with advertisements shoved into their hands by handbill passers in New York. He reports that most of those who dropped them did so *after* they had at least *tried* to spot a waste can, and that they often carried them several blocks in search of one.

2. Interestingly, both The Block and The Combat Zone are experiencing the fate of many skid rows; they are sitting in the shadow of downtown, the land they sit on has become very valuable, and the future of both is threatened by real-estate developers (*Wall Street Journal,* August 26, 1987).

References

AARONSON, D.E., DIENES, C.T., and MUSHENO, M.C. (1984). *Public Policy and Police Discretion: Processes of Decriminalization.* New York: Clark Boardman Co.

ALINSKY, S. (1971). *Rules for Radicals.* New York: Random House.

ALTSCHULER, A. (1965). *The City Planning Process.* Ithaca, NY: Cornell University Press.

ASHER, H.B. (1983). *Causal Modeling.* Newbury Park, CA: Sage Publications.

BABA, Y., and AUSTIN, D.M. (1986). "Determinants of perceived neighborhood safety." Unpublished paper presented at the annual meeting of the American Society of Criminology (Atlanta).

BACH, R.L., and SMITH, J. (1977). "Community satisfaction, expectation of moving, and migration." *Demography,* 14, pp. 147–78.

BALDWIN, R., and KINSEY, R. (1982). *Police Powers and Politics.* London: Quartet Books.

BASSUK, E.L. (1984). "The homelessness problem." *Scientific American,* 251, pp. 40–46.

BENNETT, S.F., FISHER, B.S., and LAVRAKAS, P.J. (1986). "Awareness and participation in the Eisenhower neighborhood program." Unpublished paper, Center for Urban Affairs and Policy Research, Northwestern University.

BIDERMAN, A.D., JOHNSON, L.A., MCINTYRE, J., and WEIR, A.W. (1967). *Report on a Pilot Study in the District of Columbia on Victimization and Attitudes Toward Law Enforcement.* Washington, DC: U.S. Government Printing Office.

BITTNER, E. (1967a). "Police discretion in emergency apprehension of mentally ill persons." *Social Problems,* 14, pp. 278–92.

———. (1967b). "The police on skid row: a study of peace keeping." *American Sociological Review*, 32, pp. 699–715.

BOGGS, S. (1971). "Formal and informal crime control: an exploratory study of urban, suburban, and rural orientations." *Sociological Quarterly*, 12, pp. 319–27.

BOTTOMS, A.E., and WILES, P. (1986). "Housing tenure and residential community crime careers in Britain." In Reiss, A. and Tonrey, M. (Eds.), *Communities and Crime*. Chicago: University of Chicago Press, pp. 101–62.

BRADFORD, C., and RUBINOWITZ, L. (1975). "The urban-suburban investment-disinvestment process: consequences for older neighborhoods." *Annals of the American Academy of Political and Social Science*, 422, pp. 77–86.

BROWN, D., and ILES, S. (1985). "Community constables: a study of a police initiative." In Heal, K., Tarling, R., and Burrows, J. (Eds.) *Policing Today*. London: Her Majesty's Stationery Office, pp. 43–59.

BROWN, L., and WYCOFF, M.A. (1987). "Policing Houston: Reducing Fear and Improving Service." *Crime and Delinquency*, 33, pp. 71–89.

BURSIK, R. (1986). "Ecological stability and the dynamics of delinquency." In Reiss, A. and Tonrey, M. (Eds.), *Communities and Crime*. Chicago: University of Chicago Press, pp. 35–66.

CHAMBERS, G., and TOMBS, J. (1984). *The British Crime Survey: Scotland*. Edinburgh: Her Majesty's Stationery Office.

CLARKE, R.V.G. (1980). "Situational crime prevention: theory and practice." *British Journal of Criminology*, 20, pp. 136–47.

COHEN, B. (1980). *Deviant Street Networks: Prostitution in New York City*. Lexington, MA: Lexington Books.

COHEN, S. (1973). "Campaigning against vandalism." In Ward, C. *Vandalism*. New York: Van Nostrand.

———. (1984). "Sociological approaches to vandalism." In Levy-Leboyer, C. (Ed.), *Vandalism: Behavior and Motivations*. Amsterdam and New York: Elsevier, pp. 51–62.

CONKLIN, J.E. (1975). *The Impact of Crime*. New York: Macmillan.

COOK, R.F., and ROEHL, J.A. (1982). "The urban crime prevention program: interim findings and central issues." Unpublished paper presented at the Annual Meeting of the Law and Society Association (Toronto).

COOK, T.D., APPLETON, H., CONNOR, R., SCHAFFER, A., TAMKIN, G., and WEBER, S.J. (1975). *"Sesame Street" Revisited: A Case Study in Evaluation Research*. New York: Russell Sage Foundation.

COOK, T.D., and CAMPBELL, D.T. (1979). *Quasi-Experimentation: Design and Analysis Issues for Field Settings*. Chicago: Rand McNally.

Cox, H. (1965). *The Secular City.* New York: Macmillan.

Crenson, M.A. (1978). "Social networks and political process in urban neighborhoods." *American Journal of Political Science,* 11, pp. 578-94.

――――. (1983). *Neighborhood Politics.* Cambridge: Harvard University Press.

Dahmann, D.C. (1985). "Assessments of neighborhood quality in metropolitan America." *Urban Affairs Quarterly,* 20, pp. 511-35.

Department of Housing and Urban Development. (1973). *Abandoned Housing Research: A Compendium.* Washington, DC: Department of Housing and Urban Development.

Droettboom, T., McAllister, R.J., Kaiser, E.J., and Butler, E.W. (1971). "Urban violence and residential mobility." *Journal of the American Institute of Planners,* 37, pp. 319-25.

Dubow, F., and Emmons, D. (1981). "The community hypothesis." In Lewis, D.A. (Ed.), *Reactions to Crime.* Newbury Park, CA: Sage Publications, pp. 167-82.

Dubow, F., McCabe, E., and Kaplan, G. (1979). *Reactions to Crime: A Critical Review of the Literature.* Washington, DC: U.S. Department of Justice, National Institute of Justice.

Duncan, G., and Newman, S. (1976). "Expected and actual residential moves." *Journal of the American Institute of Planners,* 42, pp. 174-86.

Emmons, D. (1979). "Neighborhood activists and community organizations." Unpublished paper, Center for Urban Affairs and Policy Research, Northwestern University.

Erbe, B.M. (1975). "Race and socioeconomic segregation." *American Sociological Review,* 40, pp. 801-12.

Federal Bureau of Investigation. (yearly). *Crime in the United States.* Washington, DC: U.S. Government Printing Office.

Felson, M. (1987). "Routine activities and crime prevention in the developing metropolis." *Criminology,* 25, pp. 911-31.

Felstiner, W. (1974). "Influence of social organization on dispute processing." *Law and Society Review,* 9, pp. 63-94.

Fields, A.B. (1984). "'Slinging weed': the social organization of streetcorner marijuana sales." *Urban Life,* 13, pp. 247-70.

Finn, P. (1988). *Street People.* Washington, DC: National Institute of Justice, U.S. Department of Justice.

Finnie, W.C. (1973). "Field experiments in litter control." *Environment and Behavior,* 5, pp. 123-44.

Fisher, C.S. (1977). *Networks and Places: Social Relations in the Urban Setting.* New York: Free Press.

FOGELSON, R. (1977). *Big City Police.* Cambridge: Harvard University Press.

FOWLER, F.J., and MANGIONE, T.W. (1982). *Neighborhood Crime, Fear, and Social Control: A Second Look at the Hartford Program.* Washington, DC: National Institute of Justice, U.S. Department of Justice.

FOWLER, F.J., McCALLA, M.E., and MANGIONE, T.W. (1979). *Reducing Residential Crime and Fear: The Hartford Neighborhood Crime Prevention Program.* Washington, DC: National Institute of Justice, U.S. Department of Justice.

FREY, W.H. (1980). "Black in-migration, white flight, and the changing economic base of the central city." *American Journal of Sociology,* 85, pp. 1396–417.

———. (1984). "Lifecourse migration of metropolitan whites and blacks and the structure of demographic change in large central cities." *American Sociological Review,* 49, pp. 803–27.

FRISBIE, D., FISHBEIN, G., HINZ, R., JOELSON, M., and NUTTER, J.B. (1977). *Crime in Minneapolis.* St. Paul, MN: Community Crime Prevention Project, Governor's Commission on Crime Prevention and Control.

FURSTENBERG, F.F., JR. (1971). "Public reactions to crime in the streets." *American Scholar* 40: 601–10.

GANS, H. (1962). *The Urban Villagers.* New York: The Free Press.

GARDNER, C.B. (1980). "Passing by: street remarks, address rights, and the urban female." *Sociological Inquiry,* 50, pp. 328–56.

GAROFALO, J., and McLEOD, M. (1988). "Improving the effectiveness and utilization of neighborhood watch programs." *Research in Action.* Washington, DC: National Institute of Justice, U.S. Department of Justice.

GIOKARIS, V.M. (1987). "Zoning and the first amendment: a municipality's power to control adult use establishments." *University of Missouri-Kansas City Law Review,* 55, pp. 263–83.

GLADSTONE, F.J., STURMAN, A., and WILSON, S. (1978). "Tackling vandalism." In Clarke, R.G.V. (Ed.) *Home Office Research Study, No. 47.* London: Her Majesty's Stationery Office.

GLAZER, N. (1988). *The Limits of Social Policy.* Cambridge: Harvard University Press.

GOLDSTEIN, H. (1977). *Policing a Free Society.* Cambridge, Ma: Ballinger.

GOODSTEIN, L.I. (1980). "The crime causes crime model: a critical review of the relationships between fear of crime, bystander surveillance, and changes in the crime rate." *Victimology,* 5, pp. 133–51.

GOODWIN, C. (1979). *The Oak Park Strategy: Community Control of Racial Change.* Chicago: University of Chicago Press.

GOVE, W., HUGHES, M., and GEERKEN, M. (1985). "Are uniform crime reports a valid indicator of the index crimes? an affirmative answer with minor qualifications." *Criminology,* 23, pp. 451–502.

GREENBERG, S.W. (1983). "External solutions to neighborhood-based problems: the case of community crime prevention." Unpublished paper presented at the Annual Meeting of the Law and Society Association (June).

GREENBERG, S.W., and ROHE, W.H. (1983). "Secondary Analysis of the Relationship between Responses to Crime and Informal Social Control." Unpublished report, Research Triangle Institute.

GREENBERG, S. W., ROHE, W.M., and WILLIAMS, J.R. (1982). *Safe and Secure Neighborhoods: Physical Characteristics and Informal Territorial Control in High and Low Crime Neighborhoods.* Washington, DC: National Institute of Justice, U.S. Department of Justice.

_____. (1984). "Informal Citizen Action and Crime Prevention at the Neighborhood Level: Synthesis and Assessment of the Research." Unpublished report, Research Triangle Institute.

HACKLER, J.C., HO, K., and URQUHART-ROSS, C. 1974). "The willingness in intervene: differing community characteristics." *Social Problems,* 21, pp. 328–44.

HALLER, M. (1976). "Historical roots of police behavior: Chicago, 1890–1925." *Law and Society Review,* 10, pp. 303–24.

HANNERZ, U. (1969). *Soulside.* New York: Columbia University Press.

HARRING, S. (1983). *Policing a Class Society: The Experience of American Cities, 1865–1915.* New Brunswick, NJ: Rutgers University Press.

HARTOG, H. (1985). "Pigs and positivism." *Wisconsin Law Review,* 1985, pp. 899–935.

HEATH, L., and SWIM, J. (1985). "Perceived control and the genesis of fear." Unpublished paper presented at the annual meeting of the American Society of Criminology, San Diego, CA.

HENIG, J.R. (1978). "Coping a cop: neighborhood organizations and police patrol allocation." *Journal of Voluntary Action Research,* 7, pp. 75–84.

_____. (1982). *Neighborhood Mobilization.* New Brunswick, NJ: Rutgers University Press.

_____. (1984). "Citizens against crime: an assessment of the neighborhood-watch program in Washington, DC." Unpublished manuscript. Washington, DC: George Washington University, Center for Washington Area Studies.

HINDELANG, M.J., GOTTFREDSON, M.R., and GAROFALO, J. (1978). *Victims of Personal Crime.* Cambridge, MA: Ballinger.

HIRSCHMAN, A.O. (1970). *Exit, Voice and Loyalty*. Cambridge, MA: Harvard University Press.

HOPE, T. (1988). "Support for neighborhood watch: a British crime-survey analysis." In Hope, T. and Shaw, M. (Eds.), *Communities and Crime Reduction*. London: Her Majesty's Stationery Office, 146–63.

HOPE, T., and HOUGH, M. (1988). "Area, crime, and incivility: a profile from the British Crime Survey." In Hope, T. and Shaw, M. (Eds.), *Communities and Crime Reduction*. London: Her Majesty's Stationery Office, 30–47.

HOPE, T., and SHAW, M. (1988). "Community approaches to reducing crime." In Hope, T. and Shaw, M. (Eds.), *Communities and Crime Reduction*. London: Her Majesty's Stationery Office, 1–29.

HUGHES, P.H., and JAFFE, J.H. (1971). "The heroin copping area: a location for epidemiological study and intervention activity." *Archives of General Psychiatry*, 24, pp. 394–400.

HUNTER, A. (1974). *Symbolic Communities*. Chicago: University of Chicago Press.

———. (1978). "Symbols of incivility: social disorder and fear of crime in urban neighborhoods." Unpublished paper presented at the Annual Meeting of the American Society of Criminology.

JACOB, H. (1984). *The Frustration of Policy: Responses to Crime by American Cities*. Boston: Little, Brown.

JACOBS, J. (1961). *The Death and Life of Great American Cities*. New York: Vintage.

JAYCOX, V.H. (1978). "The elderly's fear of crime: rational or irrational." *Victimology*, 3, pp. 329–33.

KASL, S.V., and HARBURG, E.W. (1972). "Perceptions of the neighborhood and the desire to move out." *Journal of the American Institute of Planners*, 38, pp. 318–24.

KATZMAN, M.T. (1980). "The contribution of crime to urban decline." *Urban Studies*, 17, pp. 277–86.

KELLING, G. (1987). "Acquiring a taste for order: the community and police." *Crime and Delinquency*, 33, pp. 90–102.

KENNEDY, L.W. (1978). "Environmental opportunity and social contact: a true or spurious relationship?" *Pacific Sociological Review*, 21, pp. 173–86.

———. (1984). "Residential stability and social contact: testing for saved versus liberated communities." *Journal of Community Psychology*, 12, pp. 3–12.

KENNEDY, L.W. and SILVERMAN, R.A. (1985). "Perception of social diversity and fear of crime." *Environment and Behavior*, 17, pp. 275–95.

KENNY, D.J. (1987). *Crime, Fear, and the New York City Subways*. New York: Praeger.

KIDD, R.F., and CHAYET, A.F. (1984). "Why do victims fail to report: the psychology of criminal victimization." *Journal of Social Issues*, 40, pp. 39–50.

KLEIN, M. and MAXSON, C. (1989). "Street gang violence." In Weiner, N. and Wolfgang, M. (Eds.), *Violent Crime, Violent Criminals*. Newbury Park, CA: Sage Publications, pp. 198–234.

KOBRIN, S., and SCHUERMAN, L.A. (1981). *Interaction Between Neighborhood Change and Criminal Activity*. Los Angeles: Social Science Research Institute, University of Southern California.

————. (1983). "Crime and urban ecological processes: implications for public policy." Unpublished paper presented at the Annual Meeting of the American Sociological Association.

KOHFELD, C.W., SALERT, B.S., and SCHOENBERG, S. (1983). "Neighborhood associations and urban crime." In *Community Crime Prevention*. St. Louis: Center for Responsive Government.

KRAHN, H., and KENNEDY, L.W. (1985). "Producing personal safety: the effects of crime rates, police force size, and fear of crime." *Criminology*, 23, pp. 697–710.

LANE, R. (1968). "Urbanization and civil violence in the 19th century: Massachusetts as a test case." *Journal of Social History*, 2.

————. (1980). "Urban police and crime in nineteenth-century America." In Morris, N. and Tonrey, M. (Eds.), *Crime and Justice: An Annual Review of Research, Vol. 2*. Chicago: University of Chicago Press, pp. 1–44.

LASKA, S., and SPAIN, D. (Eds.) (1980). *Back to the City: Issues in Neighborhood Renovation*. New York: Pergamon Press.

LAVRAKAS, P.J. (1981). "On households." In Lewis, D.A. (Ed.), *Reactions to Crime*. Newbury Park, CA: Sage Publications, pp. 67–86.

————. (1985). "Citizen self-help and neighborhood crime prevention policy." In Curtis, L. (Ed.), *American Violence and Public Policy*. New Haven: Yale University Press.

LAVRAKAS, P.J., and HERZ, E. (1982). "Citizen participation in neighborhood crime prevention." *Criminology*, 20, pp. 479–98.

LAVRAKAS, P.J., HERZ, E., and SALEM, G. (1981). "Community organization, citizen participation, and neighborhood crime prevention." Unpublished paper presented at the Annual Meeting of the American Psychological Association.

LEE, B.A. (1980). "The disappearance of skid row: some ecological evidence." *Urban Affairs Quarterly*, 16, pp. 81–107.

LEWIS, D.A. (1979). "Design problems in public policy development." *Criminology* 17: 172–83.

LEWIS, D.A., and MAXFIELD, M.G. (1980). "Fear in the neighborhoods: an investigation of the impact of crime." *Journal of Research in Crime and Delinquency*, pp. 160–89.

LEWIS, D.A., and SALEM, G. (1981). "Community crime prevention: an analysis of a developing perspective." *Crime and Delinquency*, 27, pp. 405–21.

———. (1986). *Fear of Crime: Incivility and the Production of a Social Problem*. New Brunswick, N.J.: Transaction Books.

LEWIS, D.A., GRANT, J.A., and ROSENBAUM, D.R. (1985). "The social construction of reform: crime prevention and community organizations: draft final report, volume II." Evanston, Ill.: Center for Urban Affairs and Policy Research, Northwestern University.

———. (1988). *The Social Construction of Reform: Crime Prevention and Community Organizations*. New Brunswick, NJ: Transaction Books.

LEY, D., and CYBRIWSKY, R. (1974). "Urban graffiti as territorial markets." *Annals of the Association of American Geographers*, 64, pp. 491–505.

LIND, E.A., and TYLER, T.R. (1988). *The Social Psychology of Procedural Justice*. New York: Plenum.

LURIGIO, A.J., and ROSENBAUM, D.R. (1986) "Evaluation research in community crime prevention: a critical look at the field." In Rosenbaum, D. (Ed.), *Community Crime Prevention: Does It Work?*. Newbury Park, CA: Sage Publications, pp. 19–45.

LYONS, A., MCCOURT, K., and NYDEN, P. (1986). *Preserving Home Values in Chicago Through a Home Equity Guarantee Program*. Chicago: The Chicago Neighborhood Organizing Project.

MACCOBY, E., JOHNSON, J.P., and CHURCH, R. (1958). "Community integration and the social control of juvenile delinquency." *Journal of Social Issues*, 14, pp. 38–51.

MARGULIS, H.L. (1977). "Applied geography: rat fields, neighborhood sanitation, and rat complaints in Newark, New Jersey." *Geographical Review*, 67, pp. 221–31.

MARKOWITZ, S.J. (1977). "Statute proscribing loitering for the purpose of prostitution is not unconstitutionally vague." *Fordham Urban Law Journal*, 6, pp. 159–67.

MAWBY, R.I. (1984). "Vandalism and public perceptions of vandalism in contrasting residential areas." In Levy-Leboyer, C. (Ed.), *Vandalism: Behavior, and Motivations*. Amsterdam and New York: Elsevier, pp. 235–46.

MAXFIELD, M.G. (1984a). *Fear of Crime in England and Wales*. London: Her Majesty's Stationery Office, Home Office Research Study No. 78.

_____. (1984b). "The limits of vulnerability in explaining fear of crime: a comparative neighborhood analysis." *Journal of Research in Crime and Delinquency,* 21, pp. 233–50.

_____. (1987). "Incivilities and fear of crime in England and Wales, and the United States: a comparative analysis." Unpublished paper presented at the annual meeting of the American Society for Criminology (Montreal).

MAYHEW, P. (1981). "Crime in public view: surveillance and crime prevention." In Brantingham, P.J. and Brantingham, P.L. (Eds.) *Environmental Criminology.* Newbury Park, CA: Sage Publications, pp. 119–34.

MCDONALD, S.C. (1983). *Human and Market Dynamics in the Gentrification of a Boston Neighborhood.* PhD dissertation, Department of Sociology, Harvard University.

_____. (1986). "Does gentrification affect crime rates?." In Reiss, A. and Tonrey, M. (Eds.), *Communities and Crime.* Chicago: University of Chicago Press, pp. 163–202.

MCPHERSON, M. (1978). "Realities and perceptions of crime at the neighborhood level." *Victimology,* 3, pp. 319–28.

MCPHERSON, M., and SILLOWAY, G. (1980). *Planning Community Crime Prevention Programs.* Minneapolis, Minnesota Crime Prevention Center.

_____. (1981). "Planning to prevent crime." In Lewis, D.A. (Ed.) *Reactions to Crime.* Newbury Park, CA: Sage Publications, pp. 149–66.

MCPHERSON, M., SILLOWAY, G., and FREY, D. (1983). "Crime, Fear, and Control in Neighborhood Commercial Centers." Unpublished report, Minnesota Crime Prevention Center, Inc.

MEDEA, A., and THOMPSON, K. (1974). *Against Rape.* New York: Farrar, Straus and Giroux.

MERRY, S. (1979). "Going to court: strategies of dispute management in an American urban neighborhood." *Law and Society Review,* 13, pp. 891–925.

_____. (1981). *Urban Danger: Life in a Neighborhood of Strangers.* Philadelphia: Temple University Press.

MILLER, R.J. (1982). *The Demolition of Skid Row.* Lexington, MA: Lexington Books.

MOLOTCH, H. (1972). *Managed Integration.* Berkeley: University of California Press.

MONKKONEN, E. (1981). *Police in Urban America, 1860–1920.* Cambridge: Cambridge University Press.

MOORE, M.H., and KELLING, G.E. (1983). "To serve and protect: learning from police history." *The Public Interest,* 70, pp. 49–65.

MORRIS, P., and HEAL, K. (1981). *Crime Control and the Police*. London: Her Majesty's Stationery Office, Home Office Research Study No. 67.

MUKHERJEE, S., and WILSON, P. (1987). "Neighbourhood watch: issues and policy implications." In Wilson, P. (Ed.), *Trends and Issues in Crime and Criminal Justice*, No. 8. Canberra: Australian Institute of Criminology.

MURRAY, E.F. (1979). "Anti-prostitution laws: new conflicts in the fight against the world's oldest profession." *Albany Law Review*, 43, pp. 360–87.

NEWMAN, O. (1972). *Defensible Space: Crime Prevention Through Environmental Design*. New York: Macmillan.

———. (1980). *Community of Interest*. Garden City, NY: Doubleday.

O'KEEFE, G.J., and MENDELSOHN, H. (1984). *Taking a Bite Out of Crime: The Impact of a Mass Media Crime Prevention Campaign*. Washington, DC: National Institute of Justice, U.S. Department of Justice.

ORBELL, J.M., and UNO, T. (1972). "A theory of neighborhood problem-solving." *American Political Science Review*, 66, pp. 471–89.

PATE, A. (1986). "Experimenting with foot patrol: the Newark experience." In Rosenbaum, D. (Ed.), *Community Crime Prevention: Does It Work?*. Newbury Park, CA: Sage Publications, pp. 137–56.

PATE, A., MCPHERSON, M., and SILLOWAY, G. (1987). *The Minneapolis Community Crime Prevention Experiment: Draft Evaluation Report*. Washington, DC: The Police Foundation.

PATE, A., WYCOFF, M.A., SKOGAN, W.G., and SHERMAN, L. (1986). *Reducing Fear of Crime in Houston and Newark: A Summary Report*. Washington, DC: The Police Foundation and the National Institute of Justice.

PEARL, J. (1987). "The highest paying customers: America's cities and the costs of prostitution control." *Hastings Law Journal*, 8, pp. 769–800.

PENNELL, F.E. (1978). "Collective versus private strategies for coping with crime." *Journal of Voluntary Action Research*, 7, pp. 59–74.

PERKINS, D.D., RICH, C.R., CHAVIS, D.M., WANDERSMAN, A., and FLORIN, P. (1986). "The limited role of community organization in crime prevention and the promising role of crime prevention in community organization." Unpublished paper presented at the annual meeting of the American Society for Criminology (Atlanta).

PODOLEFSKY, A.M. (1983). *Case Studies in Community Crime Prevention*. Springfield, Ill: Charles C. Thomas Publishers.

———. (1985). "Rejecting crime-prevention programs: the dynamics of program implementation in high need communities." *Human Organization*, 44, pp. 33–40.

PODOLEFSKY, A., and DUBOW, F. (1981). *Strategies for Community Crime Prevention*. Springfield, IL: Charles C. Thomas Publishers.

POLICE FOUNDATION. (1981). *The Newark Foot Patrol Experiment*. Washington, DC: The Police Foundation.

POYNER, B. (1983). *Design against crime: beyond defensible space*. London: Butterworths.

RECKLESS, W.C. (1961). "The distribution of commercialized vice in the city: a sociological analysis." In Theodorson, G.A. (Ed.), *Studies in Human Ecology*. Evanston, IL: Row, Peterson and Co., p. 57.

REINER, R. (1985). *The Politics of the Police*. New York: St. Martins.

REISS, A.J. (1971). *The Police and the Public*. New Haven: Yale University Press.

––––––. (1984). "Consequences of compliance and deterrence models of law enforcement for the exercise of police discretion." *Law and Contemporary Problems*, 47, pp. 81–122.

––––––. (1985). *Policing a City's Central District: The Oakland Story*. Washington, DC: U.S. Department of Justice, National Institute of Justice (March).

RIFAI, M. (1976). "Criminal victimization of the older adult." Unpublished paper presented at the Second International Symposium of Victimology. Boston.

RIGER, S., GORDON, M.T., and LEBAILLY, R. (1982). "Coping with urban crime." *American Journal of Community Psychology*, 10, pp. 369–86.

ROSENBAUM, D.P. (1987). "The theory and research behind neighborhood watch: is it a sound fear and crime reduction strategy?" *Crime and Delinquency*, 33, pp. 103–34.

––––––. (1988). "A critical eye on neighborhood watch: does it reduce crime and fear?" In Hope, T. and Shaw, M. (Eds.), *Communities and Crime Reduction*. London: Her Majesty's Stationery Office, 126–45.

ROSENBAUM, D.P., LEWIS, D.A., and GRANT, J. (1985). "The impact of community crime prevention programs in Chicago: can neighborhood organizations make a difference? (draft final report, volume I)" Center for Urban Affairs and Policy Research, Northwestern University.

––––––. (1986). "Neighborhood-based crime prevention: assessing the efficacy of community organizing in Chicago." In Rosenbaum, D. (Ed.), *Community Crime Prevention: Does It Work?*. Newbury Park, CA: Sage Publications, pp. 109–36.

ROSSI, P.H. (1989). *Down and Out in America: The Origins of Homelessness*. Chicago: University of Chicago Press.

ROSSI, P.H., FISHER, G.A., and WILLIS, G. (1986). "The condition of the homeless of Chicago." Report distributed by the Social and Demographic Research Institute, University of Massachusetts, and the National Opinion Research Center, University of Chicago.

SAMPSON, R., and COHEN, J. (1988). "Deterrent effects of the police on crime: a replication and theoretical extension." *Law and Society Review,* 22, pp. 163–90.

SAVITZ, L.D., LALLI, M.D., and ROSEN, L. (1977). *City Life and Delinquency: Victimization, Fear of Crime, and Gang Membership.* Washington, DC: National Institute for Juvenile Justice and Delinquency Prevention, U.S. Department of Justice.

SCHNEIDER, A.L. (1986). "Neighborhood-based antiburglary strategies: an analysis of public and private benefits from the Portland program." In Rosenbaum, D. (Ed.), *Community Crime Prevention: Does It Work?.* Newbury Park, CA: Sage Publications, pp. 68–86.

SCHNEIDER, A.L., and SCHNEIDER, P. *Private and Public-Minded Citizen Responses to a Neighborhood-Based Crime Prevention Strategy.* Eugene, OR: Institute of Policy Analysis.

SCHUERMAN, L.A., and KOBRIN, S. (1986). "Community careers in crime." In Reiss, A., and Tonrey, M. (Eds.), *Communities and Crime.* Chicago: University of Chicago Press, pp. 67–100.

SENNETT, R. (1970). *The Uses of Disorder: Personal Identity and City Life.* New York: Knopf.

SHERMAN, L.W. (1983). "After the riots: police and minorities in the U.S., 1970–1980." In Glazer, N. and Young, K., *Ethnic Pluralism and Public Police.* Lexington, MA: Lexington Books, pp. 212–35.

_____. (1986). "Policing communities: what works?" In Reiss, A., and Tonrey, M. (Eds.), *Communities and Crime.* Chicago: University of Chicago Press, pp. 343–86.

SHOTLAND, R.L., and GOODSTEIN, L.I. (1984). "The role of bystanders in crime control." *Journal of Social Issues,* 40, pp. 9–26.

SHUMSKY, N., and SPRINGER, L. (1981). "San Francisco's zone of prostitution, 1880–1934." *Journal of Historical Geography,* 7, pp. 71–89.

SILLOWAY, G., and MCPHERSON, M. (1985). "The limits to citizen participation in a government-sponsored community crime prevention program." Unpublished paper presented at the annual meeting of the American Society of Criminology, San Diego.

SILVER, A. (1967). "The demand for order in civil society." In Bordua, D. (Ed.), *The Police: Six Sociological Essays.* New York: John Wiley, pp. 1–24.

SILVERMAN, R.A., and KENNEDY, L.H. (1985). "Loneliness, satisfaction and fear of crime." *Canadian Journal of Criminology,* 27, pp. 1–13.

SKOGAN, W.G. (1977). "Public policy and the fear of crime in large

American cities." In Gardiner, J. (Ed.), *Public Law and Public Policy*. New York: Praeger, pp. 1–18.

———. (1981). "On attitudes and behaviors." In Lewis, D.A. (Ed.), *Reactions to Crime*. Newbury Park, CA: Sage Publications, pp. 19–45.

———. (1983). "Disorder, crime, and community deterioration: a test of the Wilson-Kelling hypothesis." Unpublished paper presented at the ninth International Congress on Criminology (September).

———. (1986a). "Disorder, crime and community decline." In Hope, T., and Shaw, M. (Eds.), *Communities and Crime Reduction*. London: Her Majesty's Stationery Office, 48–61.

———. (1986b). "Fear of crime and neighborhood change." In Reiss, A., and Tonrey, M. (Eds.), *Communities and Crime*. Chicago: University of Chicago Press, pp. 203–30.

———. (1987). "Disorder and Community Decline." Unpublished report, Center for Urban Affairs and Policy Research, Northwestern University.

———. (1988). "Community organizations and crime." In Tonrey, M., and Morris, N., *Crime and Justice: An Annual Review*. Chicago: University of Chicago Press, pp. 39–78.

SKOGAN, W.G., and MAXFIELD, M.G. (1981). *Coping With Crime: Individual and Neighborhood Reactions*. Newbury Park, CA: Sage Publications.

SKOLNICK, J., and BAYLEY, D.A. (1986). *The New Blue Line*. New York: Free Press.

———. (1988). "Theme and variation in community policing." In Tonrey, M., and Morris, N. (Eds.), *Crime and Justice: An Annual Review*. Chicago: University of Chicago Press, 1–38.

SMITH, SUSAN J. (1987). "Fear of crime: beyond a geography of deviance." *Progress in Human Geography*, 11, pp. 1–23.

———. (1988). "Social relations, neighbourhood structure, and the fear of crime in Britain." In Herbert, D.T., and Evans, D. (Eds.), *The Geography of Crime*. London: Croom Helm, in press.

SOUTHGATE, P. (1985). "Police output measures." In Heal, K., Tarling, R., and Burrows, J. (Eds.), *Policing Today*. London: Her Majesty's Stationery Office, pp. 30–42.

SPEARE, A. (1974). "Residential satisfaction as in intervening variable in residential mobility." *Demography*, 11, pp. 173–88.

SPELMAN, W., and ECK, J.E. (1987). "Problem-oriented policing." *Research in Brief*. Washington, DC: National Institute of Justice, U.S. Department of Justice.

STARK, R. (1987). "Deviant places: a theory of the ecology of crime." *Criminology*, 25, pp, 893–910.

STERNLIEB, G., and BURCHELL, R.W. (1983). "Fires in abandoned buildings." In Rapkin, C. (Ed.), *The Social and Economic Consequences of Residential Fires*. Lexington, MA: Lexington Books, pp. 261–70.

STINCHCOMBE, A.L. (1968). *Constructing Social Theories*. New York: Harcourt, Brace, and World.

STINCHCOMBE, A.L., ADAMS, R., HEIMER, C., SCHEPPELE, K., SMITH, T., and TAYLOR, D.G. (1980). *Crime and Punishment in Public Opinion*. San Francisco: Jossey-Bass.

SUTTLES, G.D. (1968). *The Social Order of the Slum*. Chicago: University of Chicago Press.

SYMANSKI, R. (1981). *The Immoral Landscape: Female Prostitution in Western Societies*. Toronto: Butterworths.

TAUB, R.P., SURGEON, G.P., LINDHOLM, S., OTTI, P.B., and BRIDGES, A. (1977). "Urban voluntary associations: locally based and externally induced." *Amerian Journal of Sociology*, 83, pp. 425–42.

TAUB, R.P., TAYLOR, D.G., and DUNHAM, J. (1981). "Neighborhoods and safety." In Lewis, D.A. (Ed.), *Reactions to Crime*. Newbury Park, CA: Sage Publications, pp. 103–22.

———. (1984). *Paths of Neighborhood Change: Race and Crime in Urban America*. Chicago: University of Chicago Press.

TAYLOR, R.B., and GOTTFREDSON, S.D. (1986). "Environmental design, crime and prevention." In Reiss, A., and Tonrey, M. (Eds.), *Communities and Crime*. Chicago: University of Chicago Press, pp. 387–416.

TAYLOR, R.B., GOTTFREDSON, S.D., and BROWER, S. (1980). "The defensibility of defensible space." In Hirschi, T., and Gottfredson, M. (Eds.), *Understanding Crime*. Newbury Park, CA: Sage Publications, pp. 53–72.

———. (1981). "Informal Control in the Urban Residential Environment." Unpublished report, Center for Metropolitan Planning and Research, Johns Hopkins University.

———. (1984). "Block crime and fear: defensible space, local social ties, and territorial functioning." *Journal of Research in Crime and Delinquency*, 21, pp. 303–31.

———. (1985). "Attachment to place: discriminant validity, and impacts of disorder and diversity." *American Journal of Community Psychology*, 13, pp. 525–42.

TAYLOR, R.B., SCHUMAKER, S.A., and GOTTFREDSON, S.D. (1985). "Neighborhood-level linkages between physical features and local sentiments: deterioration, fear of crime, and confidence." *Journal of Architectural Planning and Research*, 1985, pp. 261–75.

TEPLIN, L. (1983). "The criminalization of the mentally ill." *Psychological Bulletin*, 94, pp. 54–67.

———. (1984). "Managing disorder; police handling of the mentally ill." In Teplin, L. (Ed.), *Mental Health and Criminal Justice.* Newbury Park, CA: Sage, pp. 157–75.

TITUS, R. (1984). "Residential burglary and the community response." In Clarke, R., and Hope, T. (Eds.), *Coping with Burglary.* Boston: Kluwer-Nijhoff, pp. 97–130.

TOBY, J. (1957). "Social disorganization and stake in conformity." *Journal of Criminal Law, Criminology and Police Science,* 48, pp. 12–17.

TROJANOWICZ, R. (1983). "An evaluation of a neighborhood foot patrol." *Journal of Police Science and Administration,* 2, pp. 410–19.

———. (1986). "Evaluating a neighborhood foot patrol program: the Flint, Michigan, project." In Rosenbaum, D. (Ed.), *Community Crime Prevention: Does It Work?.* Newbury Park, CA: Sage Publications, pp. 157–78.

TYLER, T.R. (1984). "Assessing the risk of crime victimization." *Journal of Social Issues,* 40, pp. 27–38.

UNGER, D. and WANDERSMAN, A. (1983). "Neighboring and its role in block organizations." *American Journal of Community Psychology,* 11, pp. 291–300.

URBAN-SUBURBAN INVESTMENT STUDY GROUP. (1975). *The Role of Mortgage Lending Practices in Older Urban Neighborhoods.* Evanston, IL: Center for Urban Affairs and Policy Research, Northwestern University.

VELLEMAN, P.F. and WELSCH, R.E. (1981). "Efficient computing of regression diagnostics." *American Statistician,* 35, pp. 234–42.

VERBA, S., and NIE, N. (1972). *Participation in America.* New York: Harper and Row.

WADE, R. (1969). "Violence in the cities: a historical view." In Daly, C.U. (Ed.), *Urban Violence.* Chicago: University of Chicago Press, pp. 7–26.

WALKER, S. (1977). *A Critical History of Police Reform.* Lexington, MA: Lexington Books.

———. (1983). "Broken windows and fractured history: the use and misuse of history in recent police patrol analysis." Unpublished paper.

WARD, JIM. (1975). "Skid row as a geographic entity." *The Professional Geographer,* XXVII, pp. 286–94.

WEATHERITT, M. (1986). *Innovations in Policing.* London: Croom-Helm.

WEBB, B. (1984). "Is there a place for vandalism?" In Levy-Leboyer, C. (Ed.), *Vandalism: Behavior and Motivations.* Amsterdam and New York: Elsevier, pp. 175–81.

WHITAKER, C.J. (1986). "Crime prevention measures." *Bureau of Justice*

Statistics Special Report. Washington, DC: Bureau of Justice Statistics, U.S. Department of Justice.

WHITTINGHAM, M. (1981). "Vandalism: the urge to destroy." *Canadian Journal of Criminology,* 23, pp. 69–72.

WHYTE, W.H. (1988). *City: Rediscovering the Center.* New York: Doubleday.

WIEDMAN, D., and PAGE, J.B. (1982). "Drug use on the street and on the beach: Cubans and anglos in Miami, Florida." *Urban Anthropology,* 11, pp. 213–35.

WILLIAMS, H., and PATE, A. (1987). "Returning to first principles: reducing the fear of crime in Newark." *Crime and Delinquency,* 33, pp. 53–70.

WILSON, J.Q. (1968). "The urban unease: community versus the city." *The Public Interest,* 12, pp. 25–39.

_____. (1968). *Varieties of Police Behavior.* Cambridge, MA: Harvard University Press.

_____. (1983). *Thinking About Crime.* New York: Basic Books.

WILSON, J.Q., and KELLING, G. (1982). "Broken windows." *The Atlantic Monthly,* March, pp. 29–38.

_____. (1989). "Making neighborhoods safe." *The Atlantic Monthly,* February, pp. 46–52.

WYCOFF, M., and SKOGAN, W.G. (1986). "Storefront police offices: the Houston field test." In Rosenbaum, D. (Ed.), *Community Crime Prevention: Does It Work?.* Newbury Park, CA: Sage Publications, pp. 179–201.

WYCOFF, M., SKOGAN, W.G., PATE, A., and SHERMAN, L.A. (1985a). *Citizen Contact Patrol.* Washington, DC: The Police Foundation.

_____. (1985b). *Police as Community Organizers.* Washington, DC: The Police Foundation.

YIN, P. (1980). "Fear of crime among the elderly." *Social Problems,* 27, pp. 492–504.

YIN, R.K. (1986). "Community crime prevention: a synthesis of eleven evaluations." In Rosenbaum, D. (Ed.), *Community Crime Prevention: Does It Work?.* Newbury Park, CA: Sage Publications, pp. 294–308.

YIN, R.K., M.E. VOGEL, J.M. CHAIKEN, and D.R. BOTH. (1976). Patrolling the Neighborhood Beat: Residents and Residential Security. Santa Monica, CA: The Rand Corporation.

ZIMBARDO, P.G. (1970). "The human choice: individuation, reason, and order versus deindividuation, impulse, and chaos." In Arnold W., and Levine, D. (Eds.), *Nebraska Symposium on Motivation 1969.* Lincoln, NB: University of Nebraska Press, pp. 237–307.

Index

215